WOMEN ON THE
FRONT LINE

WOMEN ON THE FRONT LINE

BRITISH SERVICEWOMEN'S PATH TO COMBAT

KATHLEEN SHERIT

AMBERLEY

DISCLAIMER

The views and opinions expressed are those of the author alone and should not be taken to represent those of Her Majesty's Government, MOD, HM Armed Forces or any government agency.

First published 2020

Amberley Publishing
The Hill, Stroud
Gloucestershire, GL5 4EP

www.amberley-books.com

Copyright © Kathleen Sherit, 2020

The right of Kathleen Sherit to be identified as the Author of this work has been asserted in accordance with the Copyrights, Designs and Patents Act 1988.

ISBN 978 1 4456 9684 3 (hardback)
ISBN 978 1 4456 9685 0 (ebook)

British Library Cataloguing in Publication Data. A catalogue record for this book is available from the British Library.

Typesetting by Aura Technology and Software Services, India. Printed in the UK.

CONTENTS

ACKNOWLEDGEMENTS

Meeting people who were central to the story is a great opportunity afforded to the contemporary historian. I must record my gratitude to all who agreed to be interviewed and who so vividly shared their recollections. I owe particular thanks to Air Commodore Cynthia Fowler and Commander Rosie Wilson, not only for their own insights into their Services, but also for brokering introductions. I am grateful, also, to Colonel Fiona Walthall for reading draft chapters from an army perspective.

Some of those I have met have also shared private papers with me. I would like to mention Squadron Leader Beryl Escott for giving me access to her collection of material on the Women's Auxiliary Air Force and Women's Royal Air Force, Mr Tony Ranson for lending me Sergeant Vera Beale's (his step-mother) logbook, Flight Lieutenant Julie Gibson for her correspondence on seeking a flying career and Captain Caroline Coates (RN) for providing access to a key report on the employment of the Women's Royal Naval Service before it found its way to the National Archive. I was most fortunate to be permitted to make use of the extensive collection of documents pertaining to the career of Air Commandant Dame Felicity Hanbury (later Peake). For this, I am most grateful to her son, Andrew Peake.

Sourcing photographs is a difficult task so I am pleased to mention individuals who have donated photographs: Lady Brown, Julie Gibson, Lord Hamilton, Catherine Jordan, Anthea Larken, Wendy Nichols, Lady Oswald, Andrew Peake, Celia Reed (née Watkins), Dot Ryder, Jo Salter, Chantelle Taylor, Lord West and Rosie Wilson.

Acknowledgements

If I have enjoyed the benefit of questioning key individuals while memory permits, the negative side of studying recent events is gathering sufficient evidence before files are released to the National Archive. My work for the later chapters has relied to an extent on applications made under the Freedom of Information Act (2000). I would like to thank all of the unsung staff in government departments who responded to my requests over a period of ten years. I would like to mention particularly Sebastian Cox, Head of the Air Historical Branch of the Ministry of Defence, the many individuals of the Royal Navy's Fleet Information Cell and Chris Farmer on the General Staff at the Ministry of Defence.

Archivists – too many to mention – have also generously shared their time and expertise. In addition to the National Archive, I have relied greatly on the extensive collection on the Women's Royal Naval Service held at the National Museum of the Royal Navy (Portsmouth), where Vicky Ingles has been wonderfully helpful. At the RAF Museum (Hendon), Peter Elliott was able to put me in touch with some of the women who qualified as pilots in the early 1990s, as well as making the Museum's collection of documents available to me. At the National Army Museum, Alastair Massie was kind enough to give me early sight of the correspondence of Brigadier Anne Field.

Endeavours have been made to identify and contact copyright holders. The publisher and the author will correct any omissions in later reprints if necessary.

The core of this book started as a PhD thesis, research for which was supported by the Arts and Humanities Research Council. In addition to benefitting from the guidance of Pat Thane and David Edgerton, the legacy of the degree was a hugely supportive network of friends whose research interests focus on twentieth-century British history. We meet regularly, share our writing and provide critical-friend commentary. Warm thanks to Christopher Knowles, who read all the draft chapters, Claire Hilton, Michael Passmore, Kathrin Pieren, Mary Salinsky and Mari Takayanagi for their unfailing support. I also appreciate the advice offered by David French who read my final draft.

Working on such a project would have been impossible without the support of family and friends. Rowena Loverance's good humour proved invaluable. Thank you all for listening, questioning and encouraging me in my work.

LIST OF ILLUSTRATIONS

1. Members of the Auxiliary Territorial Service training on predictor equipment for anti-aircraft artillery batteries. © Crown Copyright Imperial War Museum. (IWM H14972).
2. Air Commandant Dame Felicity Hanbury, Director of the WAAF/WRAF (1946-50). By kind permission of Mr Andrew Peake.
3. Brigadier Mary Tyrwhitt, Director of the ATS/WRAC (1946–51). Courtesy of the Council of the National Army Museum, London. (NAM 9407-345-8).
4. Air Quartermaster Celia Watkins. By kind permission.
5. Air Commodore Joy Tamblin, Director of the WRAF (1976–80). By kind permission of the Battle of Britain Bunker Museum, Hillingdon. © MOD/Crown Copyright 1976.
6. Female members of the Territorial Army undertaking weapons training. Courtesy of the Council of the National Army Museum, London. (NAM 1994-07-335-55).
7. Commandant Anthea Larken, Director of the WRNS (1988–91). By kind permission. © MOD/Crown Copyright 1988.
8. Captain Alan West RN. By kind permission.
9. Admiral Sir Brian Brown, Second Sea Lord. By kind permission. © MOD/Crown Copyright 1988.
10. Admiral Sir Julian Oswald, First Sea Lord. By kind permission. © MOD/Crown Copyright 1989.
11. Archie Hamilton with Anthea Larken and Rosie Wilson celebrating the 100th anniversary of the Women's Royal Naval Service, Speaker's House, Palace of Westminster. © MOD/Crown Copyright 2017.

LIST OF FIGURES

LIST OF TABLES

ABBREVIATIONS AND TERMINOLOGY

Adjutant General	Head of Army Personnel
AEW	Airborne Early Warning
AFBSC	Air Force Board Standing Committee
AFO	Admiralty Fleet Order
AFPRB	Armed Forces Pay Review Body
AGARD	Advisory Group for Aerospace Research and Development
AHB	Air Historical Branch
Air Force List	Annual publication listing all officers
ALM	Air Loadmaster (formerly Air Quartermaster)
AMP	Air Member for Personnel (Head of RAF personnel)
AQM	Air Quartermaster (subsequently Air Loadmaster)
ASW	Anti-submarine Warfare
ATA	Air Transport Auxiliary
ATS	Auxiliary Territorial Service
BAOR	British Army of the Rhine
BR	Book of Reference (Admiralty publication)
CAS	Chief of the Air Staff (Professional head of the Royal Air Force)
Category	Naval term for a trade for non-commissioned ranks

CEG	Career Employment Group (Army term for a group of trades)
CGS	Chief of the General Staff (Professional head of the Army)
ChCh	Christ Church Oxford
CNS	Chief of the Naval Staff (First Sea Lord) (Professional head of the Royal Navy)
DASA	Defence Analytical Services and Advice
DGNMT	Director General Naval Manning and Training
Director WAAF	Head of the Women's Auxiliary Air Force
Director WRAF	Head of the Women's Royal Air Force
Director WRNS	Head of the Women's Royal Naval Service
ECAB	Executive Committee of the Army Board
ECAC	Executive Committee of the Army Council
First Lord of the Admiralty	Head of the Admiralty (like Secretary of State for War or Air) before it was subsumed within the Ministry of Defence in 1964
First Sea Lord	Professional head of the Royal Navy (CNS)
FOI	Freedom of Information
HC Deb	House of Commons Debates
HMSO	Her Majesty's Stationery Office
IRT	Incident Reaction Team
IWM	Imperial War Museum, London
LHA	Liddell Hart Archive, King's College London
MARILYN	Manning and Recruiting in the Lean Years of the Nineties
MOD	Ministry of Defence
NAM	National Army Museum, London
NAO	National Audit Office
NATO	North Atlantic Treaty Organisation
NAVB	Navy Board
Navy List	Annual publication listing all officers
Navy News	Publicly available newspaper for the Navy
NCO	Non-commissioned Officer
NDA	Naval Discipline Act

NMRN	National Museum of the Royal Navy, Portsmouth
ODNB	Oxford Dictionary of National Biography
PA	Parliamentary Archive, London
PPO Committee	Principal Personnel Officers' Committee
QMAAC	Queen Mary's Army Auxiliary Corps
RA	Royal Artillery
RAC	Royal Armoured Corps
RAF	Royal Air Force
RAFM	Royal Air Force Museum, Hendon
RAF News	Publicly available newspaper for the RAF
Ratings	Non-commissioned naval personnel
Regular	Voluntarily and permanently employed service person i.e. not a wartime temporary, auxiliary or reserve.
RN	Royal Navy
SDA	Sex Discrimination Act (1975)
Second Sea Lord	Head of Naval Personnel
Soldier	Publicly available newspaper for the Army
TA	Territorial Army
TNA	The National Archive, Kew
TOR	Terms of Reference
UAS	University Air Squadron
UDR	Ulster Defence Regiment
UOTC	University Officer Training Corps
USAF	United States Air Force
VCAS	Vice Chief of the Air Staff
WAAC	Women's Army Auxiliary Corps
WAAF	Women's Auxiliary Air Force
waaf	Member of the WAAF or WRAF (colloquial)
WRAC	Women's Royal Army Corps
WRAF	Women's Royal Air Force
Wren	Member of the Women's Royal Naval Service
WRNS	Women's Royal Naval Service
X-factor	Supplement to military pay introduced in 1970

I

INTRODUCTION

In May 1942, Nora Caveney was killed by a bomb splinter as she operated equipment that tracked in-coming German bombing raids and predicted the flight path for anti-aircraft artillery batteries. Her task being critical to the effectiveness of the guns at this south coast site, her place was taken immediately by another woman 'who continued to follow the raider, and the guns were able to continue firing without a moment's delay'.[1] Nora and her colleague worked with the Royal Artillery on anti-aircraft artillery batteries, a role that was opened to the Army's female corps – the Auxiliary Territorial Service (ATS) – in May 1941. Distinction was made between aiming guns, which women were permitted to do, and firing them, which officially they were not. In September 1943, more than 9,000 women worked on gun sites with the Royal Artillery in anti-aircraft fire control.[2]

In 1941, Air Marshal Gossage (Commander-in-Chief Balloon Command) agreed to employ airwomen of the Women's Auxiliary Air Force (WAAF) on his barrage balloon sites. These balloons were deployed near key facilities as a means of deterring enemy bomber aircraft from pressing home attacks. Like women of the ATS, these airwomen were part of Britain's air defence forces and they also risked becoming the target as raiding aircraft sought to destroy the defences:

> Corporal Lilian Ellis was in charge of a balloon site in South Wales during a night raid in May 1943. ... Bombs were falling all around. Corporal Ellis ordered everybody to take shelter while she completed the operation [order] ... Just then a bomb fell a few feet away, killing three airwomen and wounding four, including Corporal Ellis.

In spite of her injuries, she insisted on the other members of her crew receiving attention first. She was awarded the British Empire Medal for her gallantry.[3]

At the peak of the Second World War in 1942, more than 1,000 barrage balloons were operated by all-female crews.

Members of the Women's Royal Naval Service (WRNS), known as Wrens, also took part in work far removed from the nostalgic image of attractive young women plotting shipping movements in operations' rooms. Under the innocuous title of 'boom defence', a cohort of Wrens stationed in East Anglia attached incendiary devices to hydrogen balloons that were floated over to continental Europe when the wind was favourable. Too small a section to warrant the provision of men to guard them, these Wrens were trained to use firearms.[4]

Then there were some exceptional servicewomen who were dropped into occupied territory to operate with resistance movements, primarily as radio operators. Many fell into the hands of the Gestapo and were sent to concentration camps where some were executed.[5]

But servicewomen in the Second World War were regarded as non-combatants, as they had been in the First World War (then known as the Great War), with no explanation of the term or definition of a combat role being necessary. Indeed, the Royal Warrant that brought the ATS into existence in 1938 described its purpose as non-combatant duties. However, wartime expediency allowed for wide interpretation that could stretch the meaning of non-combatant. As General Pile (Anti-Aircraft Command) remarked in his post-war memoir:

> we were quite ready to let them fire light anti-aircraft guns, but there was a good deal of muddled thinking which was prepared to allow women to do anything to kill the enemy except actually press the trigger.

He personally dismissed the idea that ATS women assigned to the Royal Artillery were not in combat, writing: 'British girls were the first to take their place in a combatant role in any army in the world.'[6] His perspective was not the official position.

As General Pile suggested, it was nonsense to claim that women did not participate in some types of combat in the Second World War. But acknowledging the fact, even in the midst of a war that threatened national existence, was politically difficult and publicly unacceptable. It is no surprise that when servicewomen were offered military careers following the war, the practice of treating women as non-combatants continued. This limited status was not dictated by international law; it was a matter of British policy determined within the Admiralty, War Office and Air Ministry by senior male officers. No longer driven by the imperative of winning a war, these policymakers took a narrower view of what work was suitable for servicewomen.

The non-combatant principle had important consequences for these new, post-war careers in what is termed regular service as distinct from women's wartime, temporary employment in auxiliary services. It governed the number of women who could be recruited, roles they could be trained for, postings, promotion chances, pay and pensions. Being non-combatant also affected their status in the eyes of servicemen as they could not fulfil the complete range of duties that fell to men. In particular, they could not take a share of armed guard duty as they were excluded from training in the use of weapons.

Being in the armed forces was not only about employment, it also came with expectations about lifestyle. The authorities wanted young men to join, follow their early careers without domestic ties, then marriage and children for those men destined for long careers. Through allowances additional to pay and some provision of housing, married men were expected to meet their family obligations while still fulfilling military commitments of serving where and when needed. Homosexual relationships were unacceptable. Although the Sexual Offences Act (1967) began the process of making homosexuality legal, it remained an offence in the armed forces until the year 2000.[7]

Servicewomen did not fit neatly into the ideal model. Like homosexuality, lesbianism was unacceptable and women suspected of that leaning were dismissed. Married women could serve but marriage placed demands on the system of postings that for decades the Services were not inclined to tackle. They tended to leave without completing the period of years for which they had signed up. While marriage was acceptable, motherhood was deemed incompatible with service as a mother's first duty was regarded as being to her husband and children. Consequently, pregnant women were dismissed and mothers of school-age children were not permitted to join the peacetime Services. This policy ignored earlier experience. Although pregnant women had to leave, mothers had been accepted during the war, notably including mother of three children Commandant Vera Laughton Mathews who was the Director of the WRNS from 1939 to 1946. (*See* Appendix 1 for a list of rank titles and Appendix 2 for names of the Directors of the women's Services).

Dismissal of pregnant women was not exceptional in employment policy in Britain's early post-war period. There was a societal preference for mothers to remain at home rather than going out to work. However, over the following decades, civilian attitudes changed while those of the armed forces did not. Senior officers, women as well as men, clung to the old ways, believing that the armed forces had a right to be different from society. As a result, regular service careers were not only constrained by the non-combatant principle, but also by the exclusion of mothers. By design, a long-term career was for childless women and, consequently, predominantly for single women. Not combatants and not mothers. Today, all roles are open to women: seagoing in warships and submarines, flying all aircraft types in each of the Services and land warfare roles. Women who choose to have a family can do so, while continuing with their careers. This is an account of how the armed forces came to accept that some women, like some men, are motivated to take on the challenges of military life.

Previous histories of women's participation in the armed forces have mostly told the story of one of the Services.[8] A common perspective emerges that women's employment was due to a shortage of men. Also, as recruitment posters sometimes emphasised, by undertaking the more mundane tasks, servicewomen released men for combat roles. These ideas, valid during the two World Wars, have persisted as explanations of the expansion of women's roles in peacetime even as the size of the armed forces declined and the need for recruits reduced. My account of women's path to combat roles suggests a wider range of factors influencing change. By looking at all three Services, I bring out differences and interactions between the armed forces; the relationship of men, as well as women, to combat; contradictions in policy that developed between reserve units and regular forces; social factors affecting retention of personnel, not just recruitment; and the influence of policies adopted by allied nations.

Combat is the essence of armed forces. To be effective, they depend on far more than those personnel who fire weapons. Service personnel have primary roles (e.g. seamen, infantry, aircraft technician) and additional duties (e.g. guard duty). Men's primary duties may not require them to be routinely armed (e.g. sailors, engineers in army repair depots, aircraft technicians). However, the combatant nature of men's employment was underpinned by their obligation in the last resort to take up weapons and face the enemy. Being eligible to carry a weapon did not necessarily imply a person had combatant status. Medical personnel, non-combatant with protected status under the Geneva Conventions, were entitled to be armed in order to defend themselves and their patients.[9]

While men could be unarmed combatants in their daily work or armed non-combatants as medics, the situation in respect of women was dictated by gender. Excluded from seagoing, flying, land warfare and training in the use of small arms (sub-machine guns, rifles, pistols), servicewomen were deemed to be non-combatants because they were women.

Combat roles differ between the armed forces and it is helpful to understand some distinctions. Characteristics of combat roles include responsibility for killing the enemy in direct or close contact (e.g. infantry action or tanks of the armoured corps) or at a distance (e.g. air or naval action); offensive action (seeking out the enemy); and defensive action (including defending a base area and self-defence); risk of death, injury or capture. These latter risks are often shared by populations at large. Each of these characteristics featured in discussions on whether or not to widen women's military roles over the second half of the twentieth century. Over time, exclusion narrowed down to the acceptability or otherwise of women confronting an enemy face-to-face.

The Royal Navy (RN) uses a concept described as 'all of one company'. All members of a ship's company were recognised as sharing risk and all sailors were regarded as being in combat roles, whatever their actual job aboard ship. The WRNS was a shore-based support organisation, separate from the RN, and not under military law until 1977. Opinion of the value of the WRNS veered between releasing men from shore jobs so that they could go to sea (the classic explanation of using men for higher value work), or unhelpfully blocking shore jobs needed to give men respite from seagoing. Rather than necessarily reducing the need for sailors, Wrens were sometimes seen as helpfully lessening the need for hard-to-recruit civilian staff in some areas of the country. Being separate from the RN, the WRNS was vulnerable when cuts had to be made. Its existence was precarious, a factor that played an important part in 1989 when seagoing policy was developed.

The Army has a complex pecking order of regiments and corps according to war fighting roles, compounded by precedence reflecting centuries of Army history. Thus, the Household Division of cavalry and guards regiments remains at the pinnacle. Then come infantry and armoured corps regiments, their position in the order of precedence enshrined in the King's or Queen's Regulations for the Army. Corps such as Royal Signals and Royal Engineers follow on from the combat regiments. In twenty-first century terminology they are called combat support corps. The third category is called combat service support. Although not a term used in the immediate post-war period, this would have embraced the Royal Army Pay Corps, Royal Army Education Corps, etc. There is a sense in which these categories (combat, combat support and combat service support) suggest a differentiation between those actively engaged in battle with a primary purpose of killing the enemy, those who enable effective operations such as signallers or engineers – but who may also be part of operational patrols – and those to the rear of the fight. Irrespective of role, all male soldiers trained in the use of small arms. The complexity of army structure leads to it being described as a 'federated' organisation, leading to inconsistency in how policy is interpreted and implemented, as will become apparent.

Where did women fit into this male hierarchy? As in the Second World War, women were recruited into a gender-based corps. The ATS was renamed the Women's Royal Army Corps (WRAC) in 1949. Unlike Wrens, female soldiers were subject to military law under the Army Act. Whereas men trained for the role of the corps or regiment they joined (e.g. Royal Signals, Royal Army Pay Corps or Royal Corps of Transport), members of the WRAC could train in a variety of trades (e.g. as signallers, clerks or drivers) and then be farmed out to work with other corps according to the needs of the Army. However, female soldiers enjoyed identifying with their employing corps, just as members of the ATS serving in anti-aircraft batteries identified themselves as gunners. In choosing to maintain this hybrid of a gender-based corps operating in parallel with trade-based employment, the War Office created conflict within its systems and for its female soldiers. This was only resolved when the WRAC disbanded in 1992 and women joined their employing corps.

Of all the women's Services, employment of women in the Army had the strongest connection to the availability, or otherwise, of men. It was further constrained by geographic rules on postings. The Army Board decreed that women could only fill a job in peacetime if they could also do it in war. Not wanted in operational theatres due to their lack of combat training, this meant that they were also barred from units in Britain that deployed to such areas on the outbreak of war. These polices were more easily controlled in the regular Service than in the Army's reserve – the Territorial Army – as became apparent in the 1980s and 1990s.

Introduction

The Royal Air Force (RAF) was different from the other Services. From February 1949, women joined the RAF. 'Women's Royal Air Force' (WRAF) was an administrative label, used to determine pay and allowances, accommodation, uniform and postings. However, it retained some of the trappings of organisation inherited from the wartime WAAF. I use the term WRAF as a convenient means of referring to airwomen and because this was the terminology used within the Service. However, readers are asked to bear in mind that most women joined integrated RAF trades from the inception of regular service in 1949.

The Air Ministry embarked on a philosophy of integration of women into ground trades and they came under the Air Force Act in the same way as men. Unlike the gender divide of the other Services, the RAF made a different distinction that also separated the majority of men from its elite core: ground staff versus aircrew. Pecking order of aircrew depended on the type of aircraft flown and also between rear crew and flight deck. Pilots of fighter and ground attack jets (fast jets) were at the top of the pyramid, with higher standing than crews of multi-engine aircraft and helicopters. Within fast jet squadrons, flying single-seat aircraft (crewed only by a pilot rather than also having a navigator, as in other fast jets) afforded the greatest status. This hierarchy proved important in the story of women's encroachment into flying roles, though it took decades for the RAF to catch up with its Volunteer Reserve which had female pilots for a short time in the late 1940s and early 1950s.

During the Cold War, the RAF operated predominantly from fixed bases that could be hundreds of miles away from the enemy's forces. Nevertheless, such bases were vulnerable to attack, from terrorists or an enemy's special forces, as well as air attack. Bases were defended by the RAF Regiment, akin to an army regiment. In the event of an attack, the Regiment could be supplemented by other RAF personnel from ground trades, trained to use small arms. Airmen's potential liability to undertake armed action in defence of their location, and women's exclusion from that task, was the basis for describing ground-based airmen as having a combat liability not shared by airwomen.

With the use of weapons in defence of a base being low in the combat hierarchy, there is a need to differentiate it from other types of combat. I use the term main combat roles to describe land warfare, seagoing and flying roles in order to distinguish them from the use of small arms in defence of a base or self-defence.

The cascade of opening of main combat roles from 1989 has been attributed to wider reasons than the classic 'shortage of men' explanation. However, that demographic feature was still a concern to policymakers because there was a decline in numbers in the late-twentieth-century youth cohort. It was this age group that supplied recruits. Other social factors, such as public attitudes towards gender roles, women's attitudes towards careers, and legislation, have been recognised as contributing to a climate for change. It has also been suggested that views of policymakers of the 1990s were shaped by their own younger days in the 1960s and 1970s, leaving them more open to widening women's participation. In addition, technological advances reduced the reliance on physical strength making it possible for women to do more jobs.[10]

Change was not universally sought or well received where it occurred. Exploration of the interactions between decisions arrived at within the separate Services reveal the tensions. In the 1990s, it was not so much a question of embracing an agenda of equality, rather it was recognition of the quality of female recruits that was an important factor. The key domino to fall – the RN and seagoing – owed much to the Navy's failure to retain its men, the falling standard of male recruits, the persistence of one particular politician and his advisors, and the inability of the Navy to take the piecemeal approach that the RAF had been able to adopt in opening some flying roles to women. Army leadership gave ground slowly in the 1990s opening roles in engineering, flying and the Royal Artillery. It resisted opening infantry and armoured corps' roles, developing a more precise definition of a combat role to justify women's exclusion. Ultimately, the Army Board's position was undermined by operational experience in Iraq and Afghanistan, decisions made in the USA and political pressure in the Ministry of Defence.

This book traces policy developments from unacknowledged participation in combat in the Second World War to the opening of all roles to women. It explains why regular service was offered after the war, the struggle to establish careers, the importance of the decision to train servicewomen in the use of small arms in the late 1970s, why the Royal Navy opened seagoing in warships to women in 1990 and the consequences for the RAF and the Army. It also shows the growing gulf between legislative developments on women's employment rights from the 1970s and armed forces' policies. Unwillingly introducing maternity leave in late 1990, a crack appeared in the armed forces' assertion that they had a right to be different from society. This made a crucial difference to servicewomen who then had the opportunity to continue with their careers or to leave, as they chose. I suggest that widening of employment opportunities for servicewomen also contributed more widely to a changed approach to personnel issues (ethnicity, bullying, sexuality) within the armed forces in the late twentieth century.

There were other women employed in support of the armed forces. Each Service had its own nursing corps – army and naval services date back to the nineteenth century. In addition, in the twentieth century, female officers began to be employed in specialist work under the umbrella title of professionally qualified. For example, these included doctors, dentists and lawyers. They were not part of the women's Services, but joined the same branches as their male colleagues. Their history is not featured in this book.

Unusually for an historical account, I bring the story up to the time of writing (2019) because of the Ministry of Defence's announcement in 2016 that it would open armoured corps and infantry roles to women in 2017 and 2018, respectively. However, that inevitably means there is much less evidence, and so more tentative conclusions, for these later developments. Nor is it possible to judge the success or otherwise of the new policies. Such an assessment must await the passage of time and the writing of an account that focuses less on policy change and implementation, and more on operational experience.

The early chapters rely predominantly on archival sources. Exploration of policy on seagoing, flying, changes to terms and conditions of service for women and the abandonment of separate designation of women in the Services, covers developments in the late 1980s and early 1990s. Even before the thirty-year rule for the release of official files to archives became a twenty-year rule, the Ministry of Defence had a backlog of files awaiting review as to whether they should be retained in the National Archive or destroyed. While most of the events described here occurred more than twenty years ago, only a small number of relevant files tracing the evolution of policies from the 1980s onwards had been made available at the time of writing. In addition to open sources for the period, I have used requests to government departments under the Freedom of Information (FOI) Act (2000) which came into force in 2005, interviews with participants in key events, and with some of the women who seized these new opportunities.

One such interviewee was Catherine Jordan. She joined the Royal Navy in the autumn of 1993 as a university cadet just six weeks before the WRNS disbanded. She was one of the new type of female recruit – women who were committed to serve at sea. Believing that naval flying was more challenging than that on offer with the RAF, she trained as an aviator. In naval parlance, she became an observer, responsible for navigation and operation of weapon systems on Lynx helicopters. She went on to qualify as a principal warfare officer and, subsequently, commanded the frigate HMS *St Albans*. Promoted to captain in 2019, she went on to command the Royal Navy's largest training establishment – HMS *Collingwood*. She is also the mother of three children. This history is about the pathway that enabled this officer, among many others, to fulfil her ambitions.

2

'DOUBTFUL WISDOM'

Announcing the continuation of conscription for men on 30 May 1946, George Isaacs (Minister for Labour and National Service) told the House of Commons that:

> In order to lessen the needs of the Services for men ... [it had] also been decided to continue the WRNS, the ATS and the WAAF on a voluntary basis as permanent features of the Forces of the Crown.[1]

Commandant Vera Laughton Mathews (Director of the WRNS 1939–46) expected 'splash headlines' for what she considered to be a 'revolutionary change', but recollected that 'not a paper gave it a headline'.[2] Actually, Mathews was mistaken. The story did appear on the front page of the *Daily Mail* under a headline 'Plan for Girls', but she had a point about this being a revolutionary change. In introducing peacetime service for women, the British government responded differently from its post-First World War stance when it disbanded women's Services. It was also ahead of allied nations. Australia and Canada initially demobilised their women's Services, then re-established them in the early 1950s. The USA, which had fewer servicewomen than Britain, reduced numbers from 266,000 to 14,000 (approximately 1 per cent of its armed forces) by 1948 when it decided to retain women's corps.[3] Britain made its policy decision in 1946, introduced interim arrangements and brought in regular, peacetime service on 1 February 1949.

Linking the announcement to that of peacetime national service for men pre-empted potential criticism about women no longer being subject to conscription, as they had been during the war. Although young men were seen as being disadvantaged in career terms by the obligation of national service, there was little support for women also being required to serve. However, lessening the need for men was a publicly recognisable justification for women's military service. Women were portrayed during the war as undertaking supporting roles, thereby releasing men for more hazardous duties. This idea was epitomised in wartime recruitment posters, with strap lines such as 'join the Wrens and free a man for the fleet'.[4]

The idea that women served because of shortfalls of men was a standard explanation for policy, contributing to a perception that women's participation was something that required constant justification in the light of the state of male recruitment. Yet the argument for the creation of peacetime careers for women was more complex than simply an assessment of the available work force. Indeed, rather than perceiving women as helpfully reducing the need for men, some senior officers saw them as leading to the loss of an equivalent number of more useful servicemen, as overall numbers of service personnel would be capped. Preferring to revert to an all-volunteer, male Navy, the Admiralty regarded the whole concept of peacetime women's Services as 'doubtful wisdom'.[5] However, War Office and Air Ministry assessments of the strategic situation and wartime lessons learned were to prove crucial in overturning arguments against retaining servicewomen. There was a determination to avoid the mistakes made at the end of the First World War and at the beginning of the Second World War.

The Great War

Women's Services were initially formed during the Great War, the War Office taking the lead in creating the Women's Army Auxiliary Corps (WAAC) in March 1917. It was renamed Queen Mary's Army Auxiliary Corps (QMAAC) in April 1918 to honour its support to the Army in France when the German spring offensive broke through the front line. By the time the last woman was demobilised in September 1921, about 57,000 women had served in the Corps. The WRNS, formed in November 1917, supported the Royal Navy in shore-based jobs. Over the two years of its existence, 7,000 women served in its ranks. On 1 April 1918, the Royal Air Force was created by merging components of the Army's Royal Flying Corps and the Royal Naval Air Service. The WRAF came into being on the same day. Initially, it drew 10,000 women from those already serving in the WRNS or the WAAC. In total, over 32,000 women served in the WRAF between 1918 and 1920.[6]

In losing their jobs after the war, servicewomen shared a fate common to women who had taken up war work. Nevertheless, there was some discussion about whether they should be retained. In drawing up peacetime plans, the Air Ministry considered employing a permanent female component of about 6,000 women. Women had proved adept at a variety of domestic, catering, clerical and telephony duties. More than 1,000 were deployed with the Air Force of Occupation in the Rhineland, based in Cologne. Women continued to be recruited in 1919 to facilitate early demobilisation of men. President of the Air Council John Seely's view was that employing women permanently would be 'in keeping with the spirit of the times' (votes for women over the age of thirty had recently been agreed by Parliament).[7]

Those who favoured keeping the WRAF argued that women were better than men in some jobs and more economical because their pay and allowances were less than men's. A small contingent would provide a nucleus for future expansion, releasing men for fighting units. The case against retaining servicewomen challenged the cost argument as they would need barracks and ablutions for their own use and female doctors would have to be specially employed. Women could not be held to a set length of service, as men were, due to factors such as marriage and pregnancy. There was no precedent for women as permanent members of fighting forces and Parliament would probably not approve. As the peacetime RAF would be significantly smaller, every member needed to be combatant; women were not deemed to be combatant. As for the idea of the WRAF being a nucleus for expansion, another war of the magnitude of the Great War was 'not likely to recur', so there would be no such requirement.[8]

This Air Ministry debate from 1919 encapsulates arguments that would feature again in policy discussions.

There is no clear record of why the Air Ministry dropped the proposal. However, the War Office and the Admiralty were opposed to permanently losing control of air power. In 1919, they made accusations of financial extravagance against the Air Ministry in a bid to undermine it. A women's section in peacetime would probably have been regarded as proof of a lack of prudence.

Nevertheless, the War Office took the lead in exploring whether women could make some contribution in the future. It established a committee, with wide-ranging membership, to explore the potential for a reserve organisation for women. The need for a reserve hinged on how quickly women might be needed in a future war or whether there would be sufficient time to regenerate forces at the time. Reserve organisations would entail costs for uniforms, equipment and training staff. To enable call-up to service to be enforced, women would need to be enlisted under military law rather than having the lesser status of being enrolled as they had been in the war. For female officers, this would mean they would hold the King's commission and so have the same status as male officers, an idea that seemed ridiculous at the time.

Leaders of the wartime female Services – Dame Katherine Furse, WRNS; Dame Florence Leach, QMAAC; and Dame Helen Gwynne-Vaughan, WRAF – who were members of the committee, argued for a reserve on the basis that it would avoid 'the expensive experiments and delays involved in the improvisation of a corps of women'. They urged the need for officers and non-commissioned officers to be trained. The committee's report suggested that readiness on mobilisation could 'best be assured by the formation of a reserve in peace' but its associated costs would have to be justified in competition with 'other services of a more immediate and effective nature'.[9]

The views of Army Council members were divided. Lieutenant General Sir George Macdonogh (Adjutant General – head of personnel) was in favour. Lieutenant General Sir Travers Clarke (Quartermaster General – supplies, logistics and accommodation) was opposed due to the cost. Lieutenant Colonel The Honourable G. F. Stanley (Secretary for Finance) perceived the thin end of a wedge, fearing that enlisting women would lead to demands for equality. In June 1921, the Council decided a Reserve was 'not desirable at the present time, but that it would suffice to draft a scheme embodying the experience gained in the war'.[10]

The Army Council decision was in keeping with post-war defence policy, which was based on an expectation of a ten-year warning period before any future major war. Meanwhile, regular services were expected to suffice. Funding of men's reserves was reduced, the intention being to expand these auxiliary forces in response to a crisis. In this climate of budget cuts, new reserve organisations for women would have needed more whole-hearted support than they received.

The Second World War

Hopes that war on the scale of the conflict of 1914–18 would not occur again were dashed. The need to reconstitute women's Services was acted upon in 1938. Based on the territorial system for men, the War Office created the ATS for women in September of that year. Rather than setting up its own separate scheme, the Air Ministry was initially content for companies in support of the RAF to be part of the ATS. The WAAF was formed in June 1939 when these companies transferred to Air Ministry control. Initially the Admiralty was reluctant to follow the example of the other Services, believing that it could attract enough women once hostilities started. However, fearing that it was losing the best candidates to the other Services, the Admiralty re-established the WRNS in April 1939.

The year's start on preparations proved inadequate. Across the Services, there was a lack of clarity about where women were to be employed and in what roles, inadequate training facilities, lack of uniforms and unsuitable accommodation. Military administration depended on regulations but, being incomplete, these had not been issued. As the official history of the ATS described the situation in 1939:

> although in some cases the standard was extremely high, more often the ATS were pushed into [any accommodation] that could be obtained. The conditions, especially in the more scattered parties, had to be seen to be believed, disused stables, condemned cottages, village halls with no sanitation, and under canvas with outdoor cookers exposed to every weather and in muddy fields miles away from civilization and hot water.[11]

To which one might say, well that's Army life. But these conditions were compounded by the lack of uniforms and equipment, also deficient due to the absence of regulations. Women depended on the goodwill of the local quartermaster. If he was hidebound to his regulations, then women had to find their own bedding to go with the issued straw mattresses. Some ATS companies depended upon what their own officers could buy, and women sometimes provided their own crockery.

The WAAF and the WRNS experienced similar struggles, compounded in the case of the Wrens by having been declared in an Admiralty Order to be under the control of the civilian establishment rather than the Navy's personnel area in 1939. In her memoir, Commandant Mathews felt that the Wrens had been dumped on the civilian branch and there was no sympathy for her Service's naval aspirations. In practical terms, nobody had responsibility for the provision of uniforms. Eventually Admiral Sir Geoffrey Arbuthnot (Fourth Sea Lord – Chief of Naval Supplies) intervened, ordering that uniforms were to be issued. Lack of uniform was remembered with much amusement by former Chief Officer May Bell Davies, recollecting a visit by King George to Portsmouth in 1940:

> I think we had about 300 Wrens by then, with only a quarter kitted up. We scratched our heads, and with the Commodore's permission drew them up in two lines, the fully kitted ones in front, and the ones

in mackintoshes and hats in the rear lines. We prayed for at any rate a cloudy day, but it was a hot day of brilliant sunshine. His Majesty was much amused, though a little horrified that the uniforms were taking so long to appear.[12]

One of the biggest problems in establishing hierarchical organisations from a standing start was the absence of experienced women to fill officer and non-commissioned officer (NCO) posts. The first to tackle the problem was the ATS. No women could be recruited into its companies until female officers had been appointed, but:

> The number of capable women able and willing to give up the necessary time in peace without having even their expenses paid was limited, particularly when they had to undertake to give full-time service in the event of war. In some cases, County Commandants were forced to nominate officers whom they knew to be unsuitable because there was no-one else who would take the job. ... the probable duties of an ATS officer at that time were vague, yet the War Office and [Territorial -Army] Associations were both insistent that establishments should be filled as soon as possible.[13]

The key problem was not so much that these women were appointed in 1938 but that there was no subsequent mechanism for dismissing those who turned out to be incompetent.

Ignoring the advice contained in Air Ministry and War Office files from 1919/20, servicewomen were again enrolled rather than enlisted for the duration of the emergency. Consequently, the full powers of military law did not apply, and discipline was underpinned by a voluntary statement that women would accept punishment for misdemeanours. As their terms were effectively those of civilians, the military authorities had no power to prevent women from leaving. Faced with the muddle of the early stages of the war, many thousands returned home or took different jobs. Ten per cent of ATS women left in the first five months of 1940. The WAAF reported a loss of 27 per cent of its recruits from September 1939 to May 1940. It was difficult to distinguish how many women simply walked away from their jobs as many cases were simply recorded as 'compassionate discharge'.[14] The Official History of the WRNS, produced in 1956, recorded figures from December 1940 to March 1941: 37 women were said to have 'deserted', a term commonly used by naval authorities even though the offence did not exist for Wrens as they were not under military law, 164 left on compassionate grounds, 112 at their own request and 285 were discharged during a two-week probationary period for WRNS recruits.[15]

The ATS and WAAF were brought under military law in April 1941. In part, this move was expected to stem this outflow of women because now, as deserters, they could be arrested. Leaving at their own request would have to be on compassionate grounds only. Military law was also seen as necessary because of the intent to introduce conscription for women, ultimately introduced in March 1942. Women pressed into service were expected to be of lower personal standards of behaviour and less willing to accept the constraints of Service life than volunteers. Accordingly, a legal basis for discipline was deemed essential. More positively, military status was seen as paving the way for women's operational employment. Despite the best efforts of Commandant Mathews, the WRNS remained on civilian terms as the Admiralty still expected to meet its needs through voluntary recruitment and it saw no need to bring the Service under the Naval Discipline Act.

Despite the shortcomings of the early years, the reliance on women's contribution grew. In the WRNS, officers could join 47 branches and ratings 81 'categories' of work over the period 1939 to 1945, compared with 10 and 21 respectively in the First World War.[16] In addition to domestic and clerical work, roles included technical duties at unskilled or semi-skilled levels, operator work for new technologies such as radar, and keyboard work of all descriptions. The Command at Plymouth initiated employment of women as crew for harbour craft. Duties included transferring personnel and mail between the shore and ships at anchor, as well as the maintenance of the boats. This role was favoured in publicity campaigns, although only a small proportion of Wrens were employed as boat crew.

Female officers with degrees in scientific or mathematical disciplines could work on weapons trials and train submarine crews in torpedo attack. About 26 per cent of officers were employed on cipher duties, maintaining confidential books, and coding and decoding signals. A few served in troop ships crossing the Atlantic, as did some female ratings (a generic term for naval non-commissioned personnel) who worked as shorthand typists.[17] In 1944, the WRNS reached its peak of 73,500 women, 8.5 per cent of total naval forces' strength (see Figures 2.1 and 2.2, page 32, for comparative strengths of the Services).

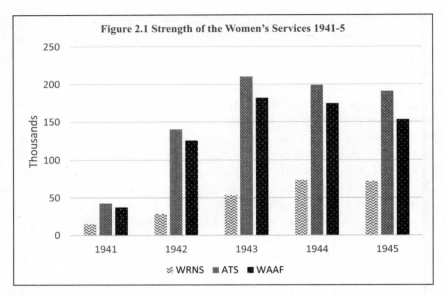

Source: At 30 June. *Annual Abstract of Statistics*, Vol. 88 (1938 – 1950), (London: HMSO, 1951), Table 125.

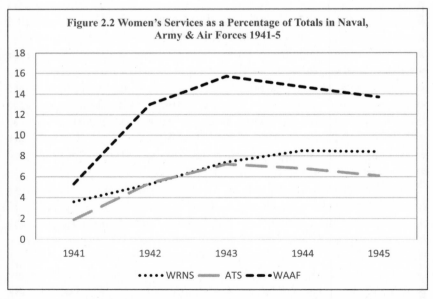

Source: At 30 June. *Annual Abstract of Statistics*, Vol. 88 (1938 – 1950), (London: HMSO, 1951), Table 125.

In the WAAF, women could join 23 branches for officers and 93 trades for non-commissioned ranks between 1939 and 1945, compared with 5 and 53 respectively between 1918 and 1920.[18] Airwomen served on operational stations alongside men. Like the WRNS, they were employed in domestic, clerical and operator trades. In engineering, some roles were initially reduced in scope so that women could undertake part of the work. However, where they proved their competence, some sub-divisions of trades were dropped and women undertook the full roles. Examples included engine flight mechanics, electricians and instrument repairers. If there were perceived shortcomings in women's ability to sustain long hours or heavy work, more women might be employed than if the task was undertaken by men. Barrage Balloon Squadrons were a case in point where twelve women were used in place of nine men. This was known as a substitution ratio. Likewise, the overall number of women that could be employed in any trade was limited to ensure that enough men were available to meet the needs of operational deployments from which women were excluded or if the trade included heavy work.[19] This was called the dilution factor. The WAAF recorded its greatest strength in 1943 as 181,800 (15.7 per cent of total air force strength).

Although the Air Force relied on the greatest percentage of women, unsurprisingly the Army employed the most. In mid-1943, the official history recorded 5,785 officers and 204,523 other ranks (just over 7 per cent of Army strength). By that date, 113 employment categories were open to women. About half of the officers served in ATS specific roles, while the others undertook duties in air defence, signals, the Royal Army Service Corps, Royal Army Ordnance Corps, the Royal Electrical and Mechanical Engineers and the Intelligence Corps. Work with anti-aircraft artillery batteries was the most controversial.

Women mostly served in the United Kingdom but as the war progressed, servicewomen were posted away from the UK. In the WRNS, women under the age of nineteen were permitted to serve close to where they lived. About one-third were serving on these 'immobile' terms in late 1942. On the outbreak of war, the ATS closed its local service scheme, which it had operated as a reserve organisation. Members of the ATS and WAAF were required to serve where sent. Women also served overseas, though the initial requirement was met by enrolling women locally. The naval authorities sent a first draft of Wrens to Singapore in January 1941.[20] Initially voluntary, compulsory liability for overseas drafting was introduced for Wrens aged over twenty in November 1943.[21]

Although airwomen could be posted to bases overseas, the Director of the WAAF did not press the issue. Such postings were agreed 'when the shortage of manpower in certain trades or branches made it virtually essential'. Air Ministry authorities foresaw difficulties such as 'the possible effect of climatic conditions, the concern of parents, ... security, both physical and psychological, the provision of special kit, ... accommodation in troopships, medical arrangements and living conditions.'[22] Initially, small numbers of officers were sent to the USA or countries in the Dominions and, from July 1942, to the Middle East. Airwomen enrolled in the UK served overseas only from 1944. Compulsory service abroad was avoided as the requirement was met through volunteers. Fewer than 9,000 members of the WAAF served abroad during the war.

The ATS sent a contingent to the Middle East in the autumn of 1941. By December 1943 there were about 5,000 women in the Command of whom 80 per cent had been locally recruited. Women were deployed to France in July 1944. By the end of the year there were five mixed anti-aircraft artillery regiments deployed in Belgium because of their experience against flying bombs. By June 1945 there were nearly 400 ATS officers and over 9,000 non-commissioned women in north-west Europe.[23]

Violet Markham and the Assheton Committee

Violet Markham (1872–1959), a life-long contributor to public service in a number of capacities, was an enthusiastic supporter of the women's auxiliary services. Her initial involvement came in the First World War when she was secretary to a committee of inquiry into stories of gross immorality among members of the WAAC serving in France. She observed that 'the scavengers in rumours' dustbin found women in uniform an easy target for gossip'. When the same fears surfaced in the early years of the Second World War, she was again called upon to investigate conditions in the women's Services. this time chairing the committee of inquiry. In her autobiography, again with a vivid turn of phrase, she recorded that 'There were whispers of gross immorality and of hospitals compelled to add as many wings as those of the Seraphim to cope with illegitimate births.'[24] The investigation revealed no such cause for alarm. Indeed, Markham found that pregnancy among unmarried servicewomen was less prevalent than in the equivalent age group of the civilian population.

Going beyond her terms of reference, Markham suggested servicewomen would be needed after the end of hostilities to assist with the forces of occupation in Continental Europe. While she thought that the 'Army [was] very unlikely in the future to provide a permanent career for women', she proposed women should be employed in the task of reconstructing liberated or occupied countries, making use of skills developed in the war.[25] Although she acknowledged that many women would want to return to civilian life, she thought there would be great interest in this outlet for further service. Perhaps she was in a good position to offer such advice as she had accompanied her husband to Cologne in 1919 when he was appointed as Chief Demobilisation Officer for the Army on the Rhine. She spent over a year in Germany.

Markham's recommendation prompted a further study, led by Ralph Assheton, the Financial Secretary to the Treasury. He was asked to consider the future of the women's Services, not just the scope for their employment in post-war reconstruction. Assheton's work came too early for the Service Ministries to have any clear idea on future policy.

The Admiralty saw 'no room for any permanent organisation comparable to the existing WRNS'. It wanted to re-establish the pre-war pattern of men's postings which rotated between shore-based jobs in the UK, ships in UK waters, or foreign service. Not being allowed to go to sea, women would mostly fill UK shore jobs. The Admiralty argued that every woman would mean one less man available for ships in an emergency. At most, it might want a small permanently employed nucleus of women to organise and train a larger reserve. The War Office declined to say what it wanted in the absence of information on its budget, whether compulsory service for men would feature in peacetime, what form the Territorial Army would take and the number of regular servicemen it was to be allowed. Echoing views from 1919, it thought 'even a nucleus [of women] for further expansion might need to be dropped in favour of other prior claims'. If it had enough money it might ask for a permanent nucleus of women and a reserve. The RAF was thought to be different because women worked alongside men on operational stations. As in its 1919 deliberations, the Air Ministry thought it 'very desirable' to have a regular women's Service. If money was tight, though, it too would opt for a nucleus of employed women plus reservists.[26]

The Directors of the WRNS, ATS and WAAF did not serve on the committee but were called to give evidence. Unsurprisingly, they championed the cause of continuing service. Less constrained by their departmental lines urging caution on budgets and numbers, they assured the committee that many women hoped that permanent careers would be offered. They stressed the need for peacetime organisations as a means of facilitating wartime expansion. Air Commandant Jane Trefusis-Forbes (Director WAAF 1939–43) argued that women should be employed in a wide range of work in order to maintain the trust of the RAF in women's capacity to undertake technical work. Permanent cadres of women would be a more effective nucleus for future expansion than reserve organisations if the need arose.[27]

Ralph Assheton sided with the caution expressed by the Service Ministries. He concluded that all three Services would need to employ women in a future major war and observed that nobody wanted to contemplate 'the delays and difficulties experienced at the start of the present war, which would be bound to recur if the women's Services had to be started from scratch'.[28] However, he thought it was too soon to take decisions. Future policy would need to be formulated in the context of restructuring the armed forces for peace, taking budgets into account. Nevertheless, a step forward could be made by announcing that women would participate in post-war reconstruction roles as suggested by Violet Markham. Accordingly, in July 1943, Prime Minister Winston Churchill announced in the House of Commons that women's auxiliary Services would be needed 'for some time after hostilities [had] ceased ... to accompany Forces of Occupation'.[29] Work passed to post-war planning committees.

Planning for the Post-Second World War Era

As in 1919, there were competing arguments in the Air Ministry over the future of the WAAF. Those in favour of regular service for women argued the need to organise in peace on the pattern required in a major war. Women had proved themselves capable of a wide range of duties and were considered better than men in some. Thus, the argument went, there would be an efficiency gain in employing women. Proponents also urged that airwomen would expect the opportunity of regular service. They suggested there was a risk of being unable to recruit sufficient men of the required quality to sustain an Air Force expected to be three times the size of the pre-war force after demobilisation.

The case against regular servicewomen was also argued on the basis of wartime experience: problems of administration, training and accommodation; the high wastage rate through women leaving after marriage; limitations on overseas posting; airwomen not undertaking the full range of work done by men; and the potential for resentment by men of working for women, which was accepted under war conditions but was a potential source of friction in peace. The difficulty of finding sufficient women for NCO and officer ranks was a major objection.[30]

Drawing on reports from various RAF Commands, the Air Ministry's evidence to the Royal Commission on Equal Pay (1943 to 1946) cautioned that wartime experience should not be generalised. Women in sedentary jobs were said to benefit from comparisons with men of 'very inferior quality to the male personnel who would be employed in peacetime'.[31] Women were perceived to perform better than men in code and cipher duties, as telephonists, fabric workers, clerks, waitresses and nursing orderlies. However, this work was described as mundane. Men were said to need more stimulating work to show their talents. Compared with men, women were reportedly more prone to sickness and absenteeism, less likely to exercise authority or initiative, or to take responsibility. While men's poor performance was attributed to the intrinsic nature of the job, for women it was perceptions of personal failings that were to the fore.

In early 1945, there was strong opposition to retention of airwomen. Air Marshal Sutton, in his final weeks as Air Member for Personnel (AMP), urged colleagues to bear in mind the financial implications of the high turnover of women compared with men. Rather than women lessening the need for men, he feared that employing women would entail the 'loss of the equivalent number of highly trained airmen'. The post-war planning committee, chaired by Air Chief Marshal Sir Douglas Evill (Vice Chief of the Air Staff), shared Sutton's views. Emphasising costs, difficulties in obtaining female officers and NCOs, the loss of men who would be 'most urgently required as basis for expansion in a future emergency' and potential legal and disciplinary difficulties, the committee assumed that there would be no regular WAAF. Such a force would only conceivably be necessary if it proved impossible to recruit enough men, however, 'this possibility could be disregarded for the time being'. The committee concluded that only a women's reserve force would be needed.[32]

Air Marshal Sutton was replaced in March 1945 by Air Marshal Sir John Slessor, a future Chief of the Air Staff. Slessor disagreed with his predecessor, suggesting that 'the WAAF was very largely ineffective during the first year of the war because it had no foundation of experience, organisation or training'. Regular service would be needed to provide a core of women in appropriate trades around which future mobilisation could be built. In addition, regular servicewomen would be needed for administration, organisation and training of reservists. He dismissed financial objections by arguing that, while 'women might not do as much as men and they might cost more than men', but that '[was] not the point'. He elaborated that '... in any future war a substantial proportion of the Service [would] consist of women (which no one contests)' and that the RAF should be organised in peace 'to prevent war not merely to win it in the third or fourth year'.[33]

There was still opposition at the Air Council to the concept of regular service for women and, as the policy would have implications for the Army and the Navy, the matter would need to go to the Cabinet for approval. As an interim measure, it decided to create an extended service scheme for the WAAF, pending a decision about peacetime service. Slessor was directed to consult Army and Navy opinion on commissioning a study into the long-term need for servicewomen.[34]

The Army Council's thinking was ahead of the Air Ministry's. By the beginning of 1944, the War Office's post-war problems committee came down in favour of a regular corps of women as a nucleus for wartime expansion and a reserve to provide trained women for future mobilisation. The argument in 1944 was based on operational need in a future war. Setting aside financial considerations, it proposed a regular cadre of 2,000 and a reserve of 10,000.[35] There was still some reluctance at the Army Council, which was concerned about the cost of a women's corps in the light of women being less employable than men. However, when the case was put to the Executive Committee of the Army Council in August 1945, the analysis had developed two distinct strands. First, and deemed uncontroversial, was the need to be prepared for a future war. The reliance on women in wartime was seen as obvious. The suggested figures for the nucleus were now 3,000 regular servicewomen and a reserve of 16,000. Women would be trained and employed in jobs that did not directly relate to civilian employment, with significant numbers in work for the Royal Signals and the Royal Army Ordnance Corps. It was assumed that women for so-called easy trades (clerks, cooks and orderlies) would be recruited when needed from civilian life where they would have acquired the necessary skills. Second, and described as more controversial, was the idea that women should be employed because of a shortage of men.[36]

Planning figures fluctuated wildly. At one point the need for 30,000 women was suggested as fears grew that the Army would not attract sufficient male volunteers and that, if conscription was retained, the period men served might not be adequate. Then doubts about the ability to recruit enough women of the necessary quality resulted in a more realistic figure of 15,000. Once budget constraints were considered, then men were seen as offering better value for money than women because they could do the full range of work and could be sent anywhere in the world. Self-imposed limits on where women could serve implied that they were less useful than men. The Army Council decided to accept the need for peacetime service but deferred a decision on numbers.[37] When the Air Ministry proposed a further study, the War Office rejected the approach because its plans were more advanced. It intended seeking government approval to employ regular servicewomen rather than delay by commissioning further investigation.[38]

Meanwhile, the Admiralty was reluctant to commit to keeping the WRNS and welcomed the idea of a further study.[39] At a time of great uncertainty concerning its budget, the number of men it was to be allowed, the value for money of employing Wrens, and the potential for the Royal Commission on Equal Pay to increase women's pay, the Board was not ready to make a decision. Officials seemed lukewarm about women's contribution. In evidence given to the Royal Commission, the Admiralty's assessment of Wrens was expressed in damning terms as being up to 25 per cent less effective than men in most trades and never more than 10 per cent superior where they were deemed to perform better. While the derivation of these percentages was not explained, inferiority was attributed to:

> lack of physical strength and inability to stand up to prolonged strain, ... inferior mechanical aptitude, lower capacity for the application of knowledge, inclination to get flustered in emergency and more easily discouraged when up against difficulties; lack of capacity for improvisation; unwillingness to accept responsibility and inability to exercise authority.[40]

Given this judgement, it was not surprising that the Admiralty resisted the continued employment of women – although the evidence to the Commission may have been chiefly intended to highlight differences in roles, responsibilities and output to undermine any case for equal pay. During the war, servicewomen were paid two-thirds of the rates for single servicemen.

In December 1945, with projected budgets being less than anticipated, the Admiralty Board asked planning staff to look into completely demobilising the WRNS by 31 March 1947.[41] However, three months later the personnel department's perception of women's utility was veering away from the stance that they blocked shore appointments towards the idea that they released men for higher value work at sea. Rear Admiral Denny, the Assistant Chief of Naval Personnel, wrote to Admiral of the Fleet Viscount Cunningham (First Sea Lord – professional head of the Royal Navy) arguing that there could be an advantage in using women in shore-based jobs to avoid men having too much time ashore compared with time at sea.[42]

Deciding on Peacetime Service

With War Office plans already advanced, the delaying device of a further study was dropped. Air Marshal Slessor recommended regular service for women in a paper for the Air Council in January 1946. He made two key points. First, he cautioned against a peacetime organisation which lacked a necessary wartime component in case the government of the day failed, or was unable, to give the go-ahead to correct the deficiency before a war started. Second, by now Slessor doubted the RAF could obtain enough men in peacetime for an Air Force expected to be about 300,000 strong. Addressing objections that insufficient women were capable of exercising authority in NCO and officer ranks, he proposed long service as a means of developing women's skills. Rather than questioning women's ability to fill more senior ranks, he turned this objection into a reason for employing regular servicewomen. As he saw it, women would gain experience over a career in the same way as men, rather than being plucked from civilian life and dropped into senior roles in an emergency. He also saw women continuing to work alongside men as a means of overcoming the potential for prejudice. Working with women was to become a 'natural incident of service life'.[43]

At the Air Council meeting, Marshal of the Royal Air Force Lord Tedder (Chief of the Air Staff from the beginning of 1946) supported Slessor's case. He argued, 'In the event of another war, we might not have a year's grace which we had at the beginning of the last war.' Also in favour, Lord Henderson (a government whip in the House of Lords) suggested that 'the public was now attuned to the idea of women in the Services.' Sir William Brown (Permanent Under-Secretary) raised concern about the financial implications. He doubted that peacetime service would appeal to women.[44] His was now a minority view. Slessor's recommendation was agreed.

While the Air Council made its case for a 10,000-strong women's Service to be employed in as wide a range of duties as possible and the War Office wanted to employ at least a nucleus of 3,000 servicewomen, the Admiralty Board still thought of doing without the WRNS.[45] The First Lord of the Admiralty, A. V. Alexander, was known to be an admirer of naval traditions, so it is no surprise that he sided with the senior admirals and thought that it was 'doubtful wisdom to attempt to maintain active Women's Services in peacetime'.[46] He acknowledged that if the others retained servicewomen, there would be strong pressure on the Admiralty to adopt the same policy, but he believed the Cabinet would reject the idea. He complained about the pressure to make a decision before the outcome of the Royal Commission on Equal Pay was known. However, a rough estimate provided for the Board suggested that even if equal pay was introduced, women would still be marginally cheaper to employ than men primarily due to women's lesser entitlement to allowances.[47]

In March 1946, General Lord Ismay (Ministry of Defence) advised Prime Minister Clement Attlee that a decision on the women's Services was urgently needed. With the War Office and the Air Ministry ready to proceed, Ismay informed Attlee that they had been 'unable to get the Admiralty to make up their minds'.[48] Attlee put pressure on the Admiralty through the Defence Committee, bringing the matter to a head.[49] Alexander remained reluctant to keep the WRNS, complaining that Wrens were not as productive as men and attracted additional costs for women's accommodation. He argued that the Admiralty 'should not be too ready to follow the other Services in this matter'.[50]

Alexander was on an official visit to India when the issue needed a decision at the Admiralty Board. In his absence, the Board concluded that a reserve, without a regular component, would not provide the basis for expansion in a future war. It recommended to him that the Navy should keep the WRNS, with a permanent nucleus of up to 5,000 women and a reserve.[51] Although not fully convinced, Alexander conceded. The Admiralty put its name, alongside the War Office and the Air Ministry, to the proposal to create regular service for women.

Alexander's opinion that the idea would be rejected at Cabinet was ill-founded. The paper that went to the Defence Committee set out the case in terms of preparation for a future war, with a nucleus of regular servicewomen and reserve organisations. It suggested a WRNS of 2–3,000, or possibly 5–6,000, an army contingent of at least 3,000 and an air force component of 8,000. The extent to which women could be employed as a means of lessening the need for men was a supplementary factor requiring more work.[52] The Committee accepted the proposals, though James Chuter Ede (Home Secretary) was concerned that the armed forces would take women that he wanted to have available for home defence plans.

The minutes recorded a desire for servicewomen to be trained in roles such as typing, bookkeeping and domestic trades which the Committee deemed would be useful when the women returned to civilian life. Acknowledging that the Services might want to employ more women than proposed as the cores for expansion in war, the Defence Committee concluded that 'Subject to consultation with the Treasury, [the Services' Ministries could] recruit as many women as could usefully be employed in substitution for men.'[53]

Conclusion

The optimism of 1919 that the Great War would be the last such conflict was absent in the immediate aftermath of the Second World War. The Chiefs of the armed forces accepted that a future major war was possible. It was common ground that servicewomen would be needed in such a conflict. The question to be resolved was how to prepare for that eventuality. Would reserve forces be adequate or was there merit in maintaining regular cadres? The War Office was the first to reach a position that peacetime service was needed. It initially derived its stance from an assessment of the need to be ready for a major war. As doubts grew about the ability to recruit enough male volunteers, and fears over an inadequate period of conscription developed, so the secondary argument of women lessening the need for men emerged.

It is likely that the Air Ministry would have reviewed its 1945 decision not to retain the WAAF in peacetime once the War Office's plans became known. However, it arrived at the same policy through the intervention of Air Marshal Slessor who overturned Air Marshals Sutton and Evill's preference for a reserve only. Slessor's main argument was based on the need for all components of the RAF to be ready at the start of hostilities and lessons of the early war years' problems in creating women's corps from scratch. Military need overcame residual objections concerning lack of value for money. As the challenge of maintaining the size of the RAF became clearer, lessening the need for men was an additional argument in favour of employing women.

But the Admiralty was reluctant. It had been less reliant on women during the war. Being smaller than the other two Services, it was confident that it could sustain its peacetime strength through voluntary male recruitment. It was a matter of judgement as to whether women released men for sea duty or blocked the shore jobs needed to give men respite tours of duty. In the end, the dithering A. V. Alexander was put under pressure to approve the joint paper for the Cabinet Defence Committee.

As with national service, it went along with the other Services, although it would have preferred to revert to an all-male, volunteer Royal Navy.

Analysis in the Service Ministries and in the paper for the Defence Committee emphasised the need to prepare for a future major war. Making the announcement in the context of continuing conscription for men, Clement Attlee gave prominence to servicewomen lessening the need for men rather than the need to be prepared for the next war. With varying degrees of optimism, each of the Directors of the women's Services at the end of the war – Commandant Vera Laughton Mathews WRNS, Chief Controller Leslie Whateley ATS and Air Chief Commandant Lady Welsh WAAF – hoped that peacetime service would be established. They had little influence in the decision-making process other than in reassuring their superiors that enough servicewomen wanted the opportunity to make the idea viable. Once the decision was made, they and their successors made important contributions in determining what careers for women in the regular armed forces would look like.

3

NO 'LITTLE OLGAS'

Announcing peacetime service for women in May 1946 was the easy part. Deciding what a military career for women would entail was more difficult. Although urged on by senior female officers, it took nearly three years for the Service Ministries to resolve issues on organisation, status, titles and employment – or more importantly for women's prospects, exclusions from the essential military functions of land warfare, seagoing, flying and training in the use of small arms. The common founding principle was that women would be regarded as non-combatants. For more than thirty years, this principle would govern servicewomen's careers, as would organisational and military environment factors that led to very different philosophies on women's employment between the three Services.

The starting point for policymakers was the positions women occupied at the end of the war. But what was acceptable for permanent employment as opposed to roles carried out for the duration of the war? Should women still have operational jobs? Could they undertake the full duties where wartime practice had been to split trades into smaller component parts? Was it acceptable for men to work for women in peacetime? Where were women to fit in the mix of regular servicemen, national servicemen and civilian workers?

Against a backdrop of demobilisation, forces of occupation in Germany and Austria, policing the Empire, the start of the Cold War and shortages of adequate male recruits, the Service Ministries' aspirations for women's employment grew. By December 1948, target strengths were 26,000 for the WRAF, 18,000 for the WRAC and 7,500 for the WRNS.[1] However, the wartime legacy was being squandered. Women were leaving in droves (*see* Figure 3.1), in part because they had done their bit and wanted to return to civilian life, partly due to better opportunities in civilian work, but also because of uncertainty about what a future in the Services would offer. While strength still exceeded the original 1946 targets, by the start of regular service in February 1949 each Service was well below the new figures being touted within the Defence Ministries.

Extended service schemes were introduced from November 1946 to stem the outflow of women and appeals to rejoin were made to those who had already left. Playing on the uncertainties of settling back into civilian life, with its tribulations of obtaining the necessities of life as rationing bit deeper in the immediate post-war years, Air Commandant Felicity Hanbury (Director of the WAAF from 1946) wrote to former airwomen:

> The WAAF has a great future which will be established upon the traditions we all helped to build in wartime. As soon as legislation can be introduced, it will be re-formed on a regular basis, moving forward with the Royal Air Force and sharing in its plans ... to train, house, clothe and feed its members under the finest conditions possible. ... We need ...trained and enthusiastic women to whom the job well done, the spirit of fellowship and the orderly life appeal ... If you wish for a career, as interesting and worthwhile as any civilian occupation, the Extended Service Scheme gives you the best possible chance of doing so, for you will be able to apply in due course to transfer to the permanent WAAF.[2]

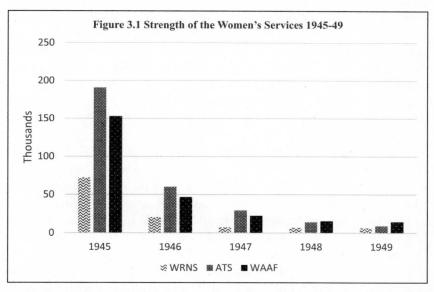

Figure 3.1 Strength of the Women's Services 1945-49

Source: At 30 June. *Annual Abstract of Statistics*, Vol.88 (1938-1950), (London: HMSO, 1951), Table 125.

The offer failed to impress one recipient. She sent the letter back with one word scrawled across it in large letters – 'NUTS!!' [original emphasis]. Hanbury's general promises needed to be backed up by firm details if women were to commit to new careers.

Organisation and Status

The organisation of women's regular service was of fundamental importance to what followed. It determined how women were to be regarded and, over the years, it shaped women's perceptions of where they fitted into their respective Services. It also set the parameters within which senior women officers operated and the extent of their influence over policies. Wartime legacy influenced decisions.

Enthusiastic about the contribution that women could make and determined that women and men would be interchangeable in approved work, the Air Ministry intended the RAF to be integrated. Rather than persisting with its separate organisation, women were to be attested (swearing an oath of allegiance) or commissioned into the RAF. They would come under the Air Force Act, with modifications to clauses only where deemed essential. With the same commissions as men, female officers would exercise powers of command over men and women alike. There would initially be some limits to this integration. Discipline, welfare and basic training were seen as issues that should come under the jurisdiction of female officers. Also, senior women would be needed to advise Air Ministry and RAF Headquarters' staff on matters affecting women. Thus, it was necessary to retain a senior female officer appointment – the Director – established at the one-star rank of air commandant. She would have a small staff to support her work, the duty to visit women wherever they were stationed and the right of direct access to members of the Air Force Board, a privilege not normally extended to a one-star officer.[3]

The Admiralty's solution was at the opposite end of the spectrum. It was content to let the WRNS continue as it was – a self-contained entity, officially described as 'an integral part of the naval organisation'.[4] Military status and the disciplinary code were more contentious issues, as they had been in the war. Commandant Mathews, Director WRNS, had argued since 1940 that women should be brought under the Naval Discipline Act (NDA). Her case was that women replaced men and worked alongside men who came under military law; men and women committing an offence jointly were subject to different procedures; some women were engaged in secret work and work verging on combatant; and wartime numbers were vastly greater than originally envisaged and so greater disciplinary powers were needed. With the introduction of conscription for women, she again urged the case, saying that the voluntary code of conduct would be at risk with women being recruited from 'all classes' and so 'the same standard of good behaviour [could] not be relied upon'. She saw status under the NDA as a boost to efficiency and morale. However, Sir Henry Markham (Permanent Under-Secretary at the Admiralty) regarded 'the idea of extending their Lordships' commission to WRNS officers [as] distasteful.' The Admiralty Board sided with him.[5]

Mathews continued to battle, spurred on by the difference in standing between her Service and the others. She tried again in 1942, without support. In 1944 she added new considerations, the most important of which were the spectre of large numbers of Wrens leaving the Service as their husbands returned from overseas and the difficulty of controlling demobilisation without the threat of charges under military law. She now had support from some major naval Commands who were likewise concerned about what they called desertion. However, the Admiralty still regarded the NDA as unnecessary, that it probably would not solve the problems Mathews raised and its introduction would create a lot of paperwork.[6]

The formation of the peacetime service provided an opportunity to review the policy. In 1946, Mr Samuel (Head of Naval Law) favoured the introduction of the NDA for women, not because the WRNS could not continue to be run as before, but on the grounds that it would be 'the correct status for a body which [was] an integral part of the Navy'.[7] Nevertheless, the Admiralty Board declined this legal advice. Yet again, it cited the standing of the WRNS in public opinion as the best of the women's Services. With the smaller number of women required in peacetime, it would be able to select the best volunteers. As a consequence, good discipline did not require the safeguard of law.[8]

While this reasoning became the official explanation, there were other considerations. First, the NDA was thought to be harsh compared to the Air Force Act and the Army Act because it was written with the maintenance of discipline at sea as its essence. As women were not to serve at sea, much of it would not be applicable. Second, it was suggested that Wrens might leave the Service rather than accept this more stringent disciplinary code. Third, it was assumed that if a Wren was subject to a court martial, then a WRNS officer would have to be appointed as a member of the court.[9] This was the advice of Mr Samuel who thought it would be 'unacceptable [for the court] to be composed entirely of men' and that there would be 'repercussions from the public' if that were the case.[10] At the time, only seamen officers served on courts martial. The Admiralty Board was concerned that opening this function to female officers would set a precedent for other male officers, a view shared by Mr Samuel.[11] It would seem that the Board was also intent on preserving the elite standing of seamen officers.

The Admiralty also disliked the powers of command that the RAF intended giving its regular service female officers and NCOs. Officers would hold the King's commission, which required them to 'exercise and well discipline in their Duties such Officers, Airmen and Airwomen as may be placed under [their] orders' and instructed subordinates 'to Obey [the officer] as their superior'.[12] The outward symbol of this authority was the obligation on lower ranks to salute officers in recognition of the King's commission. However, the Admiralty Board was appalled by the idea of compulsory saluting of female officers by lower-ranked men. It preferred that the practice 'should be governed by courtesy and not prescribed by regulation.'[13] Deploring the widening gap between the Navy and the other two Services, the Board lamented that it could not stop them from taking this step. WRNS officers were to be given a 'Board commission', which required them to obey orders from their superiors, but did not grant powers of command. This should not be taken to mean that men of lower rank did not work for female superiors; they did so by virtue of an Admiralty Fleet Order.

Although the decision was dressed up as acknowledging the WRNS as the superior organisation, its officers felt keenly the distinctly lower status conferred on them compared with their counterparts. Commandant Woollcombe (successor to Mathews in 1946) urged her officers to accept the decision loyally, saying that '... the Service must do its best to fill the place allotted to it.'[14] Nevertheless, the issue of status would not die away, not least because of the goading of Wrens by other servicewomen that they were mere civilians. Noting that this description was commonly used in the press and by the public, Admiral Sir Robert Burnett (Commander-in-Chief Plymouth) believed that the Wrens' apparently lower status compared to army and RAF women contributed to the increase in 'desertion' being experienced.

'Parents and prospective employers, husbands and sweethearts' had an impression that service in the WRNS was like 'any other civilian job which may be terminated at the best by a week's notice, at the worst by downing tools, and walking out'.[15]

Burnett did not urge reversing the NDA decision, which he described as being 'intended as a compliment, and loyally understood and accepted as such by the Service'. Rather, he suggested the need to describe the WRNS as part of the Royal Navy.[16] Mr Samuel ascribed taunting of Wrens by other servicewomen to 'feelings akin to an inferiority complex vis-à-vis the WRNS'. Taking up Admiral Burnett's suggestion, he proposed that the WRNS be described as 'part of the permanent organisation of the Royal Navy' in place of its weaker description as 'an integral part of the naval organisation'.[17] The Admiralty Board accepted his advice. Nevertheless, not coming under military law, Wrens remained a uniformed corps of civilians.

Women having been under the Army Act since 1941, the War Office saw no difficulty in maintaining that policy in peacetime. Organisation was more a matter of debate throughout 1946. Should it adopt the model of integration as the RAF intended or should it retain a separate corps for women? The argument in favour of integration was based on cost savings as fewer senior women would be needed compared with the hierarchy needed to run a separate corps. Integration would eliminate dual channels of communication and conflicts of allegiance as had been evident between the ATS and those of its members who served with anti-aircraft artillery units. Finally, being part of an army corps with a long tradition and history would be good for women's morale.[18] Major General Vulliamy (Director of Signals) was a keen supporter of integration in order to have stability within his units rather than women being subject to postings to other corps if they were short of personnel.[19]

The case for retaining a separate corps for women was based on the need for flexibility. Recruiting women into specific corps would lock them into those organisations and therefore prevent women from being employed wherever need arose. Countering the idea that a separate corps would be expensive, it was argued that integration would require female officers and senior NCOs to be employed widely in training depots and units to provide the necessary welfare and disciplinary support. Additionally, women's promotion prospects in competition with men in an integrated service would not be as good as the opportunities afforded by a women's corps. Lack of career opportunities would thus deter the best women from joining.[20] Vulliamy backed down.

In December 1946, the Army Council settled for the status quo of a separate female corps. Its purpose was to 'provide replacements for male officers and men in such employments as may be specified by the Army Board of the Defence Council from time to time.'[21] Unlike men who joined a regiment or corps according to intended employment, women were recruited into a corps on the basis of gender. This was not a trivial matter. For ranks of lieutenant colonel and below, regimental duty was described as mainstream employment. For men, this would imply specialisms such as infantry, armoured warfare, engineering, signals and intelligence – and attracted associated advanced training courses. Women's mainstream employment was as women in a female corps, rather than in specialist work. Thus, a conflict was embedded for women from the outset. Their field of employment could be with men's corps, but promotion chances might depend upon undertaking mainstream appointments in the WRAC. From the definition of the WRAC's purpose, women's employment depended on the state of the rest of the Army.

Titles

The women's Services were created as reserve organisations before the outbreak of the Second World War and two of them used 'auxiliary' in their titles. The term, along with 'territorial' used in the Army, was commonly applied to reserve formations, trained as units and available for service in the event of war. Thus, its application to companies in the ATS and the WAAF was in keeping with standard military terminology. In 1941, the word auxiliary was adopted in the Army as the feminine of soldier, to refer to non-commissioned members of the ATS.[22]

The word auxiliary proved to be a problematic term when it came to regular service. The Admiralty had no issue to address as there was nothing in the title Women's Royal Naval Service that caused difficulty. Having decided to keep women separate from the RN, retaining the title was seen to have the advantage of continuity with its successful wartime predecessor. However, Auxiliary Territorial Service and Women's Auxiliary Air Force would not be accurate titles in the military sense of the word auxiliary. Nevertheless, Prime Minister Clement Attlee favoured retaining these names that had 'gathered ... a great amount of goodwill and honour'. While he acknowledged that use of auxiliary would be militarily incorrect, he did not regard that as a conclusive reason for change.[23] Use of the term auxiliary was problematic in a general sense as well as in military language. When applied to servicewomen, it was seen as indicating their lower status compared with servicemen. Ben Parkin (Labour MP for Stroud who served as an RAF officer during the war) urged that auxiliary be dropped from the title to be adopted in the post-war service for airwomen. He described it as having an 'honourable connotation' but 'a relic of the time when [women] were brought in as odd drivers, orderlies or generally decorative adjuncts to an office.'[24]

Despite Clement Attlee's sentimental attachment to the wartime titles, the Air Ministry and the War Office were determined to adopt new ones. The argument rumbled on until 1948. The Air Council believed that any title should reflect women's integration into the Service. Consideration was given to designating women as RAF with a signifier of gender such as RAF(W) or RAF (Women's Division).[25] A. V. Alexander (now Minister for Defence, formerly at the Admiralty) put forward 'RAF (Women's Section)' to Attlee on the basis that airwomen would be 'fully integrated with the RAF proper' and, therefore, would 'not be in any sense auxiliary'. Attlee favoured 'Women's Royal Air Service'. However, Lord Tedder (Chief of the Air Staff) and Sir James Barnes (Permanent Under-Secretary at the Air Ministry) 'attach[ed] the greatest importance to embodying the words "Royal Air Force" in any proposed title' as those for the other women's Services embodied Royal Navy and Army. The Air Council preferred '... "Women of the Royal Air Force" as the accurate and logical title' but was prepared to compromise by reverting to the First World War designation of Women's Royal Air Force.[26] Royal assent was given in December 1948. The new title came into use on 1 February 1949.

The Army Council believed that the title for their women's organisation should be short, inoffensive, self-explanatory, traditional, and lend itself to a collective noun. This provided a good reason for rejecting a proposal that 'Royal' should simply be added to the existing title as it would lead to the unfortunate acronym of RATS. The Princess Royal's Own was mooted, but dropped because of fears that the abbreviation PRO might have an 'obscene significance in the vulgar tongue'. What about Royal Army Women's Corps? This was unobjectionable and had a 'euphonious abbreviation [RAWC] with a faintly ornithological suggestion that compared suitably with Wren'. But then there was the misfortune of its abbreviation ending with WC which would be bound to lead to nicknames. Princess Mary, the Princess Royal, suggested shuffling the words to Women's Royal

Army Corps (WRAC). Armed with a nod of royal approval, the name was put forward by the Army Council and Clement Attlee 'did not object' – a rather grudging consent.

Belatedly, the Women Comrades Association weighed in to say that they were proud that the previous title had not included the word women, unlike the other Services, and they hoped the new title would also avoid 'women's anything'. The objection was too late. The formal submission had already been sent to the King. WRAC was agreed.[27] Aspirations to avoid a lewd interpretation were thwarted; the title was pronounced 'rack' by soldiers, referring to something that could be 'screwed against a wall'.

With the demise of ATS, the wartime practice of calling women auxiliaries was no longer appropriate. The next dilemma was what word to use that would be the equivalent of the Navy's 'Wren' and the Air Force's official usage of 'airwoman'? (Colloquially, women in the RAF were still called 'waafs', as had been the wartime custom). General Sir Richard O'Connor (Adjutant General) offered his colleagues a choice between 'soldiers' or 'women', neither of which he thought particularly suitable. The Army Council opted for women.[28] There is no record of their discussion, but it is hard to conclude otherwise than that they were reluctant to grant women the status of being soldiers at the outset of regular service.

Ranks

Non-commissioned women's ranks in wartime Services had mainly conformed to titles used in equivalent men's Services. The WRNS added the word wren to the most junior non-commissioned ranks such as leading wren to equate to leading seaman. Likewise, in the RAF, aircraftwoman was used in place of aircraftman. From 1941 non-commissioned titles in the Army were the same for men and women. However, officers' ranks were different from men's and this caused confusion because the standing of women's titles was not well understood. For example, the ranks equivalent to the male army rank of lieutenant were third officer (WRNS), subaltern (ATS) and section officer (WAAF). For colonel, women's ranks were respectively superintendent, controller and group officer.

Senior Controller Mary Tyrwhitt, Director of the ATS from May 1946, was particularly keen to address the issue because 'The Army used to pretend they didn't know what our ranks meant and they called us "Miss" and refused to use our titles.'[29] This was not only an Army matter. In records of meetings within the Service Ministries, it was commonplace to refer to female officers as Miss or Mrs, perhaps in addition to their military title, but often omitting rank. Although supported by the Army's post-war problems committee, Tyrwhitt stood no chance against the Chief of the Imperial General Staff, Field Marshal Montgomery's opposition. He summarised his argument against using the same ranks for men and women with a question: 'How could two majors get married?'[30] Her ideas were more welcomed by his successor, Field Marshal Slim. She also had the backing of the Princess Royal, by now appointed to the honorary position of Controller Commandant WRAC. This more favourable climate saw the measure through the Army Council. In March 1950, a year after the introduction of regular service, rank titles were made the same across the Army. Brigadier Mary Tyrwhitt achieved what the other female Directors declined to attempt. Only Clement Attlee was left grumbling that nobody had consulted him.[31]

In 1948, the Air Council decided to change the two least understood titles of assistant section officer and section officer which were used for the most junior female officers. It replaced them with pilot officer and flying officer, the ranks in use for men. As there was an intention at the time to create a flying branch for women (see below), using the same rank titles as junior male officers was seen as a good idea. However, the more senior titles were retained as they were deemed sufficiently close to those of men's to be understood (e.g. wing officer rather than wing commander). In addition, women at those ranks were expected to be employed in women's administration rather than in posts also open to men. Believing that senior female officers would not be required to exercise as much authority as men of equivalent rank, the Air Council decided against further changes.[32]

With the War Office ready to make its formal submission on identical rank titles to the King in early 1950, the Service Ministers' Committee asked the Air Council to reconsider the matter. Senior RAF members remained against the idea on the grounds that 'the Service in general [might regard] it as being a little ridiculous for male rank titles to be applied to women officers.' Air Chief Marshal Sir John Slessor, now Chief of the Air Staff, thought men might resent the move. Discussion also revealed a wider anxiety. Air Chief Marshal Sir George Pirie and Air Marshal Sir Victor Goddard thought RAF rank titles inappropriate for all ground-based officers, male or female. Titles created in 1918 reflected the fact that then nearly all officers flew aeroplanes or commanded formations of aeroplanes. The continuation of wartime specialist ground-based roles such as RAF Regiment, secretarial and accounting, equipment, catering and technical, left the anomaly of non-aircrew men also holding ranks suggestive of flying duties. Addressing the question of rank titles of ground-based officers was deemed too contentious. The Air Council shelved the issue. Arthur Henderson, Secretary of State, was unwilling to override RAF members of the Council but lamented that the Service, which he regarded as pioneering the integration of women, was now to lag behind the Army.[33]

Rather disparagingly, Air Marshal Sir Leslie Hollinghurst (Air Member for Personnel) described the Navy as having 'contracted out as usual.'[34] It did not come under pressure to change rank titles because the Service Ministers' Committee agreed it was in a 'special position, since they were a civilian service'.[35] Commandant Woollcombe did not press the case. Despite her colourful description of WRNS' officer ranks as 'rather an unhappy blend of the Merchant Navy, the Railway and the Asylum', she thought it 'undesirable and sometimes inconvenient that men and women officers should bear the same rank titles.'[36] She was against any change and there the matter rested. The WRNS also maintained its distinctive rank braid. While the WRAC and WRAF used the same rank insignia as the Army and RAF, albeit with the WRAC having its own distinctive cap badge, WRNS officers' rank braid was made from blue lace rather than the gold used by RN officers. This reinforced the WRNS's sense of a separate identity.

The Non-Combatant Principle

Responding to a request for comments on a proposal that women should be trained to use small arms for self-defence, Major General Richard Hull (Director of Staff Duties at the War Office and later Chief of the Imperial General Staff) wrote:

> The WRAC should neither be armed nor trained in the use of arms. ...it would be psychologically unsound and an expensive waste of equipment, ammunition and training time to train women in the use of personal arms. The fact that 'little Olga' is trained to kill and prides herself on the number of notches cut on her revolver butt is no reason why we, too, should cry 'Annie get your gun'. It is still the soldier's duty to protect his womenfolk whatever they are wearing. Even in these days when war means total war let us at least retain that degree of chivalry.[37]

Hull clearly identified members of the WRAC primarily as women not as military personnel. Perhaps he did not observe the insult contained in his words, asserting that training the WRAC was unsound and a waste of resources but acknowledging the competence of Soviet female soldiers.

The issue that the War Office was attempting to resolve was the question of the appropriate war role for the WRAC. Should they, like members of other support corps, be trained to take up arms as a last resort? If so, would this be voluntary or compulsory for women already serving and, likewise, for new recruits? At the other extreme, should they be treated like civilian women and bundled out of the way if time allowed? Or should they all be trained in some additional useful skill such as first aid? They could then be employed in that traditional female role of caring for the wounded rather than trespassing on male turf of confronting the enemy.

The War Office was in the lead on the issue of small arms training for servicewomen. In 1948, a draft paper supported by Major General McCandlish (Director of Personnel Army) suggested that the WRAC could be trained for self-defence and possibly to guard their locations. Legal advice was explicit that nothing in UK or international law dictated that women were non-combatants. This was only a matter of British policy. The law did not define combatant duty.

Senior Controller Mary Tyrwhitt was clear that women should be trained in small arms. Servicewomen were soldiers and should be an asset in war and not seen as a liability needing to be found a safe place away from an enemy or in need of protection by male colleagues. She believed that while policy could dictate that women would not be sent to seek the enemy, there was no guarantee that women could always avoid enemy troops. Then, she remarked, women would 'rather trust to their skill with a rifle' than the finer feelings of an uncivilised enemy.[38]

Tyrwhitt was expressing views consistent with those of some earlier female Directors. In 1941, Air Commandant Trefusis-Forbes wanted airwomen to be trained to use firearms as part of the wartime initiative to provide more defence forces for airfields. She claimed that the other female Directors were against the idea of women using lethal weapons because they perceived a psychological difference between 'women having immediate responsibility for the killing of men and being indirectly responsible'. She believed that they thought 'it would be detrimental to the "womanliness of women" to be actually responsible'.

However, she asserted that airwomen were bright enough to realise that the distinction between direct and indirect killing was 'not worth considering'.[39] Whether or not this was an accurate reflection of Commandant Mathews' view in 1941, by 1943 she was in favour. Arguing her case that women should come under the Naval Discipline Act, she pointed out that the Admiralty Board had approved the training of some Wrens in the use of guns.[40]

Not much is known about the views of the Admiralty and Air Ministry in 1948. McCandlish speculated that the Navy would regard the WRNS as non-combatant shore-based employees while the RAF might train women for defensive duties as part of its philosophy of integrating women into the Service. However, at a meeting to discuss War Office proposals the reverse positions were taken by Admiralty and Air Ministry representatives. Mr Bird, from the Admiralty, claimed that it was probable that compulsory training for defensive purposes would be introduced. This seems doubtful as hitherto the Admiralty had not been at the forefront of policy. The Air Ministry, represented by Group Captain Jackman from the Directorate of Personnel Services, said the question had not yet been considered. He reported that the 'Air Ministry had no intention of introducing compulsory weapon training for the WRAF at present.'[41] This reflected the position of the previous Secretary of State, Philip Noel-Baker. In a letter in 1947 to his War Office counterpart, he recorded his view that he hoped women would never have combatant status.[42]

The RAF's attitude towards weapons training and defence duties was also problematic for the majority of airmen who were employed in ground-based trades. From 1937 to June 1940, most airmen trained only to drill with weapons, not to fire them. With the threat of invasion, airmen were then expected to use small arms to supplement army detachments which guarded airfields. Following the fall of Crete, where there was a failure to defend a key airfield, defence of RAF bases transferred from the Army to the RAF. The RAF Regiment, akin to an army regiment, was created for this purpose and other airmen were trained in support of the task. Post-war, training all airmen in ground combat proved contentious because of the cost of ammunition and diversion of men from their normal duty. This was of particular concern in highly skilled trades, such as engineering, where the priority was to employ men in their primary role. A policy of two hours training per week, introduced in 1946, was not sustained. It was replaced by a policy of up to forty-eight hours training per annum in

1951.[43] Men's obligation to train to use weapons was the essence of the difference in commitment made by airmen and airwomen.

By the middle of 1949, McCandlish appeared to be in favour of the WRAC being trained for self-defence purposes. However, his promise of sending a paper to the Executive Committee of the Army Council (ECAC) was not fulfilled. Servicewomen were not to be trained to use small arms and were to be still regarded as non-combatants. The exclusion of airwomen from use of firearms was subsequently embodied in the Queen's Regulations for the RAF.[44]

The WRAC was described officially as a non-combatant corps. Army terminology on this point was complicated. Usage until the 1940s had been to divide men's corps and regiments into combatant or non-combatant for the purpose of determining powers of command of officers and pay. It did not signify the absence of training in the use of firearms. The war had seen many previously non-combatant corps gain combatant status. Thus, post-war the terminology was seen as outdated. But the ECAC had severe difficulty in trying to resolve the tangle. It took eight papers on the subject over the period from 1945 to 1959 without achieving a satisfactory outcome.[45] As far as the WRAC was concerned, though, the position was clear. It was a non-combatant corps, meaning that its officers could not command by right male officers of combatant corps.

Non-combatant policy, however subsequent generations of policymakers chose to interpret it, became enshrined as the foundation stone of women's regular service in each of the armed forces.

Exclusions from Essential Roles

Writing to Charles Portal (Chief of the Air Staff) in 1944, Air Chief Marshal Leigh Mallory (Commander-in-Chief of the Allied Expeditionary Air Force) suggested that women, as an integral part of the RAF, should also be 'part of its essential function – flying'.[46] Some female pilots were employed during the war. They delivered military aircraft between airfields. These pilots worked for the Air Transport Auxiliary (ATA) under the Ministry of Aircraft Production. This Ministry urged the Air Ministry to create a WAAF flying section whose pilots could then be seconded to the ATA in the same way as RAF pilots were. In 1943 a call was made for volunteers, and 150 women were short listed from nearly 2,000 who applied. However, the initiative was opposed by Air Marshal Sutton (Air Member for Personnel). Sutton thought it would be administratively inconvenient to have a small number of WAAFs working for another Ministry. In addition, ATA women and the WAAF had different terms of service.[47] Women in the ATA enjoyed equal pay from 1943, whereas airwomen were paid only two-thirds of single men's pay. Resolving whether women were to be paid on ATA or WAAF terms would certainly have been problematic. Although Portal was enthusiastic, seeing female ATA pilots as a basis for a WAAF flying branch in the future, Sir Archibald Sinclair (Secretary of State for Air) accepted Sutton's argument and blocked the idea. Thirty-one women left the WAAF to join the ATA as ferry pilots.[48] At least in refusing to have members of the WAAF train as pilots, the Air Ministry was being consistent. In 1943, it had also blocked Admiralty aspirations to have female pilots to fly some passenger aircraft.[49]

Women were not only excluded from piloting aircraft but they were also denied most rear-crew roles, including those for which the aircraft were remote from contact with the enemy. For example, women were excluded from training as drogue operators, who were responsible for trailing targets from aircraft so that fighter pilots could practise gunnery, on the grounds that they were 'physically unsuitable to the work'.[50] They were also barred from the trade of being pigeon keepers. Five airwomen trained for the job but then were not posted to the role because duties included training flight crews in how to release birds into the slipstream of an aircraft. Some airwomen did eventually make it into the air in the traditional women's role of nursing. The need for medical orderlies to attend wounded personnel being evacuated by air gave rise to the Flying Nightingales.[51] Less heralded were the short trips undertaken by female mechanics who participated in air testing of repaired equipment.[52]

After the war, support for a female flying branch grew. In 1947 Philip Noel-Baker, Secretary of State for Air, announced in the House of Commons that women aircrew would be trained 'when circumstances permitted'.[53] Despite attempts by successive Secretaries of State (Arthur Henderson having taken over from Noel-Baker in October 1947) to bring about a WRAF flying role, circumstances never were quite right. Objections were raised about cost, the lack of capacity in the training system, the waste of places needed for men and a lack of suitable roles.[54] A review was promised in 1951, but no record of such work has been traced. The Air Council finally decided to drop the idea in December 1954.[55] However, female pilots from the ATA could join the RAF Volunteer Reserve, as could other female pilots if they had sufficient hours of flying experience. In 1952, out of a total of 5,126 reserve force pilots, 59 were female. The scheme closed to new entrants in July 1953 when the budget for Reserve flying schools was cut.[56]

The argument that it was a waste of resources to train women as they could not be employed operationally as pilots was actually a gender-based argument rather than a matter of principle that all pilots must be operational. There were two categories of men who received flying training without giving full value for money through subsequent operational flying. Some male officers in the Technical Branch were trained to 'wings' standard although they would undertake no productive flying. It was thought to be good for the RAF if male ground branch officers had a connection with flying as it would give them a common outlook with their aircrew colleagues. In contrast to the argument about women aircrew, an objection about wasted resources was dismissed because cutting the programme would not achieve great economies.[57] Selected national servicemen also trained as aircrew up to basic flying training standard, with a commitment to keep current at this level for their period in the Reserve.[58] By July 1950, the RAF was training 300 national servicemen per annum as pilots.[59] Some members of the Air Council suggested it would be better to train regular members of the WRAF than national servicemen but their view did not prevail.

The Admiralty did not spend the same energy as the Air Ministry on its policy. In 1943, in reply to a question in the House of Commons during the naval estimates debate, Captain Pilkington (Civil Lord of the Admiralty) said that '... the principle of WRNS serving afloat [was] not objected to by the Admiralty ... But the real difficulty about this proposal [was] accommodation on board.' He went on: '... if, when and where it [was] found practicable to employ Wrens afloat that [would] certainly be done.'[60] Such professed optimism about the role that women could play was absent from the 1946 policy proposal for regular Service. Without equivocation it declared that 'it [was] not, of course, intended to employ WRNS on board ship.'[61] Reluctant as it had been to continue with the WRNS, it would have been remarkable had the Admiralty considered seagoing in warships for women at that time.

Unlike other Army corps, the WRAC did not have a defined functional employment. Women were to be posted to work with other corps as need dictated. The defining principles for such employment were that, first, jobs would only be open to women in peacetime if they could also perform them in war. Second, women would not be employed in small numbers as the necessity for female supervisors for welfare and discipline and the provision of facilities for women, would result in disproportionate costs. Third, women would undertake jobs in lieu of male soldiers, meaning that they were not to do jobs that civilians could undertake.[62] Embedded within these principles was the crucial exclusion that women were not to be employed in theatres of war and so were not to work in corps areas overseas. This entailed some debate as wartime practice had seen women of the British Red Cross Society and of the Council of Voluntary War Workers employed in areas from which the ATS were banned, much to the resentment of the ATS. A proposal that there be some flexibility on the policy, leaving it to Commanders-in-Chief to decide, was rejected by the Executive Committee of the Army Council. While some sympathy was expressed for the idea, it decreed that the proper time to decide on any relaxation of policy would be on the outbreak of war.[63]

The linking of women's exclusion from jobs in peace that they could not also fulfil in war, together with their exclusion from corps areas overseas, had the further implication that women could not work in units in Britain if the mobilisation role required deployment to a theatre of war. This geographic limitation was a constraint on women's employment that was to persist for decades. It had an adverse impact on career prospects as opportunities were denied on the basis of this policy. The best jobs were closed to women and numbers who could be employed were limited.

It went without saying that the WRAC would not be employed with combatant corps and regiments with one exception left over from the war – anti-aircraft artillery. The ECAC agreed that women could continue their work on heavy anti-aircraft artillery batteries, but they thought that the public would only find this acceptable if the women were stationed in the UK in defence of home territory. Women were not to be posted overseas in this role.[64] The policy was relaxed briefly when postings to a battery in Gibraltar were introduced in 1952. The role survived until the disbandment of Anti-Aircraft Command in 1955.

Employment

Post-war employment policy for women was part of broader restructuring as the armed forces restored regular service career patterns for men and planned peacetime national service. Reviews were initiated to rationalise working methods and cut costs. Expecting to be about 30 per cent larger than its 1938 strength, the Navy wanted to revert to regular service volunteers, backed up by a substantial trained reserve. The Admiralty Board believed that 'conscription would not on balance be to the advantage of the Navy'. Although it recognised that it would need to 'take its share of conscripts', in fact, the Navy took comparatively few national servicemen (*see* Table 3.1).[65] The RAF planned for the increased importance of air power. At nearly three times its 1938 size, it would be significantly dependent on national servicemen. The Army was to be heavily reliant on national service intakes and significant numbers of regular servicemen would be employed on training these men.

For women's employment, there were some common policies. Women's welfare and discipline was to be overseen by female NCOs and officers. This implied the need for junior women to be employed in sufficient numbers at a location to make the overhead worth the expense. Middle ranking and senior female officers were expected to work predominantly in the running of their Service rather than in jobs open to male officers. Junior rank women were excluded from roles that required long or expensive training. Unlike some wartime practice where substitution ratios varied (for example three female cooks replacing two men), women were to be employed in place of servicemen predominantly on a one-for-one basis.[66] Each Service adapted these common positions according to its own needs.

In the WRNS only 27 of the 81 wartime categories of work were expected to remain open to non-commissioned women. The proposed allocation of ratings had a traditional look, with over 42 per cent of the jobs being in catering and domestic duties and a further 24 per cent in clerical work.[67] Wrens' work within the Fleet Air Arm was in doubt, being dependent upon the decision on how men's work was to be organised. One study advocated more integration of Fleet Air Arm categories with

Table 3.1: National Servicemen – Allocations 1947–50

	Number of Men		
Year	RN	RAF	Army
1947	12,700	48,600	122,100
1948	3,700	46,700	100,500
1949	8,100	43,100	115,400
1950	1,300	52,300	120,600

Source: *Ministry of Labour and National Service: Reports*, Cmd. 7559 (Nov 1948), Cmd. 8017 (Aug 1950), Cmd. 8338 (Aug 1951), (London: HMSO).

men's seagoing categories, which would have reduced opportunities for Wrens. A second study favoured the wartime system of specialist categories for aircraft work. This specialist solution prevailed. As a consequence, men in these roles would spend the bulk of their careers in shore-based work.[68] This decision re-opened the work to Wrens, themselves shore-based.[69] Abolition of other roles was also partially reversed in the late 1940s. Operator jobs in telegraphy and telephony were restored to the list and cinema operators were likewise reprieved. The target strength for the WRNS kept changing. When it was set at 9,500 ratings in 1947, about 14 per cent were expected to be employed in domestic and administrative work for the WRNS. This was described as slightly higher than the equivalent in the RN.[70]

There was some discussion about whether female officers were to be entered into separate, specialist branches or to form one branch. Commandant Mathews favoured the former idea for junior officers, with senior officers coming together as one branch as they would not be employed in place of men, but only on WRNS work. However, a meeting chaired by Rear Admiral Denny (Assistant Chief of Naval Personnel) decided in favour of one branch for all rather than sub-dividing a small cohort. All junior officers were to be capable of being employed on a mixture of specialist work and female administration duties.

Branches of the Navy were invited to consider where they could employ WRNS officers in place of men. Bids were received for 201 female officers of whom 67 were to replace warrant rather than commissioned officers. This was regarded as a 'most unhealthy sign' as it would limit the opportunities for promotion for male ratings seeking the highest non-commissioned rank.[71] The list was cut to reduce the number of warrant officer replacements. No observation was made about the reduced standing of junior female officers substituting for non-commissioned rather than commissioned men. The requirement for cipher officers, a large field of wartime work, was dropped. Machines operated by ratings were being introduced instead. Specialist roles open to female officers included meteorology, safety equipment, air radio, communications, secretariat, pay and cash, air stores, catering, clothing and victualling.[72]

Plans for the integrated RAF anticipated that the majority of trades would remain open to women, though some roles were no longer needed, for example barrage balloon work. Others, such as air movements assistant roles and five clerical trades, were initially reserved for national servicemen whose time spent in training was to be kept at under four months on average.[73] Women were preferred to national servicemen as radar and wireless assistants because they would give longer service. Women were now excluded from the wartime role of armament assistants because it involved weapon handling. This was seen as incompatible with their non-combatant status.[74] A paper on the future of the technical branch noted that airwomen would not be trained to the highest standard as apprentice training was too long and females would not be allowed to join at the young age specified for the scheme.[75]

Unlike the WRNS which adopted a single branch, WRAF officers could join the majority of branches open to non-flying personnel. The technical branch planned to take only a third of its strength as graduate entrants; the majority of places were to be filled by those commissioning from the ranks. However, with few women taking appropriate degrees and airwomen not eligible for apprenticeships and so not reaching the top echelon of engineering trades quickly, there would be limited opportunities. In addition, women were deemed incapable of managing a section comprised predominantly of men. The wartime practice of employing female officers to supervise airwomen working in signals and radar operations was discontinued. Thus, available technical branch jobs were reduced to a handful in statistics and analytical work.[76] This unwelcoming approach led to the near demise of the female technical officer, with just two appearing in the *Air Force List* of 1948. Nevertheless, the technical branch remained open to female officers. There was an important structural difference between the WRAF and the WRNS. The WRAF would not administer itself but would be integrated into RAF systems. Consequently, it was estimated that only 1.4% of women would be in jobs exclusively for the running of the WRAF.[77]

The list of trades open to non-commissioned members of the WRAC employed in place of male soldiers was similar to those of the other Services: clerks, cooks and stewards, drivers, keyboard operators, orderlies, store-women and telephonists. Where women worked in specialist units, for example as drivers with the Royal Signals, there was an intention to avoid posting them away as drivers for other units. Major General Vulliamy (Director of Signals) was keen for women to develop expertise in support of his units rather than being seen as a pool from which others could fish.

WRAC officers were all initially to be employed on regimental duty, i.e. in a role only open to female officers, in the administration of the WRAC or in a women's unit. In subsequent tours of duty junior officers would be eligible to work in mixed units where they would again be responsible for administration of women but could also hold an operational or technical job in place of a male officer. Openings were expected to be available in the anti-aircraft artillery regiments, signals regiments and Royal Army Service Corps transport companies. Beyond those unit appointments, female officers could also expect staff appointments in other support corps.[78]

Conclusion

Regular service for women was established on three different organisational patterns: the RAF with no separate women's Service but a philosophy of integration; the Admiralty retaining a separate women's Service, stopping short of military status; and the War Office with its military women in their own gender-defined corps and the lesser status associated with being a non-combatant corps. Although the WRAF did not exist as an organisation – the label was intended for administrative purposes – the idea of the WRAF being distinct from the RAF persisted, as did the habit of calling women waafs.

These organisational decisions reflected the corresponding military environments. Air Force work divided more naturally into aircrew and ground crew rather than by gender. Operating for the most part from fixed bases, it could provide facilities and work environments appropriate to mixed workforces. Throughout the war, it had gained experience of having women working alongside men and undertaking the same primary duties. To gain the benefit of retaining servicewomen, the Air Council opted to integrate women into the RAF rather than maintaining a separate female Service. But it chose to exclude women from flying duties. For the Admiralty, there was no merit in seeking to integrate women into the RN as the majority of branches and trades could not be opened on an equal basis without women being eligible to serve in ships.

Either of these models of integration or separation could have been implemented by the War Office. However, it stayed with what it knew – a military Corps for women. It rejected the RAF model of integration for fear of creating small pockets of women in various Corps. Instead, it accepted the additional overheads of running a Corps for women, expecting to gain more from the flexibility of being able to employ its members in support of whatever corps or services were short of men. Land warfare had no obvious boundary equivalent to flying or seagoing in the other two Services so the Army Council established a geographic rule to define the limits of women's employment. They were not to be exposed to the rigours of field employment or to be vulnerable to enemy action in a theatre of war.

While women's careers would develop within these different organisational constraints, a common principle was established that was to limit numbers, roles and opportunities for decades. This was the principle that women were to be regarded as non-combatants. Women were excluded from jobs on this basis.

4

'THEY ARE AFTER ALL WOMEN'

A Wren who joined the WRNS in 1946, walked out of her job in 1948 saying that she had been offered her former position as a cashier in a dairy on 'a very good wage'. She wrote:

> I have found it impossible to save the amount of money which I must have for my wedding … I see no other way out, as I fully realise I have no grounds for compassionate release. All my uniform can be found in my chest of drawers in Stanshaw Camp, I believe I have left all the kit required. … I am returning railway warrant, liberty ticket and Pay Book.[1]

Not being under military law as the WAAF and the ATS were, Wrens could not be arrested and returned to their units. This Wren, having been careful not to make off with naval property, was free to return to civilian life. The senior WRNS officer at Portsmouth could only lament that 'Better paid jobs are easily available on shore [meaning in civilian employment], and desertion from the Service appears to be no handicap in obtaining them.'[2]

The young Wren's letter encapsulates two key issues on terms and conditions of service: pay and marriage. By 1948 the Service Ministries and the Treasury had been arguing for more than two years. Delay was undermining the best efforts to make peacetime service attractive. Before negotiating with the Treasury, whose approval was needed on pay and pensions, the Service Ministries needed to agree a common policy. While the latter were determined to adopt military norms, modified as they thought necessary for women, Chancellor Sir Stafford Cripps saw servicewomen as female workers who should be treated like civilians. The other major issues vexing the Ministries were marriage and motherhood. Married women, including those with school age children, had served in the war. Was this still acceptable or should married women be excluded as had been commonplace in pre-war government employment?

While senior female officers had little influence on the decision to create regular service, they came to the fore as policies on terms and conditions of service were drafted. These women rose to the top of their Services during the course of the war. In 1946, they held one-star ranks, equivalent to brigadier in the army. Whereas a regular service brigadier in the War Office would typically have at least 20 years' army experience behind him and possibly staff college training in which he would have developed the skills needed to work in planning and policy roles, these women had advanced to the top of their pyramids on the basis only of their wartime service.

The Directors and Their Roles

Drafting a history of the WAAF after the war, Group Officer Constance Woodhead assessed the problem of finding women for senior officer posts:

> Our ages varied from twenty-five to near fifty ... one of us, at least, bore an ancient and noble name, many were from 'good county' families [original emphasis], some from the professional classes, some from the world of commerce ... but hardly one career woman, not a single University don or teacher, hardly a woman with serious experience of public or business life behind her. ... women already launched on a successful career were naturally, in all but a few cases, unable or unwilling to give up that career for a nebulous future in anything as new as a women's military service. It was left to a handful of inexperienced women ... to guide and control the very big service which the WAAF became.[3]

Her assessment echoed that made earlier by Chief Controller Helen Gwynne-Vaughan, the first Director of the ATS. Observing that initially women officers tended to be 'leisured women', she wrote:

> ... the officers who would be best worth having in war were by no means always those who could give most time in peace. ... The result, in spite of brilliant exceptions, was too large a proportion of the type of officer who was not accustomed to regular or exacting work.[4]

Despite these misgivings, the women who helped to shape the regular Services emerged from those recruited at the start of the war.

In 1939, the Admiralty appointed Vera Laughton Mathews as Director of the WRNS. Born in 1888, the daughter of a senior naval officer and a Spanish-born Italian mother, she worked as a journalist and was active in the women's suffrage movement. After serving as an officer in the First World War, she maintained her WRNS' connections by taking the role of Vice President of the Wrens' Association which was established in 1920.[5] With the ideal combination of service culture in her family and previous experience, she put her own name forward for consideration for a role in the reformed WRNS.[6] Married with three school-age children, she was surprised not to be questioned about her family responsibilities.[7] She went on to serve throughout the war and into the early phase of preparation for the introduction of the permanent Service.

The field of candidates to succeed Mathews in 1946 narrowed because Angela Goodenough, senior officer for Wrens in the East Indies, tragically contracted a fatal illness while serving in Ceylon (now Sri Lanka). Jocelyn Woollcombe, Deputy Director responsible for recruitment and training since 1943, was selected. She, too, came from a family rich in experience of Service life. Her father was a naval officer and her mother the daughter of a colonel. Woollcombe had worked as a clerk in Naval Intelligence from 1916–1919 and joined the WRNS in 1939. She took over in November 1946 and held the Director's role for four years, relinquishing the post in 1950.[8]

While the WRNS thrived under the leadership of Commandant Mathews, the War Office experience was less fortunate as it tried three very different ATS leaders. A post-war saying summarised the experience:

> Helen Gwynne-Vaughan dug the foundations, so deep that everyone fell in; Jean Knox put up the curtains, before the windows were in; and Leslie Whateley put on the roof and finished the job.[9]

Helen Gwynne-Vaughan having been a driving force in the re-establishment of women's Services, it is unsurprising that the War Office confirmed her as the Director in 1939. She came to the post with a formidable background and strong views based on her experience in the First World War, initially with the Army and then as Director of the WRAF from September 1918. She wanted women to be treated as soldiers, subject to military law. Although she had supported a separate organisation for army women, she changed her mind and thought it would be better for them to join the corps appropriate to their trade.[10] Her vision for what servicewomen could contribute outstripped her capacity to deliver an efficient organisation. With criticism of the ATS mounting and the need for expansion becoming critical, she was forced to retire in July 1941. The public reason was on grounds of age (she was sixty-two) but within the War Office, and widely in the ATS itself, she was seen as a fearsome old woman, part of the problem rather than a leader capable of transforming her Service.

The appointment and subsequent retirement two years later of her successor, Jean Knox, has been the subject of much speculation. Without reliable sources, it is difficult to judge events. In 1941 there was an urgent need to expand the ATS from a ceiling of 40,000 to a maximum of 200,000 to help to alleviate the army's losses of 1940.[11] However, it was struggling to recruit due to a poor public reputation. The War Office was keen to present a more positive image of the ATS. Older officers were overlooked with the selection of thirty-three-year old Senior Commander Jean Knox. She was given a few months' experience as Inspector of the ATS in the rank of Controller but, in effect, she was promoted four ranks to the acting rank of Chief Controller (the equivalent in male ranks would have been from major to major general) in the space of six months. She was to provide a glamorous image for public consumption in the recruitment campaign. Leslie Whateley, a more able administrator, was appointed as her deputy and undertook most of the work at the War Office, while Knox travelled at home and abroad to promote the ATS.[12] Knox stepped down in October 1943, ill-health being given as the reason.

In a memorandum assessing possible successors to Knox, the crop of controllers and senior controllers were variously dismissed as uninspiring, lacking leadership qualities or indecisive. Controller Baxter-Ellis had a strong write up, but she was set aside having had a serious operation which left a question mark over her health. The obvious choice was Knox's deputy, Senior Controller Leslie Whateley who was described as 'intensely loyal, level headed and [having] character'.[13] Aged forty-four, she was an experienced administrator from an army background. On leaving school she worked as secretary to her field-marshal and Victoria Cross holding grandfather. Twice married, she had a son from her first marriage. She joined the ATS when the first call went out for volunteers in September 1938. Her war service had been largely in War Office appointments and having deputised for Knox, she had an understanding of what was needed. With the ATS numbering over 200,000 as she took over, Whateley saw her task as supporting her officers so that they, in turn, could look to the welfare and well-being of the junior ranks. The success of her period in office can be gauged by the subsequent accolades: a DBE (Dame Commander of the Most Excellent Order of the British Empire) in 1946; Chevalier of the Légion d'Honneur and Croix de Guerre with silver star from France; Order of Merit from the USA; and the first non-royal woman to become honorary colonel of a regiment (668th battery, heavy anti-aircraft regiment, Royal Artillery).[14]

Whateley retired from the ATS in May 1946, just before regular service for women was announced. The work involved in the transition to permanent, regular service fell to the next Director, Mary Tyrwhitt. A single woman, born in 1903, Tyrwhitt came from a naval family. Her father was an admiral of the fleet and her brother was also a naval officer. She joined the ATS as an officer in November 1938 when she was invited to raise a platoon at Cranbrook in Kent. During the war, after a brief period as a company commander in charge of cooks, clerks and orderlies at Chatham, she moved into the organisation and delivery of training for officers and NCOs. Her talents as a staff officer led to her becoming a Deputy Director to Whateley who assessed her as 'possessing a marked sense of justice, the deepest spirit of service and great moral courage'.[15] Tyrwhitt took over in May 1946.

Air Ministry experience was also turbulent. Jane Trefusis-Forbes, a successful business woman who had been a company commander for an RAF section in the ATS from 1938, was appointed in 1939. Born in 1899 in Chile, where her father was working as a civil engineer, she served during the First World War in the Women's Volunteer Reserve.[16] Trefusis-Forbes' tenure ended in crisis, the catalyst for which was Violet Markham's report on welfare in the women's Services. Markham considered the WAAF to be over-centralised, with too much authority vested in the Director. She made a number of recommendations for delegation of powers to Headquarters and Air Ministry departments. Trefusis-Forbes and Air Marshal Sutton (Air Member for Personnel) disagreed over the report and her relationship with her superiors never recovered. She noted at the time that Sutton had told her that she was 'down the drain with the Air Council'.[17] Perhaps unwilling to dismiss her, having suffered controversy in 1918 over the sacking of Violet Douglas-Pennant as head of the WRAF after just three months in office, Trefusis-Forbes was promoted and dispatched to Canada, which had requested a visit to mark the anniversaries of its women's Services. She relinquished her appointment as Director at the end of September 1943 in order to 'carry out "this very important special duty".'[18]

Needing to recommend a successor to Sir Archibald Sinclair (Secretary of State), Air Chief Marshal Portal asked Sutton to suggest candidates. Sutton listed the nine most senior female officers, dismissing five of them as not having strong enough physiques to cope with the demands of the job. Another was rejected as temperamentally unsuited, leaving three officers to consider.[19] Portal turned to his usual confidant, Wilfrid Freeman, for advice. Freeman, formerly Vice Chief of the Air Staff, was running the Ministry of Aircraft Production. However, he took a close interest in the WAAF in which his wife, Elizabeth, was an officer. In his parting shot as Vice Chief, he sent a paper to Air Council members including a diatribe about the quality of WAAF senior officers. He believed that 'the wrong people are in high places' and this was leading to a decline in efficiency.[20] Noted for being forthright, he now marked the women's card. Two were dismissed as 'dear old things' and another pair as 'weak'. One was described as 'mannerless and hopeless', the next as 'ill … presumably suffering from the change of life'. Of the three names left on Sutton's list, he thought one was 'weak' and another 'hopelessly weak and tarred with the same brush as the present Director'. The one left standing was Wing Officer Wynne-Eaton, whom Freeman saw as a candidate for the post of deputy rather than Director.[21]

Portal and Freeman favoured a less senior officer who did not feature on Sutton's list. This was Felicity Hanbury, a friend of Elizabeth Freeman. She seemed to fit to perfection the model of an officer. Public school educated and presented at Court, her father had been a colonel in the army and her mother was the daughter of a politician. Having learned to fly as a civilian, but with insufficient solo hours to satisfy the Air Transport Auxiliary, she made a successful career in the WAAF. Widowed early in the war, she was decorated with the MBE (military division) for her work at Biggin Hill during the Battle of Britain. In 1943 she was a squadron officer at Headquarters Bomber Command. In August of that year, she was promoted to acting wing officer and appointed to run the women's officer training school at Windermere.[22]

Having had his list of contenders rejected, Sutton put forward the next most senior female officer. Freeman's advice now was to 'lock up [Sutton] in an asylum' as his recommendation was 'the pleasantest but certainly the least fitted [WAAF officer] to be head of any Service.'[23] Forwarding Sutton's brief to Sinclair, Portal added his own recommendation of Felicity Hanbury. In defence of her age and lack of seniority (she was thirty years old and, having just been promoted to wing officer, she was two ranks below the level at which the appointment would be made), he cited the War Office's appointment of Jean Knox in 1941. He claimed that this had been a remarkable success.[24] However, the War Office was about to dispense with Jean Knox's services.

Sinclair was not persuaded by Portal's case for Hanbury. Instead, he opted for Lady Welsh. Mary Welsh was in uncertain health and Portal expressed doubts as to whether she would stand the strains of the role. However, she had been successful as Inspector for the WAAF. Her appointment was also seen as politically sensitive because she was married to Air Marshal Sir William Welsh who was serving as Head of an RAF delegation in the USA. Portal was conscious of the potential for accusations of nepotism, but he was prepared to defend the selection. Mary Welsh took up the job in October 1943, holding the post for three years.

Portal wanted a Director who would 'clear out with a ruthless hand the deadwood at the top'.[25] In this respect, Welsh's performance disappointed. Freeman concluded in 1945 that he had been 'utterly wrong about Welsh' and lamented that he had recommended her for the job. Felicity Hanbury remained the favoured officer. Portal asked to be informed about plans for her postings and insisted she be given jobs that would prepare her to take over from Welsh. Crucially, he intervened in 1944 to prevent a case being made against her for inefficiency in her job at the officer training school where she fell out with Squadron Leader Brew, the station commander. Headquarters' staff, including the senior WAAF officer, sided with Brew. But Hanbury had a host of impressive supporters, Violet Markham and Helen Gwynne-Vaughan among them. Portal, alerted by Hanbury herself and by Freeman, called for the papers and dismissed the case as unfounded.[26] Not only talented but able to call on the patronage of the Chief of the Air Staff, Hanbury continued upwards and was given postings at home and the Middle East which put her in the leading position when Welsh retired. This time there were no objections to her appointment; she took over on 1 December 1946. At last, the Air Council had found a female leader from a Service family, educated at public school and with 'belly fire' that seemed to be the model for an officer.

The roles of the Directors were affected by decisions already taken about organisation. Hanbury's tenure was the highpoint of the influence of the Director WRAF as integration of women into the RAF over the following years reduced the scope of the job. Working in the Air Member for Personnel's department under the Director General Personnel, her position was mainly advisory. Recognising that women being employed in a predominantly male service might need special consideration, Air Ministry departments were obliged to consult her on policy issues affecting employment or well-being. Although responsible for basic training for officers, NCOs and junior ranks, the Director did not have a remit for specialist training or the subsequent technical efficiency of women. Nor was she responsible for discipline. Her executive authority was limited to the disposal of compassionate cases for postings or discharge. Her staff participated in the selection of commissioning candidates and had a say in the posting of officers. Regulations gave the Director the right to visit any station where airwomen served. The wartime practice of having dedicated female administrative officers at Command and Group Headquarters was abolished. These officers now joined the more widely employable RAF Secretarial branch and all female officers were trained to deal with women's administration in addition to their specialist function.

In contrast to the advisory role in the WRAF, the Directors of the WRNS and WRAC had executive authority as heads of their Service or Corps. In the WRNS, the Director was responsible for recruitment of ratings, the selection, appointment and promotion of officers and initial recruit training. She advised on other issues and was answerable to the Admiralty for the performance of the WRNS, its morale and its well-being. The wartime system of female administrative officers continued. The authority of the Director as head of Service conferred greater status on these officers compared with the advisory roles that pertained in the WRAF. As well as jobs at Command Headquarters, special posts were established at each unit where Wrens were employed. Known as Unit Officers, these women were responsible for training junior officers and NCOs in their general service duties, welfare, accommodation, discipline, programmes of education and vocational training, and sport. They were mostly of first officer rank and were treated as heads of department, although they were junior in rank to men who ran departments. Attending regular management meetings with men running establishments, unit officers had routine access to information and to male superior officers, giving them more authority than WRAF officers who undertook women's administration only as an additional duty. Unit Officers provided an important mechanism for encouraging and maintaining a sense of identity among Wrens and for enforcing standards of dress and behaviour.

For the Army, there was no novelty in having a separate corps, with its own way of operating within the overall regulations laid down by higher authority. The WRAC was a manifestation of what was standard practice. As with the other women's Services, the Directorate was established within the personnel area of the War Office. The Director had officers at Command and District Headquarters whose role was like that of the equivalent WRAF officers – there to advise male commanders on issues of welfare, administration and discipline. The WRAC undertook its own recruitment, selection for trades and basic training, some specialist training such as for clerks and drivers, and officer and NCO training.

Jocelyn Woollcombe, Mary Tyrwhitt and Felicity Hanbury reached the top of their organisations over a period of seven years and now had the task of negotiating terms and conditions of service for the long-term future of servicewomen. Each was indoctrinated into their parent Services' way of doing things and had views shaped by battles already fought. The WRNS was regarded as the elite of the women's Services, but it had civilian rather than military status. The WRAC was confident of its place as a military organisation, basking in the major contribution made to air defence, but with a persistent schism over whether army women should join employing corps or remain as a separate entity. Felicity Hanbury, willing to exploit her connections to achieve her aims, was faced with the challenge of integrating women into the RAF.

Pay and Pensions

It was standard practice for employers, including government departments, to pay women less than men. Men were assumed to have family responsibilities, not shared by women, with a husband expected to provide a home for his wife. Pay in the armed forces took this idea of marital duty a step further by differentiating between the pay of married and single men. Basic pay was set on the needs of single men, assuming that they lived in barracks and food was provided free. It was determined by type of employment, skilled trades receiving more than semi- or unskilled, as well as rank and seniority within a rank. An additional allowance was paid to married men if they were old enough – the regular forces discouraged early marriage believing it to be a distraction – so that they could provide for the costs of family life. From July 1946, the qualifying ages were twenty-five for officers and twenty-one for non-commissioned men. Its value was about 30 per cent of total remuneration. Non-commissioned single men's total emoluments, including benefits in kind, were below those of male, semi-skilled industrial workers whose pay did not depend upon marital status. Married men's pay came out higher. Peacetime national servicemen were paid less than regular service single men.[27]

For servicewomen, the first principle was that they would not qualify for marriage allowance. If they were married, their husbands would be responsible for providing their home. All women were treated as though they were single, irrespective of actual marital status. Thus, the starting point was the pay scale of single men. As it was customary to pay women less than men, the question to be resolved was what percentage of men's rates was appropriate. Wartime practice set the scale at two-thirds of single men's pay, plus similar benefits in kind (uniform, food and accommodation). This reflected the idea that three women would be needed to replace two men as it was anticipated that women would not be such productive workers. The link to men's pay was broken in July 1946 when women received a flat rate increase rather than a percentage of men's new rates of pay, the justification being the need to work out the detail of regular service before pay scales could be set. Consequently, women's pay fell well behind what could be earned in civilian employment.

The longer this short-term fix of 1946 persisted, the more the Directors worried about the impact on recruitment and retention of servicewomen. The Service Ministries agreed that the link to men's pay should be re-established. Recognising that women were to replace men on a one-for-one basis, they wanted a more generous percentage. Jocelyn Woollcombe supported an improved percentage rise for the majority of Wrens, but believed that pay for women above the rank of second officer, equivalent to lieutenant RN, should taper back to two-thirds. Her point was that these officers would be employed only in administration for the WRNS, thus not substituting for men.[28] Accordingly, the Admiralty's negotiating position was a rate of 80 per cent of single men's pay for the majority, with a lesser rate applying to senior officers.

The Air Ministry started at the two-thirds rate. Two factors militated against equal pay: women's exclusion from the use of weapons and the burden of overseas postings which would fall on airmen to a greater extent than women.[29] However, the latter reason was subsequently judged to be hazardous as 'if this was admitted, then the Army could claim higher rates [for men] than the RAF' as more soldiers served abroad.[30] On considering the Admiralty's proposals, it supported the idea of the 80 per cent rate. However, it rejected tapering back for senior officers on the grounds that all women would remain employable in place of men and senior women's administrative roles were comparable to the work of men of equivalent rank – a statement that contradicted its views when rejecting the use of RAF rank titles for senior female officers. By 1948,

Air Ministry officials wanted to establish in principle that women's pay should be equal to single men's once equal pay was implemented for the civil service. Arthur Henderson, Secretary of State, agreed.[31]

The Executive Committee of the Army Council (ECAC) moved from an initial position of two-thirds, to 75 per cent and then fell in line with the other Ministries in supporting a united front with the Treasury at 80 per cent. Although the Admiralty still favoured tapering, in September 1948 Service Ministers agreed to pursue the case for 80 per cent with no tapering at senior ranks.[32]

Air Ministry reference to equal pay arose from the findings of the Royal Commission on Equal Pay which reported in October 1946. Although the Attlee government accepted the conclusion of the Royal Commission that women should be paid the same as men for work of equal value, it deferred adopting such a policy on the grounds that the time was not right economically. Such was the developing post-war economic crisis, the government attempted to control wage inflation in the public sector through a personal incomes policy. For Sir Stafford Cripps the issue of servicewomen's pay was bound up with the related issue of nurses' pay. Each of the armed forces had its own nursing service, predating women's military service in both the Navy and the Army. From 1943, these officer-status women were paid on the same scale as civilian nurses. This link was broken in January 1946 when civilian pay increased more than pay for service nurses. The unsurprising outcome was a crisis in staffing the Services' nursing corps.

Cripps opposed re-establishing a link between servicewomen's pay and that of men, in part because female officers would receive much more than nurses. This was unacceptable to him because: it would represent a startling pay rise at a time of wage restraint policy; female officers, who could be appointed at a young age, would receive more money than nurses who were 'professional women engaged on women's work' (by implication, suggesting that commissioned service was not women's work); and perhaps crucially, this would lead to pay claims for armed forces nursing services which would have an impact on pay for civilian nurses.[33]

Cripps' first point was correct in a sense, but the proposed pay rise simply corrected the under payment of women that prevailed from 1946. He was also right to be wary about the impact on nursing services. The Air Council had already expressed a need for nurses' pay to be improved.[34] Cripps was also against the 80 per cent sought by the Services because this was the ratio used for female non-industrial civil servants and was seen as indicating women's work was equal to that of men. Cripps feared that, when at some unspecified date in the future, a government implemented the equal pay proposal, women in the armed forces would also expect it. Perhaps his most important objection to equal pay for servicewomen was that he regarded it as untenable that they should be paid the same as fighting men because they 'had no liability to engage in personal combat'.[35]

The idea of a link between liability or otherwise to participate in combat duties was contentious in the arena of men's pay, having been aired in the 1946 settlement. The Treasury and Service Ministries recognised that not all servicemen were fighting men.[36] For men in support roles, use of weapons was described as a contingent liability, something they might be called upon to do in the last resort.[37] Men's pay had not been directly linked to their relationship to combat roles. Men in technical trades in the Army were paid more than those in fighting units, even though they might be employed in repair depots a long way from action. The 1946 pay award attempted to address the imbalance by enabling a 'skilled fighting soldier [to] receive the same pay as a skilled tradesman'.[38] However, skilled tradesmen in the RAF continued to be better paid than its ground combat personnel. Gunners of the RAF Regiment were in the third of four groups for pay purposes. The Treasury argued that men were paid on the basis of the majority employment, i.e. as though they had the same shared risk and responsibility as those in fighting units. A. V. Alexander (Minister for Defence) countered that 'no component of men's pay could be said to relate to combat'.[39] Nevertheless, for servicewomen, pay was determined by their relationship to combat – not sharing men's contingent liability to use weapons implied lower pay.

Cripps, determined to avoid linking women's pay to men's, asked his officials to draw up a scale related to that of women in industry. The resulting proposal devised rates of pay for junior ranks on what was described as a purely arbitrary basis, while those for officers were intended to be lower than the pay of nurses. The gap between women's and men's pay was to widen with increasing rank.

The problem that quickly emerged was that, by taking industrial pay as a reference point and so not taking account of marital status as servicemen's pay did, women would be paid as highly as single servicemen. According to Treasury calculations, an unmarried trained male soldier of private rank received 42 shillings per week and benefits in kind valued at 35 shillings. This was less than average semi-skilled male industrial wages of 89 shillings. Starting from the average of 77 shillings and 6 pence per week paid to semi-skilled female industrial workers and deducting the 35 shillings ascribed to benefits in kind, servicewomen would earn 42 shillings and 6 pence per week. This was 6 pence more than a single private's pay.

Treasury officials suggested that linking women's pay to industrial wages was impractical. Devising a scheme that would be sufficiently attractive to encourage women to join, and then provide incentives to longer service and promotion, was too complex. They preferred the two-thirds ratio of single men's pay as being simpler to implement and more likely to be acceptable to the Services than a separate pay code for women.[40]

Air Commandant Felicity Hanbury feared a permanent decoupling from men's pay scales as it would lead to battles each time there was an increase for men. Doubting that official channels would be effective in winning over the Treasury, she enlisted help from two sources. First, she persuaded Air Chief Marshal Wilfrid Freeman to write to Stafford Cripps. Knowing Cripps from their time together at the Ministry of Aircraft Production, Freeman reminded him that he had once been in favour of equal pay. He described the argument that women were non-combatants as fallacious as women in the Air Force were '[almost] as combatant as a large portion of the RAF with the sole exception of aircrews.'[41] Freeman's approach was rebuffed, so Hanbury next sought help from the highly respected engineer and educator Caroline Haslett, head of the Electrical Association for Women. Haslett was a known contributor on the issue of women's pay, having given evidence to the Royal Commission on Equal Pay on behalf of the British Federation of Business and Professional Women. A friend of Lady Cripps, she used this connection to lobby the Chancellor. She urged him to avoid creating an idea of women's work being distinct from men's work.[42] Her letter was also politely acknowledged but set aside.

Undeterred, Haslett used her friendship with Isobel Cripps to go to 11 Downing Street to see Sir Stafford a week before the Cabinet was due to meet on the subject.[43] The following day, Cripps wrote on a Treasury file:

> After discussion with a number of women I am of the opinion that my pay scales though rational will not be acceptable to the women in the forces and that they would not help recruiting either. For some reason or other the women think it would be derogatory <u>not</u> [original emphasis] to get a proportion of the men's salary! The trouble is that when we get equal pay they will want five-fifths and not four-fifths ... However, I have come to the conclusion that I should not persist in the idea of a separate scale for women.[44]

Cripps' Cabinet paper set out a case for his special pay scale for women, but suggested that, if this was not accepted, then a ratio of not more than the previously prevailing two-thirds of single men's pay should be set. Alexander proposed four-fifths.[45] At the meeting, Cripps was supported by George Isaacs (Minister of Labour and National Service), Aneurin Bevan (Minister for Health), Herbert Morrison (Lord President of the Council) and Arthur Woodburn (Secretary of State for Scotland). Their key concerns were size of the pay rise at a time of wage restraint and implications for other women workers if a fixed ratio of women's to men's pay was accepted as a principle. When pressed by Attlee, Cripps admitted that, while a special scale would be theoretically better, 'they must have [a] fixed rate because of the emotion aroused on this.'[46] The Cabinet settled on a compromise rate of three-quarters of single men's pay (Tables 4.1 and 4.2). This outcome was justified on the basis of 'the prevailing relationship between men's and women's remuneration in industry; the recruiting situation; and the fact that women are non-combatant'.[47] Alexander was advised to avoid reference to non-combatant status when addressing the House

Table 4.1: Weekly Basic Rates of Pay for Women's Auxiliary Services, Women's Regular Service and Regular Single Servicemen (1946–8)

Rank	Women 1946–1948	Women on Introduction of Regular Service	Regular Single Servicemen 1948
Private	23/4 to 24/6	34/5	45/6
Lance Corporal	30/4 to 36/2	37/4	49/–
Corporal	32/8 to 39/8	47/3	63/–
Sergeant	37/4 to 47/10	63/–	84/–
Staff Sergeant	46/8 to 54/10	70/7	94/6
Warrant Officer II	49/– to 59/6	75/10	101/6
Warrant Officer I	65/4 to 74/8	86/4	115/6

Sources: *Pay and Marriage Allowances of Members of the Armed Forces (other than the Women's Services)*, Cmd.7588 (London: HMSO, Dec 1948); *Pay, Retired Pay, Service Pensions and Gratuities for Members of the Women's Services*, Cmd.7607 (London: HMSO, Jan 1949) and TNA: WO 123/91 Army Orders 1949). Pay is quoted as shillings/pence using an army representative scale. This was the cash payment; personnel also received benefits in kind. There were 12 pence to the shilling and 20 shillings to the pound. When decimal coinage was introduced in 1971, a shilling became 5p.

Table 4.2: **Female Officers' Annual Pay (£) (1946–8)**

Rank	Rate 1946–1948	Rate from December 1948
2nd Subaltern	152	177
Subaltern	176	205
Junior Commander	219	314
Senior Commander	365	479
Chief Commander	541	647
Controller	625	889
Senior Controller	726	1,053

Source: Cmd.7607. Army ranks quoted. The pay scale also applied in the Air Force. The scale for the WRNS was modified to take account of faster promotion.

of Commons.[48] This may have been intended to avoid re-opening discussion of men's differing liabilities to engage in fighting.

Pay negotiations can be seen as a victory for the Service Ministries over the Treasury, with the adoption of military rather than civilian terms of service. However, with pay being set as a percentage of that of single men and, therefore, already abated to take account of marital status, a Treasury official observed that pay policy for servicewomen was 'pretty near to applying the principle of unequal pay twice over'.[49]

Pensions were a new issue as women moved on to regular service terms rather than being wartime temporary personnel. Like pay, this also proved controversial. Men who served for more than twenty years were paid an immediate pension on retiring. Its value depended on years served and rank attained. Unlike pay, it was not related to marital status. Bachelors received the same pension as married men.[50] The Treasury regarded pension provision as generous but recognised the need, as many men were required to leave in their mid-forties, an age when their family responsibilities would be at a peak. Officials thought also that fighting men might have difficulty finding new jobs as their skills would not necessarily fit them for civilian work.[51]

Initially, the Treasury considered women's peacetime Services as a short-term experiment. Once the glamour of wartime service had worn off and the disabilities in civilian life had eased, officials doubted that women would take kindly to military service. It described women's pensionable service as 'a most un-business-like proposition'. It wondered whether, rather than retaining individuals on a long-term basis, it would be preferable to 'replace them by a fresh entry'. However, if a pension was to be offered, women should be obliged to serve for longer than men to earn it as they did not undertake equal work. Female civil servants, who received pensions at age sixty, were seen as the comparator.[52] The likelihood of women being able to find new employment after retirement was argued both ways. It was thought that women approaching fifty would have difficulty in gaining civilian work. Alternatively, as so many would have been employed in domestic trades, there would be a ready market for their experience.[53]

Stafford Cripps was concerned that setting women's pensions as a fixed percentage of men's rates would be too generous because all men's pensions were determined on the basis of married men's pay. If a ratio was agreed in principle, then it should be lower than that used for pay so that women would not benefit from the way that men's pensions were calculated.[54] In Cabinet, he argued that women would be very well off on their pensions and this would 'provoke demand for increases for men'.[55] The idea that women did not have the same family responsibilities as men was common ground. Accordingly, the Cabinet agreed to set the ratio at two-thirds of men's pensions (Table 4.3).

Doctors and dentists were an interesting exception. When these professionally qualified women were employed during the war, they worked within the medical branches, not the women's Services. Their professional associations (British Medical Association and British Dental Association) insisted that they receive the same pay as men.[56] This continued to be the case for regular service. The Air Ministry assumed that, as pay was equal, then pensions would be equal. Treasury officials' perspective was that 'women doctors are after all women and should be remunerated as such'. Conceding pensions payable at the same ratio

Table 4.3: Female Officers' Pensions 1949

Rank	Years Served	Pension (£)
Junior Commander	20	250
Senior Commander	22	320
Chief Commander	24	420
Controller	26	550
Senior Controller	28	600

Source: TNA: WO 123/91 Army Orders 1949. Subaltern ranks are not shown. They did not serve for long enough to earn these pensions.

as pay would undermine the decision to use different pay and pension ratios for other women in the Services. When they raised the issue with Sir Stafford Cripps, he suggested they should 'gracefully retire on this one!'[57] Rather gleefully, the Air Ministry noted that the Treasury had capitulated.[58]

Marriage and Motherhood

Before the war it was standard practice for employers to require female workers who married to leave. Out of necessity, this policy had been set aside for the duration of the war. The armed forces were no exception. It accepted married women, including (from 1941) mothers of school-age children.[59] Servicewomen who became pregnant were required to leave. With the introduction of peacetime service, like other employers, the Service Ministries had to decide whether employment of married women would continue post-war.[60] This had two elements: could women who married while serving remain in the forces and could married women join?

The Services needed some women to have full careers so that there would be a cadre of senior officers and senior NCOs to deal with matters such as policy, welfare and the training of junior women. However, the demands of a career were regarded as being in conflict with the obligations of marriage. Air Ministry deliberations stand as an example of the discussions. Examining the idea of regular service, its post-war manning policy committee initially favoured discharging women on marriage. Countering this view by arguing the need to populate senior posts, Air Commandant Lady Welsh successfully proposed that women who married should be given an option to leave rather than automatic discharge. Accepting her suggestion, the Committee then went further by proposing that married women and widows should also be eligible to join provided they would be available for posting wherever needed, including overseas.[61]

Like the planning committee, the Air Council was divided on the issue when deciding on terms of service in 1947. Air Marshal Sir William Dickson, Vice Chief of the Air Staff, opposed commissioning of married women as officers, arguing that it was 'a great mistake, anti-social [and] introduced an element of inflexibility in posting'. It is not clear whether this latter point implied a need to post married personnel with some degree of proximity or whether the emphasis was on the undesirability of having married personnel serving at the same location. What is certain is that the posting of married women was seen as problematic.

Air Commandant Felicity Hanbury, in attendance at the Air Council meeting, suggested that 'from the administrative point of view, it would be of the greatest value to have a few married women in the Service.' Her views were not elaborated in the minutes. She may have been making the same point as Lady Welsh about retaining candidates for senior ranks. With Hanbury receiving support from Air Marshal Slessor (Air Member for Personnel), the Air Council opted to allow married women to serve, subject to 'adequate administrative safeguards' being introduced.[62] One such safeguard appears to have been the right of husbands of married applicants to object, though actual consent was not required.[63] Recruiting literature made explicit the need for married women to prove they could fulfil service obligations. The Admiralty and the War Office reached the same conclusion.

Having determined that married women could join, the issue of those with children below the school-leaving age (fifteen from 1947) also had to be addressed. Although mothers took paid work outside the home, there was an expectation that they would stay at home to take care of the children while fathers earned the family income. But employment in the armed forces brought difficulties beyond those of most work places. One key problem was self-inflicted. Believing that it would undermine discipline, married personnel were not permitted to serve on the same unit. Frequent postings to different locations and hence separation from a woman's family network, accommodation difficulties due to the shortage of married quarters and restrictions on married couples working at the same establishment made it extremely difficult for married women with children to serve on full military terms.

For Woollcombe, Tyrwhitt and Hanbury the willingness of all women to accept postings was crucial. This was a fundamental tenet of service life. If these smaller, peacetime Services were to be efficient, they could not afford cohorts that would only serve locally as had been permitted in the wartime WRNS. In addition, enforcement of compulsory service overseas for women, avoided during the war, was now essential in the RAF because the establishment for airwomen in occupied Germany exceeded the supply of volunteers. The Air Ministry preferred airwomen to national servicemen for overseas duty because tours of duty abroad needed to be for about two years duration. Conscripted men would not serve for long enough to make overseas postings economic.[64] Hanbury argued at the Air Council that women with children under the school-leaving age would be unable to make the necessary commitment to serve where needed and that they should be excluded from joining. This was adopted as policy.[65]

Rules on pregnancy were simple; discharge was automatic. This was not contentious – it was common ground that the obligations of new motherhood were incompatible with military service. However, Commandant Woollcombe feared that the consequence of such a policy would be that '"career" [original emphasis] WRNS Officers must almost inevitably be single women or at any rate women without families.' She wanted female officers to be able to rejoin and compete for senior posts when 'their family responsibilities were less onerous'. Rear Admiral Denny (Assistant Chief of Naval Personnel) was not enthusiastic. He believed 'the practice of importing a number of ex-officers in the higher ranks as a matter of course was most undesirable.' He thought that encouraging women to return should only be considered if there was a lack of suitable candidates for promotion.[66] Both the Air Ministry and the War Office were prepared to re-employ female officers who left because of marriage. On the advice of Mary Tyrwhitt, the War Office adopted promotion rules in the WRAC that would favour women with continuous service.[67]

Thus far the Ministries were mainly in agreement. It was the contentious issue of pregnancy of unmarried women where there was significant divergence between the War Office and the other Ministries. In her memoir, Felicity Hanbury recalled that dealing with the discharge of pregnant single women had always 'held a very important place in the work of the WAAF administrative officers.' In such cases, the WAAF officer guided the woman to civilian agencies that could provide assistance, advised on how to register for work, and how to claim support from the father, through the civil courts if necessary. When regulations for the regular WRAF were discussed at a meeting of the Air Member for Personnel and his senior staff, Felicity Hanbury recorded that she 'listened, spellbound, to these men discussing, apparently in all sincerity, what punishment they should mete out to any airwoman or WRAF officer who became illegitimately pregnant.' Her opinion not being sought, she apparently interjected, '"And what do you propose to do to the men involved? ... Promote them to Air Marshals, I suppose?"'[68]

Despite Air Commandant Hanbury's doubts, the Air Council did believe it had leadership obligations on moral standards and it took pregnancy of unmarried women seriously, particularly if fathers were in the RAF. Echoing a letter issued in May 1945, Air Marshal

Sir Leslie Hollinghurst (Air Member for Personnel 1949–52) wrote to Commanders-in-Chief asking them to issue orders on the subject of moral responsibility and social relationships to officers and men under their command. He acknowledged that relationships were inevitable. Where these led to marriage, he welcomed them because airwomen made 'the finest possible wives for men making a career in the RAF', having a 'steadying influence ... on their husbands.' However, relationships that resulted in pregnancy outside marriage were condemned as having a disproportionately damaging impact on the woman who had to give up her job and then cope with the social stigma and financial hardship of single motherhood. Such cases also resulted in bad publicity for the RAF and could hinder recruiting to the WRAF.[69]

Hollinghurst regarded men as 'invariably by all standards the more blameworthy' for pregnancy outside marriage than airwomen. He directed that, where a man was senior in rank and was considered to have taken advantage of a young airwoman, he was to be charged with an offence under the Air Force Act. Advice was given on talks for men on conducting proper relationships with airwomen, sex education for young airwomen, steering young women away from the perils of excessive drinking, and the process for swift posting away to another station if an inappropriate relationship was detected. A system of collecting data on pregnancy of single women by RAF station was introduced. Station commanders were warned that 'When the incidence [was] unduly high it [would] normally be held to reflect upon the power of command and leadership ... and appropriate action should follow.' The paper did not quote an acceptable average. Although the letter suggested great anxiety on the issue, it also noted that the incidence of pregnancy outside of marriage was lower than in the same age group in society. However, Air Marshal Hollinghurst believed that the RAF should have higher standards than the civilian community.[70]

Discharge from the service as a result of pregnancy was on the agenda at the conference of Senior WRNS Officers in October 1949. Apparently discussing pregnancy of single women, the notes recorded that investigations 'had produced some very horrifying figures'. Wrens' failings were attributed to 'lack of standard and moral conviction, drink and ignorance.' The merits of the talk on sex given during recruit training were called into question. Some thought it did more harm than good. Representatives from the Commands at Nore and Plymouth blamed large shared cabins (as the Navy invariably described accommodation) that allowed 'girls to listen and take part in undesirable talk'. Presumably taking idleness as a sign of degeneracy, the Plymouth representative also condemned 'the habit of WRNS ratings of lying in bed all Sunday morning'. Commandant Woollcombe undertook to review the approach to sex education in initial training and, meanwhile, urged her colleagues to do 'everything possible to improve the moral tone.'[71]

To the dismay of Mary Tyrwhitt, regulations approved by the ECAC in December 1946 had the effect of allowing pregnant non-commissioned ranks to leave the army on full retirement benefits, but for officers the regulations would only apply to married women.[72] She took up the issue at the Regular Women's Service Committee, contending that:

> unless it [was] proposed to make pregnancy out of wedlock a military offence (in which case, if the man concerned were an officer or soldier, he could of course be charged as an accessory), there [were] no grounds for discrimination between the unmarried and married officer in the matter of retirement benefits.[73]

She argued that pregnancy should not be treated as a military offence as it would give rise to undesirable publicity. When her case for equal treatment was made again to the ECAC, it was not persuaded. Although it claimed not to be passing judgement, it maintained a moralistic line in respect of unmarried, pregnant officers. Officers and other ranks could be treated differently because officers were held to higher standards of behaviour. In becoming pregnant, an unmarried officer was breaking her contract 'by her own action' and 'discounted the argument that ... pregnancy was the result of the action of two persons, one of whom would escape its consequences'.[74] This was a very different line from that taken by the Air Council which at least recognised the differential impact of pregnancy and attempted to address the moral issue of shared responsibility.

Conclusion

Unlike men's regular Services, where leaders were chosen from carefully groomed elite officers who built careers over a lifetime, Woollcombe, Tyrwhitt and Hanbury emerged to run the women's organisations on the basis of their wartime contributions. They were not necessarily the most senior in age or rank, but were selected in recognition that they were the most able to undertake the challenging work of establishing peacetime careers for women. Their influence was apparent in all aspects of terms and conditions of service.

The battle over pay was critical, not simply for the rates that were negotiated, but for the principle that women were part of the armed forces and should be paid as such. They should not be regarded, as Cripps preferred, as a female workforce assisting the military. The women's Services had suffered from the decoupling of pay from men's rates in 1946 and Hanbury foresaw future problems if women's pay was always to be negotiated separately. In a bold move, working outside of the normal channels of communication, she used her connections to influence Cripps.

Although the idea of equal pay for equal work was current in the late 1940s, it remained entirely normal for women to be paid less than men. The negative aspect of adopting military norms was that the armed forces' pay code discriminated between married and single men. As marriage allowance was connected with family responsibilities, which it was assumed women would not share, servicewomen were treated as single. They received a percentage of single men's rates and so earned less than civilian workers whose marital status did not dictate pay.

The primary reason given for not recognising servicewomen's work as equal to men's was their non-combatant status. Here the Air Ministry differed from the other Services in that it saw women's contribution as of equal value in principle to that of men employed in ground-based roles. It recognised the limited liability for combat of the majority of its personnel. However, the War Office at this time was considering defensive arming of the WRAC. The reason why that proposal was not taken to the Army Board in 1949 has not been traced. It leaves open the question of what would have happened to pay policy if the War Office had approved arming of women and whether this contributed to the decision not to proceed.

Woollcombe, Tyrwhitt and Hanbury made essential interventions when the Admiralty, Army and Air Force Boards might well have opted to exclude married women. The key arguments were the need to create a pool of contenders for senior rank and the presence of married women to guide young servicewomen working and living in predominantly male environments. Nevertheless, the Directors shared concerns about whether married women would accept the commitment of serving where sent, including overseas. They could not afford a cohort who would duck unpopular postings, which would then fall disproportionately to single women. There was an acceptance, though, that the duties of married life might well outweigh those of a career. Accordingly, they negotiated a right for women to give notice to leave if they married while in the Service. This was seen as an essential right if young women were to be persuaded to volunteer. Quick and free discharge on marriage was a critical difference in terms of service compared with servicemen who had no such right.

Regulations were brought about by a mixture of what the Directors thought prudent, adaptation of men's regulations, expectations of behaviour in the Services and norms of society at that time. Terms and conditions of service, which were hardly helpful to married personnel of either sex, were even less so for women. They went beyond the norms of British society and reflected the Services' cultures and career patterns. Dismissal on pregnancy was not controversial. Reflecting the values of the times, the Directors also surrendered the possibility of women with young children serving as they had in the war, although there was a theoretical possibility of female officers re-joining. With barriers to married service having been erected, this would be a long-term career opportunity only for those prepared to remain single or, if married, childless, as predicted by Jocelyn Woollcombe.

Treasury officials doubted that young women would find Service life appealing in peacetime. Terms of service were stacked against long-term employment. Allowed to leave on marriage and dismissed when pregnant, servicewomen were perceived as having a lesser commitment to serve than male colleagues. How could opportunities, pay and prospects be made sufficiently attractive to appeal to potential recruits? The early years of regular service were to prove challenging.

5

EARLY YEARS OF REGULAR SERVICE

Speaking at the Association of Wrens' Annual Meeting in May 1947, former WRNS Director Vera Laughton Mathews said:

> We know that the decision to keep the WRNS as a permanent Service was due very largely to the man-power situation in the country, but that will not be so for ever, and the future of the WRNS depends very much on the account that those now serving give of themselves. They must make themselves essential to the Navy.[1]

Mathews emphasised the publicly stated reason for the creation of regular service for women, namely lessening the need for men. However, she overlooked two important aims in the paper that went to the Defence Committee of the Cabinet in May 1946. First, there was to be a core of women in the armed forces to provide a nucleus around which expansion could take place in national emergency. Second, there would be reserve forces from which those reinforcements would be drawn.[2]

The key issue was whether or not women could be recruited and retained to make these aims of a core for expansion and lessening the need for men realistic. A spirit of optimism in the Service Ministries saw target numbers for women increased from about 14–17,000 in the 1946 Cabinet paper to 51,500 in 1948 plans. However, the original aims were already undermined as a period on the reserve after leaving the Services was not made compulsory. In the early 1950s, expectations of the nature of a future major war also changed. The Soviet Union demonstrated its nuclear weapons' capability, and Britain successfully tested an atom bomb in 1952 and a hydrogen bomb in 1957. The idea of a war of attrition like the First World War, or the slow build-up to land warfare experienced by Britain in the Second World War, was swept aside by the advent of nuclear weapons. Military planners assumed that if deterrence failed, a major war would start with an exchange of nuclear weapons and that the UK would be a main target for such an attack. Accordingly, 'by 1955 British planners assumed that [a global war] would be nasty, brutish, very short, and that it would have to be fought with forces in being because there would be no time to mobilise and despatch reserves'.[3]

A pivotal moment in defence policy was reached in April 1957 when Duncan Sandys (Minister for Defence) published his White Paper. He proposed significant changes to the armed forces to reflect 'these scientific advances [that] fundamentally alter[ed] the whole basis of military planning.'[4] Britain would revert to its custom of having all-volunteer armed forces. Conscription was to end. The final intake was planned for 1960, with an expectation that the last national serviceman would leave by the end of 1962. Male regular forces would be capped at 375,000, to be supported by civilian staff and contractors. Reserve forces would be earmarked for home defence duties rather than as reinforcements to be deployed to continental Europe. To the alarm of servicewomen, the WRNS, WRAC and WRAF were not mentioned.

If there was less need for men, less reliance on reserves and no time to expand the armed forces in the event of major war, what was the purpose now of women's Services? Had women made themselves essential as urged by Commandant Mathews and was there a place for them in post-national service forces as envisaged by Sandys? But first, would women volunteer for these peacetime forces and could they undertake long-term careers so that target strengths could be met?

Recruitment and Retention

Speaking in 2009, retired fighter control specialist Air Commodore Joan Hopkins said of her decision to enlist in March 1955, aged nineteen, 'I watched Swansea burn. I swore that I would never let anybody do that to my country again if I could do anything about it. ... So that's why I joined the Air Force.' From observing a ship being damaged by an explosion, to an unexploded landmine in her street and a barrage balloon descending onto the roof of her home, Joan had vivid childhood memories of the war. Her emotional recollection of seeking a Service career was accompanied by more pragmatic thoughts:

I worked for my father for the best part of a year [after leaving school]. He was a wholesale-grocer and I was humping and dumping in his warehouse. I didn't enjoy it much. I needed to get away from my family ... I had to go clear away. But at the age that I was, I couldn't live on my own. I had to find an organisation that would take me in. I opted for the Air Force. ... [My family] weren't happy. The only reason that women joined the Air Force was a sexual one ... that was – at the time – the popular impression of women in the Air Force. They were only there as comforts for the troops. I was not going to join the Air Force to be a comfort for the troops.[5]

Anthea Savill (later Commandant Larken, Director of the WRNS 1988–91) was born in August 1938 and joined the Wrens at the age of eighteen. Rather than opposition from those around her, the idea was suggested to her by a family friend and, once she had decided, she was strongly supported by her headmistress. She remembered that her mother 'was concerned about me going away. But I would have been going away anyway, wouldn't I? One way or another'. As for seeing the WRNS as a long-term career, she recollected:

I don't think I thought enough ahead as to what [I] would do. I didn't join the Wrens intending to be Director. I joined the Wrens intending to have a career, enjoy myself and see what happened. ... I don't recall meeting too many who felt they had the Director's baton in their knapsack. ... The people I was with ... were not people who sat back on their behinds and let life pass them by – they were all intelligent girls with common sense. ... I think a lot of them were looking for marriage. After all, we're talking the late 1950s and that's a lot of what one did in those days. And a lot of them did get married and left.[6]

These recollections provide some insights into attitudes in the 1950s. Anthea Savill's remarks highlight an important truth: young women were not necessarily seeking a long-term career. Hopkins revealed a mix of motives behind her decision to join: patriotism, but also the urge to make her own way in life. She also recognised a key difference between military and civilian workplaces. For her, the RAF was not just about a satisfying job, it was also a surrogate family environment. But she also remembered the reputation of servicewomen as being sexually available, reflecting morality scares from both World Wars.

Paradoxically, although seen as potential sex objects, there were fears that military service implied a lack of femininity. The recruiting system had to counter negative stereotypes and foster positive images of the Services with those who influenced career choices. The challenge was to make the armed forces sound attractive and exciting compared with civilian life and how to influence the opinions of the people who surrounded potential recruits – family members, friends, boyfriends and school teachers.

The Central Office of Information, advised by a Service Ministries' policy committee, was responsible for publicity. It placed advertisements in national and local press, including magazines. Advertisements aimed at women were keen to portray images of modernity and femininity, as well as highlighting career opportunities. However, campaigns could be constrained by other employment priorities. For example, in 1948 the committee banned the use of posters aimed at women in the north-west of England in order to protect the textile industry.[7]

Early campaigns for the WRNS ('You'll like the life in the WRNS') emphasised the glamour of the Service and its members.[8] An example from 1952 pictured a young, attractive woman, with styled hair showing

An Advertisement for the WRNS 1952 (TNA: INF 2/89).

under her cap and a modicum of make-up, suggesting the retention of femininity. No educational qualifications were demanded. It was personal attributes of character and ambition that were called for from potential recruits.

WRAF recruiting contained more information on the work and career prospects than the Navy campaign. Urged to 'Join the WRAF and give your ambition wings', integration within the RAF, working with men, and the prospect of holding rank senior to men, were to the fore. Advertisements made an appeal to discard the limitations of civilian life as women were urged to 'seize life's opportunities' and 'achieve financial independence' rather than 'sit still and watch life pass you by' or 'stay tied to anyone's apron strings'.[9] A 1951 advertisement depicted a WRAF sergeant working alongside male colleagues in an operations room and out-ranking one of them.

An Advertisement
for the WRAF
1951 (TNA:
INF 2/75).

Campaigns for the WRAC took on the people surrounding young women with advertisements including appeals to family and friends. In 1952, text highlighted the attractions of service life in contrast to the frustrations of the civilian environment:

> ... you make many new friends – friends to work with in an absorbing job, friends to share your free time. No rent or clothing to pay for, no having your meals alone, no season ticket to buy, no crowded buses or trains to face every day. Responsibility? Yes – the sort that gives you self-confidence and self-reliance.[10]

An Advertisement for the WRAC 1952 (TNA: INF 2/86).

These advertisements shared common themes of bright young women, undertaking important work, with the attractions of smart uniform, free food and accommodation, travel, companionship and exciting leisure opportunities – a chance to get on, away from the humdrum existence of home life and a job without prospects. But limitations were revealed in an Air Ministry pamphlet aimed at parents. Taking a frequently-asked-questions approach, this booklet urged the need to consider a daughter's career with the same care as that of a son. However, ambition appeared to be secondary to traditional expectations as revealed in a question on promotion. The scene was set with a remark which might be posed by parents: 'In the event of our daughter not marrying, we understand that she can make the WRAF her career.'[11] Career prospects were presented as a fallback, should the primary aspiration of marriage not be achieved. Nor was there any expectation of combining marriage and career.

An analysis of WRAF recruiting in 1949 showed that the average age of a new recruit was nineteen. A 1951 survey indicated that only a small proportion had good qualifications. The majority were from working-class backgrounds and had left school at an average age of fourteen years and eight months. All 123 in the survey were single. Typically, they had had three civilian jobs before enlisting: factory work (32 per cent), clerical jobs (23 per cent), shop work (12 per cent) or domestic trades (11 per cent). Most had at least one hobby classified as active, such as sport or dancing. A 1958 survey found that women joined for travel, companionship, to become independent, for a complete change from civilian circumstances and to get on in life.[12]

A War Office report from 1952 made similar points. As the majority of girls left school before they were old enough to join the WRAC, the report concluded that they had to target recruiting material through the press and Labour Exchanges to entice them to leave their current employers. But an effort should be made before girls left school to plant the idea that a service career was attractive. Parents were seen as a major obstacle as they expected daughters to remain at home to help with domestic work and to contribute a share of their earnings into the family budget. Boyfriends were likewise seen as obstacles as they feared competition from male soldiers. Young women themselves were perceived as less likely than young men to be willing to move away from their home area.

Noting that it was not doing as well as the RAF, the War Office blamed its own system of recruiting. Women were enlisted into the WRAC and only allocated to a trade after joining and committing themselves to serve for three years. Potential recruits were put off by the inability to choose their type of employment and feared spending their time on menial work. Neither of the other Services adopted this entirely blank-cheque approach. Although not guaranteed a specific trade before enlistment, their recruits had an indication of the type of work (e.g. technical, clerical, catering) open to them on the basis of their performance on assessment tests in the recruitment process and vacancies to be filled.[13]

The concept of the women's Services being cores for expansion in the event of a future major war was soon tested and found wanting. In response to the outbreak of the Korean War in 1950, the government increased the period of national service for men from eighteen months to two years. Consequently, the number of men in the armed forces rose from 666,000 in 1950 to 848,000 in 1952. In contrast, the strength of the women's Services was plummeting despite the War Office's 1952 aspiration to more than double the size of the WRAC.[14]

Optimistically, the Air Ministry estimated that it would need an annual intake of 19 per cent of planned WRAF strength to maintain numbers. War Office and Admiralty staff planned on figures nearer 25 per cent.[15] However, the annual outflow of trained women in the 1950s was nearly 40 per cent. Consequently, there was a net loss of women nearly every year (Figures 5.4 and 5.5). A number of factors contributed to shorter than expected length of service, the most critical of which were marriage and pregnancy. Serving if married was difficult, at a time when marriage at an earlier age was a trend in British society. The critical age category for the armed forces was twenty to twenty-four as women were mostly under twenty years old on joining and signed on for four-year engagements (reduced to three years for the WRAC in November 1949). Census returns from 1951 and 1961 show that in this age group, the percentage of married women rose from 46.5% to 56.4%. Corresponding statistics for the age group twenty-five to thirty-four rose from 78.8% in 1951 to 85% in 1961. In addition, the median interval between marriage and birth of a child was in the order of nineteen to twenty months.[16] Even if a woman stayed in the Services after marriage, there was a strong likelihood that she would leave within two years to have a child.

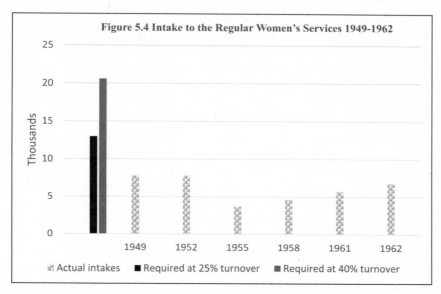

Source: Required intakes are to sustain a strength of 51,500 at turnover rates of 25% and 40% per annum. Actual intakes from *Annual Abstract of Statistics*, No.93, (London: HMSO, 1956), Tables 136 and 137 and No.103, (London: HMSO, 1966), Tables 134 and 135.

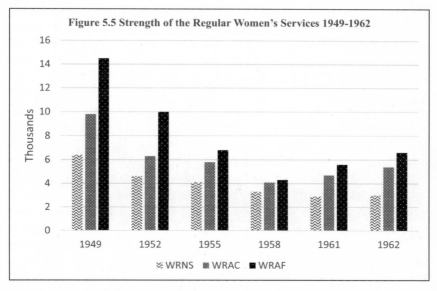

Source: *Annual Abstract of Statistics*, No.93, (London: HMSO, 1956), Tables 136 and 137 and No. 103, (London: HMSO, 1966), Tables 134 and 135.

Policies allowed for married women to serve, but the reality was difficult. There were explicit obstacles for those with husbands also in the armed forces. Army regulations stated that a married officer could not be posted to the same unit as her husband.[17] In the WRNS, married women could serve at the same establishment as their husbands provided there was no great disparity in rank between them and their work did not bring them into contact with each other. Otherwise, 'every endeavour' would be made to post a married woman near her husband. However, this was not guaranteed as the needs of the Service came first. Of course, men's seagoing necessitated separation.[18]

In the RAF, if both husband and wife were in the Services, it was at the commanding officer's discretion as to whether they could serve at the same station. If one was an officer and the other non-commissioned, they were barred from serving together.[19] In addition, not all stations had WRAF sections, so collocation was not always possible. These regulations were drawn up on an assumption that married personnel working together was to be avoided. There were also off-duty complexities in these organisations that expected personnel to socialise with work colleagues of equivalent status. Attendance at a mess or club was determined by rank. For non-commissioned ranks, a wife holding junior rank was often unwelcome at events in a Senior NCOs' mess. Likewise, attendance of non-commissioned ranks in officers' messes was problematic.

Even if collocation of couples was permitted, practical difficulties could intervene. In the 1950s, a lack of married quarters was compounded by the shortage of civilian accommodation as the country recovered from wartime damage to housing stock.[20] As all servicewomen were deemed to be single irrespective of their actual marital status, women were not eligible to take up tenancies of married quarters. Women married to civilians had to trust to civilian housing. A woman married to a serviceman had to rely on quarters being available where her husband worked, assuming that the couple had postings with the necessary proximity. So bad was the housing situation throughout the 1950s that the RAF and the Army bought caravans to use as married accommodation.

There was also a degree of ambivalence towards favourable posting of married women, which was seen as being at the expense of single women. The senior female WRNS officer at Plymouth Command headquarters complained that married Wrens ignored their commitment to being mobile, demanding the right to be posted to suit their marital circumstances. If they were dissatisfied, they '[made] threats of desertion and sometimes of correspondence with their MPs.' Concessions, if made, were 'largely at the expense of the single girls'. The author wanted Wrens to be obliged to resign on marriage, as was the case in the Queen Alexandra's Royal Naval Nursing Service. Failing that, she proposed 'powers of greater discouragement to those contemplating remaining in the Service on marriage'.[21]

The RAF appeared to be sympathetic in principle but constrained in practice. A 1959 report on WRAF commissioning policy suggested that it would be helpful if married women were 'afforded a reasonable chance of being posted with or near their husbands'. Arrangements were made for some married women to be collocated 'but these cases [were] the exception rather than the rule, and involve[d] many informal negotiations.' There was reluctance to advertise such a mechanism, as collocation could not be guaranteed. Nevertheless, the officers and aircrew manning committee decided that discreet reference could be made to the process and that requests would be considered.[22]

The engagement structure of successive short contracts also contributed to higher than planned rates of leaving. Women had to make a positive decision to re-engage for further service after they completed their initial period of three or four years; the default position was to leave. Some snapshot data is available. In 1951, 40 per cent of Wrens left having either completed their period of service or departed early due to marriage, pregnancy, on compassionate grounds or 'deserted'. In the second half of 1954, of 628 non-commissioned women in the WRAC who came to the end of their engagement, only 203 signed on for a further term. A 1957 paper for the Air Council noted that about one-third of the WRAF left each year.[23] It became a common occurrence for senior women officers to urge their juniors on stations to encourage women to sign on for further periods of service. This idea of 'internal recruitment', as it was called, also featured with servicemen as retention became a more significant problem than initial recruitment over the ensuing decades.

Developments in the Women's Services

The vulnerability of the WRNS as a shore-based, civilian-in-uniform organisation was evident immediately. A major study on the size and shape of the armed forces recommended disbanding it only four weeks after regular service started in 1949. Too many women were employed in administering women (800 out of a strength of about 7,000). The study argued that as the RN was not short of male volunteers, Wrens could be replaced by regular servicemen. These would be more flexible in the jobs they could do and would serve on average for longer. It went on to say that this was not the case in the other Services, which would have to replace women with men serving even shorter periods (i.e. national servicemen).[24] The Admiralty Board dismissed the suggestion as politically unthinkable. In addition, such a move would lead to an increase in the proportion of men ashore, contrary to the Board's manpower policy.[25]

Little wonder then that Dame Nancy Robertson (Director WRNS, 1954–58) described her objective as being 'to consolidate the permanent Service and to ensure that there was a worthwhile career open to ambitious and well-qualified girls'.[26] The theme remained the same for her successor, Dame Elizabeth Hoyer Millar, who described the difficulty of sustaining enough posts for Wrens. As bases closed in the 1950s, she said the 'problem was to find them billets [jobs] in order to keep the strength going to what was the ceiling we were allowed, and below which would have been uneconomic.'[27] This perception of there being a minimum size dictated by value for money was an anxiety shared by the other Services' Directors.

Nevertheless, WRNS Directors had a strong sense of the purpose of their Service as shore-based support for the Royal Navy. They looked for opportunities for women to take on more jobs, particularly overseas postings. Malta was the main opportunity at this time. Periodically, Wrens would spend time at NATO Headquarters. First Officer Joan Cole was given the interesting post of assisting the Women's Royal Australian Navy to start up again, it having been disbanded after the war. She held the role of its Director from November 1954.[28] However, cutbacks in the strength of the Royal Navy and its shore bases had a detrimental impact on the WRNS.

This unity of purpose was missing from the WRAC. The conflict between career prospects of specialists working for army support corps and women employed in WRAC companies was already evident in two reports that went to the Army Council in 1952. There was some feeling that women with specialist skills should join their employing corps. Brigadier Coulshed (Director WRAC) wanted to retain women under her control, suggesting that otherwise the WRAC 'would simply become a corps of housekeepers'.[29] The Army Council accepted the need to keep a women's corps but thought that working 'shoulder-to-shoulder with men' should become the norm.[30]

Sadly for women, one of the most popular jobs now seen as for men only was work with the Royal Artillery (RA) in heavy anti-aircraft artillery batteries and searchlights. This operational role persisted post-war. However, technological developments meant that such batteries were to be replaced by surface-to-air missiles and more reliance on fighter aircraft to defend British airspace. The War Office announced the demise of Anti-Aircraft Command in 1955. With its disbandment, the WRAC component was also disestablished. In 1958, when arms and corps were invited to consider how they might employ women, the reply on behalf of Major General Reginald Hobbs (Director RA) comprised two sentences:

> I have given a considerable amount of thought to the possibility of opening more trades to WRAC in the Royal Artillery. I have, however, come to the conclusion that, because of the limitations that apply to any trade which women undertake, I can offer no suggestions.[31]

This reply, which seemed to belie the idea that the matter had been given considerable thought, reflected the reality of the constraints imposed by policy that women could not undertake work in peacetime that they could not also fulfil in war, that they were excluded from working in field conditions, that they were not to be given lengthy training, they were not to be armed, work had to be within their physical capabilities, any trade in which they were employed had to offer an adequate rank and promotion structure with some overseas service, and that women were not to work in isolated groups. Light ant-aircraft batteries, intended for field deployments, were deemed unsuitable for women.

All of these conditions came into play when the Royal Signals were short of men of the required standard, particularly in support of intelligence services. Signallers had to be available for mobile roles as well as static headquarters. Even for some static jobs, there were perceived problems in women covering night shifts if they had to work predominantly with men. In West Germany, the idea of cutting the men's establishment for intelligence work and replacing them with WRAC was resisted. Women would be accepted if they were additional to the number of men allowed, otherwise there would be insufficient personnel for mobile units on the outbreak of war.[32]

Not all theatres took this view of women's unsuitability. Lieutenant General Sir Roger Bower, Commander-in-Chief Middle East Land

Forces, was keen to have more WRAC in place of men – particularly men with families who were said to create an administrative burden and were a drain on the defence budget. He proposed that soldiers' entitlement to a marriage allowance be deferred from age twenty-one to age twenty-five, bringing them into line with regulations for officers. He argued that if it was done gradually and without much publicity, it need not be politically objectionable.[33] That idea got nowhere, but it provides an interesting glimpse of attitudes. Bower was not so much an enthusiast for the WRAC, rather he opposed early marriage for men which was facilitated by payment of the marriage allowance at age twenty-one.

While the War Office struggled to expand women's employment as fully mobile regulars, it revived a wartime practice of local service that had proved successful in the WRNS. The thought was that young women were unwilling to leave home but they might be encouraged to work at their local unit. As they would live at home, the additional advantage was that accommodation and food would not be provided – reducing costs. Having only a local commitment, married women might be enticed to serve. The Army Council approved the concept in September 1952.[34]

Local service was not a great success, though it is not clear why the idea was not attractive. Perhaps it had the disadvantages of service conditions (low pay compared with civilian work) plus the cost of travel to and from work, without the advantages of camaraderie of living and socialising collectively. Roles open to locally employed women were limited to those that had short training, and promotion chances were slim. The Air Ministry followed the army's example in 1958. The quality of women joining was deemed a success but only 445 out of 1,000 posts were filled.[35] Although disappointed with poor take-up, the scheme was retained as overheads were low.[36]

The Air Ministry's policy of integration was gradually taking shape. The women's officer training school at RAF Hawkinge was closed and, in 1962, training was collocated with male officer training at RAF Jurby on the Isle of Man.[37] Staff College places for female officers were approved in principle by 1950.[38] This was an important development because it opened up more jobs at Headquarters and Defence Ministries for women. Squadron Officers Martin and Borlase were the first selected to attend the College in Andover in 1953. Squadron Officer Martin went on to become the first woman to achieve the rank of air commodore in competition with RAF officers. To the dismay of

Jean Conan Doyle (later Director WRAF, 1963–6), Squadron Officer Borlase became engaged to a fellow student on the course, married and left the Service in 1954.[39] Borlase's departure so soon after completing this prestigious course may have fuelled belief that investing in women's training was poor value for money.

A proposal from Technical Training Command in 1963 not only to collocate junior ranks' recruit training but to integrate it, came to nothing. Conan Doyle was thought to oppose the move as 'efficiency and morale would suffer if [men and women] were trained in the same place.'[40] This seems an odd stance as initial officer training had been collocated the previous year and trade training courses, which followed on from junior ranks' recruit training, was already combined. Conan Doyle may have been safeguarding a rare senior post for female officers as commander of the WRAF Recruit Training School. Integration of training would have led to the loss of this post as a male officer would inevitably have been selected to command a combined training school.

Like the War Office, the Air Ministry struggled with its policy on employing women in West Germany. The normal establishment of its 2nd Tactical Air Force – as its forces were known – initially included WRAF personnel. The wartime establishment required 819 women of whom 486 would serve on operational units, some of which would disperse from main bases to become mobile formations.[41] Air Chief Marshal Sir Robert Foster, Commander-in-Chief from October 1951 to December 1953, opposed including airwomen in operational wings as had been accepted by his predecessor. He cited accommodation and supervisory difficulties for mobile units in war. As the potential warning time prior to a Soviet attack would be too short to withdraw airwomen and replace them with men (assuming men would be available), then he could not accept women in peacetime. He saw airwomen as contributing only in headquarters, hospitals and some static formations.[42]

Air Commandant Nancy Salmon (Director WRAF) was dismayed that an important policy on women's employment could be overturned suddenly on a change in Commander-in-Chief. She pointed out that airwomen had been deployed in 1951's autumn exercises to great effect and that withdrawal from their roles just a few months later would be damaging to morale, bringing with it a suggestion that the women had failed. She dismissed arguments about the unacceptability of women being exposed to risk from attack in war pointing out that this flew in the face of the decision to employ servicewomen. They would not be immune from attack even if only based in the UK and they must accept their share of the hazards of war. She called for the Air Council to set out policy on operational employment.[43] It duly did, but it sided with Robert Foster. Avoiding the argument about hazards of war, it highlighted Foster's point that living conditions for a mobile force were 'primitive and arduous ... [and] women would be an embarrassment to which a Commander should not be subject'.[44]

In 1955, policy was reversed following a request from Foster's successor, Air Marshal Broadhurst. His problem was very practical. There was a shortage of men of suitable calibre for signals intelligence work, particularly Russian linguists. Urged on by Nancy Salmon, Broadhurst argued that fears about servicewomen being captured by the enemy were 'no longer as important as in the past' as nuclear weapons had changed the situation.[45] The Air Council agreed that airwomen could be employed as radio operators and in signals jobs in forward units of 2nd Tactical Air Force.[46] Airwomen were restored to the establishment.

After the failed promise of aircrew roles in the late 1940s, some limited opportunities were introduced for senior NCOs in the 1950s, leading to the first women to gain aircrew status in regular service in the role of air quartermaster (AQM).[47] AQM was not an established trade. The work was carried out by NCOs who volunteered for a tour of flying duty. Roles included passenger flights, transport of cargo and despatch of army paratroopers. Routine work included completion and custody of 'ship's papers' on behalf of the captain of the aircraft, checking the correct loading and lashing of freight prior to and during flight, custody of loose equipment abroad the aircraft, preparation and serving of simple meals, custody of mail, and aircraft movements at airfields without specialist ground staff. AQMs had lower status than men in aircrew trades and branches. In addition to their basic pay, they received a supplement known as crew pay (2 shillings and 3 pence a day in 1960) while non-commissioned aircrew such as air signallers received the more generous flying pay (8 shillings a day). Nor were they permitted to wear a flying badge to proclaim their status.[48]

The first jobs for airwomen came with Skyways, a civilian airline operating a contract for the Ministry of Defence for flights to Egypt. It was standard practice to give male crew members RAF reserve status and for them to wear RAF uniform in order to extend to them the safety of military status at a time of instability in the region. However, it was unclear as to whether Skyways' female stewards could also be offered reserve status. While clarity was sought, the Air Ministry agreed to allow airwomen to work with Skyways. By early 1953, three were in training and three more were awaiting their course. One such was Vera Beale who had been working as a clerk. She flew with Skyways from 26 June 1953 to 30 September 1954 when the scheme was dropped.[49]

Opportunity arose again in 1957 as the requirement for air quartermasters increased with the introduction of Comet jets into the RAF for passenger flights. These aircraft were seen as providing an opportunity to create two specialisations within AQM work: one for tactical squadrons (freight and transport for para-troops) and one for passenger flights. However, 'there was an urgent problem to attract sufficient volunteers of a high quality'.[50] Men with NCO rank tended to be married and were thought to be reluctant to take up the role because of the amount of time spent away from home. Lacking sufficient men of the necessary quality, the Air Ministry opened the role to women for passenger flights though not for freight as the work was deemed too physically demanding. It was agreed to seek eight female volunteers for passenger aircraft duty on a trial basis.[51]

Sergeant Beale again volunteered. She was accepted in July 1958, went to RAF Dishforth for training in August and then to No. 216 Squadron at RAF Lyneham in September. She was joined there by the youngest of the volunteers, Sergeant Celia Watkins. Watkins joined the RAF in 1954 at the age of eighteen, encouraged by a former RAF officer who used to give her a lift into her local town from her father's small holding in Somerset. She qualified as a physical training instructor (giving her early promotion to corporal) and, living the dream advertised by the recruiters, was soon posted to RAF Wahn, near Cologne. Promoted to sergeant, she returned to Britain, and faced the decision whether to re-engage for further service or to leave. Then she learned of an opening to become an AQM. This was all the encouragement Watkins needed to stay in the RAF.[52]

Accepting handfuls of women for the role failed to solve the problem. An additional 100 AQMs were needed in 1960. To attract more men, the officer and aircrew manning committee (manning here meant personnel) proposed that it should become an established trade with dedicated personnel and aircrew status rather than relying on volunteers from other trades.[53]

Such a move would also bring about aircrew status for female AQMs. Wing Commander Dutt of the Manning Branch protested that 'surely it [was] not intended to give women aircrew status?'[54] He went on to say that if women became aircrew there was a problem because the aircrew selection centre did not have female accommodation nor were the selection exercises suitable for women. However, the committee saw no objection to this small number of women being designated as aircrew. In February 1961 the Air Council passed a proposal for 25 women be employed in the role out of a planned complement of 310.[55] Treasury approval for aircrew status and pay for all AQMs was sought. Insisting on delay because a pay freeze was in force, it queried the award of aircrew status and pay for women because they would only serve on passenger aircraft. Aircrew status, badges and pay were finally approved in 1962. By February 1963 there were 15 female AQM aircrew.[56] Celia Watkins was one of these first women in regular service to attain aircrew status.

Reserve Forces

Reserve forces customarily comprised male civilian volunteers who undertook military training in their spare time in return for a bounty, and former servicemen whose terms of engagement could require a period on the reserve. The latter included national servicemen. As compulsory reserve liability was not part of terms of regular service, women's reserve forces had to be almost entirely drawn from the civilian community.[57] At a meeting in the Admiralty in 1947, it was assumed that a WRNS Reserve should be about 80 per cent of the strength of its active Service.[58] While there was a recruitment campaign, the WRNS reserve matched this target (Figure 5.6). Numbers fell away in the late 1950s and early 1960s. The Air Ministry decided to accept reservist women into any trade for which training could be provided, without limit on numbers.[59] However, a brief flurry of interest in the early 1950s was not sustained. The number of female reserves became insignificant. The Army, putting rather more effort into the WRAC Territorial Army (TA), was by far the most successful. Women were recruited into the TA, either into mixed platoons or into women-only companies. The former platoons were better recruited, perhaps reflecting the social dimension to territorial service. But none of these reserve schemes provided realistic means of rapidly expanding the armed forces in the event of a general war.

The War Office also led the way in seeking to attract well-qualified officers. In September 1949, at the suggestion of some universities (St Andrews, Dundee and Glasgow are named on the file), the War Office introduced WRAC(TA) companies for undergraduates in a scheme equivalent to that already established for men. These students were seen as a source of

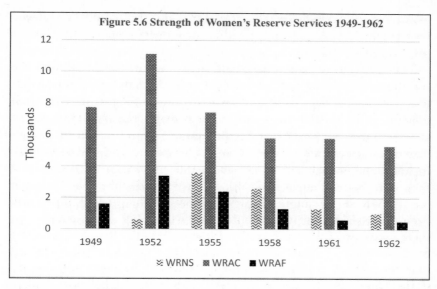

Figure 5.6 Strength of Women's Reserve Services 1949-1962

Source: *Annual Abstract of Statistics*, No.93, (London: HMSO, 1956), Tables 136 and 137 and No. 103, (London: HMSO, 1966), Tables 134 and 135.

well-qualified and motivated officers, either for regular service or for the TA on completion of their degrees. Although initially training was confined to the basics of officers' military skills (leadership, administration, military law and drill), the need to introduce some specialist training was soon recognised. Provision was dependent on what was available through their university's men's company. During a long vacation, women were required to attend the WRAC training school for a five-week course. The scheme was a success, though undergraduates preferred to identify with the men's company rather than as 'WRAC(TA)'.[60] No doubt there was a strong social element to such enthusiasm.

Transition to All-Regular Forces

In response to Duncan Sandys' Defence White Paper of April 1957, the defence correspondent of the *Daily Express* claimed that a defence committee had considered 'Proposals for the reduction and eventual abolition of the Wrens, Wrac and Wraf (sic)'.[61] He went on to ask if women performed essential tasks, or whether men or civilians could do them instead. He concluded that as 'vast reductions in manpower' were planned it was unlikely that women's Services would survive. The purpose of servicewomen was taken up by Miss Joan Vickers, MP (Conservative – Plymouth, Devonport). She claimed 'The use of women in the Services [was] extravagant' and they could be replaced by civilians.[62] This question of value for money haunted Directors of the women's Services.

The speculation had some justification within the MOD and the Admiralty. In March 1957, a brief provided for Sandys suggested that the women's Services were 'only worthwhile so long as it remain[ed] difficult or impossible to recruit enough male regulars.' However, it suggested that as the RAF and Army did not expect to recruit enough men of sufficient quality, their women's Services would still be needed. In addition, women did work which was unpopular with men and they were better than men in other (unspecified) jobs. The situation for the WRNS was more precarious as disbanding it had apparently been discussed within the Admiralty on a 'number of occasions' and there was scope for 'doing away with women in the Royal Navy apart from nurses'.[63] A draft paper produced in the Admiralty suggested that the WRNS was not economic. It would be more satisfactory if the Navy could have more men as they would be more widely employed.[64] However, the final version which went to the Chiefs of Staff Committee argued for 80,000 adult men plus a WRNS of 3,000. Nevertheless, disbanding the WRNS was one of several measures listed as potential cuts which might be needed to stay within budget. Other ideas investigated, and vigorously rejected, included disbanding the Royal Marines or the Fleet Air Arm.[65] These measures may have been little more than the Admiralty making a point about its difficulty in reducing its size.

The MOD's lukewarm attitude towards women's Services and the Admiralty's by now customary ambivalence were not apparent in either the War Office or the Air Ministry. Rather, they wanted to avoid taking the additional risk of having to find enough male volunteers to replace servicewomen as well as ending conscription. George Ward, Secretary of State for Air, and Julian Amery at the War Office made 'reassuring statements about the WRAF and the WRAC during the Estimates Debates [but] the Admiralty ... remained silent'.[66]

At the Service Ministers' Committee in July 1957, Sandys accepted the need for servicewomen. But he proposed reducing costs by creating a single women's Defence Force whose members would work with any of the Services. Putting forward this suggestion, he demonstrated a lack of understanding of how servicewomen perceived their position. They were not simply a pool of workers to be assigned. They joined a particular Service and had a loyalty to it in the same way as was inculcated into male recruits. Sandys' Ministerial colleagues rejected his idea on the grounds that it would be disastrous for recruiting.[67] It was seen as 'essential to *esprit de corps* [original emphasis] that women should feel themselves an integral part of their own Service.'[68] They went further. Faced with uncertainties about reverting to all-regular forces, commitments were made to increase the number of servicewomen.

These aspirations for growth turned out to be simply more wishful thinking as policies which hindered retention of servicewomen were not addressed. Success of the reversion to all-regular forces was critically dependent on recruiting and retaining volunteers, male and female. A paper for Service Ministers by the Defence Administration Committee claimed that recruiting trends meant that the Army and RAF '[would] not be merely somewhat under strength' but '[would] be completely unable to carry out their tasks' when national service ended.[69] A committee was established to investigate recruiting in December 1957 under the chairmanship of Sir James Grigg (formerly Permanent Under-Secretary at the War Office and Secretary of State for War 1942–45). Dame Felicity Peake (formerly Hanbury, Director of the WAAF/WRAF) also joined the committee. Grigg's report, published in October 1958, was confident that the Services could attract enough men to sustain all-regular forces. It envisaged an annual entry into non-commissioned ranks of 42,000 men over the period 1958–62 to cover the loss of conscripts, reducing to a requirement for 34,000 per annum once national service ended.[70] However, it suggested that improvements should be made to nearly all aspects of personnel policies and career structures.

As with men's recruiting, Grigg was confident that the Services could find the 5–6,000 female recruits he was told they would need annually. Indeed, this proved to be the case in the early 1960s (Figure 5.1). But this intake could only sustain women's Services totalling about 15,000 as long as outflow was still running at about 40 per cent per annum. The Ministries had ambitions to grow numbers to more than 20,000 as a hedge against shortfalls in men's recruitment. To achieve the 20,000 either more women must be recruited or policies were needed to stem the annual outflow.

A crucial difference between men and women's terms of service was women's right to leave if they married while in the Services, resulting in a 'high proportion of women not complet[ing] their engagements'.[71] Grigg's report supported this right to leave, describing marriage as 'fully as important a social duty as a career in the Women's Services'.[72]

However, having identified marriage as the key reason for the inability to retain women, he made no recommendations about making married service easier. Rather, he proposed improving allowances and pension rights to ameliorate the financial impact of leaving early and making terms and conditions of service sufficiently attractive to generate better recruitment.

Grigg did attempt to address the psychological barrier of three- or four-year engagements that required women to make a positive decision to extend their service. He proposed the introduction of open-ended terms of engagement in place of fixed-terms. After serving a minimum of two or three years, chosen as the period over which the initial cost of uniforms and training would be amortised, women would serve until retirement age with the right to give six months' notice to leave. This would make the default position one of staying in the Services. Women would have to make a decision to leave. However, the government rejected the idea on the grounds that it would have an 'adverse effect on morale and manpower planning.'[73]

Pay was a contentious issue, at least as far as the Air Ministry was concerned. There was always the idea that if more recruits were needed, then better pay had to be offered. In the Air Ministry there was keen support for women to be awarded equal pay (based on single men's pay, not married men's) on the basis that they were interchangeable with airmen and on the grounds that equal pay was now being phased in for non-industrial civil servants. However, its position was not supported by the War Office or the Admiralty who argued that women in their Services did not do the same work as men. Grigg's committee dismissed the proposal for improving pay, concluding that 'women in the Forces [were] well off financially as compared with those outside' and that equal pay 'would [not] markedly affect the rates of recruitment.'[74]

Grigg's report described women's Services as being 'accepted without question, since ... no large organisation should carry out its obligations by relying solely upon men.' Grigg went on to say that any criticism of the Services should '[not] spring from the fact that they employ women in peace-time, but from the feeling that they do not employ enough ... there [were] still far too many men operating telephone switchboards and driving staff cars.' He criticised a 'lack of emphasis on the need for Women's Services', blaming the Sandys' White Paper for 'quite erroneously [creating] an impression that women were no longer wanted'.[75] For Grigg, servicewomen were an essential part of the armed forces who could relieve men of routine work.

The women's Services emerged from the Sandys' review and the subsequent Grigg report on an apparently firm foundation, now being seen in the habitual role of making good shortages of men and undertaking mundane work so that men could concentrate on roles for which only they were suitable. A core for expansion was less evident now in discussion of the purpose of regular service. However, failure to address the well-known reasons why women left early meant that the ambitious targets to increase the strength of the Services were not met.

Conclusion

Throughout the 1950s and into the 1960s, failure to retain servicewomen undermined the public basis for the policy that they would lessen the need for men. Women's early return to civilian life was attributable to marriage and pregnancy. This coupled social norms of women marrying at a younger average age than in pre-war times with the regulatory climate in the Services. The right to leave on marriage became an entrenched principle, seen by senior female officers as an essential promise to young women if they were to be enticed to join.

In 1964, in response to a question about steps being taken to retain servicewomen, Christopher Mayhew (Minister for the Navy) described marriage as 'a great bugbear [taking] our people away'.[76] Yet means of lessening its impact were not sought. From recruiting literature suggesting careers as a fallback in the absence of marriage, through to an official inquiry into recruitment which described marriage as a social duty for women, and on to regulations which made married service problematic, there was a sense that long-term military careers were not natural for women.

The decision to end national service for men was perhaps an opportunity to terminate the employment of servicewomen. The concept of women's Services being cores for expansion had no place in the April 1957 White Paper. Reserve forces policy did not provide an adequate pool of trained women to be embodied into the Services in the event of a major war. However, reverting to all-regular forces was expected to put a strain on male recruitment. Replacing servicewomen in the all-volunteer forces envisaged for the 1960s would have required an increase in men's recruitment by at least 6 per cent. This was not a risk that either the War Office or the Air Ministry wanted to take. Although the Admiralty may have considered disbanding the WRNS as a cost savings measure, women's Services were seen as a means of mitigating the risk of shortfalls in male volunteers of the required quality. Lessening the need for men had overtaken cores for expansion as the rationale for servicewomen.

These early years also solidified the different philosophies of women's employment. The Air Ministry made progress with its intent to run an integrated Service. Women became an accepted part of the establishment on operational bases in West Germany, sharing the same risks as men if the Cold War had turned into actual war. A few female officers had access to career-enhancing staff training and a few senior NCOs broke through the barrier of ground-based employment to become aircrew, wearing flying badges to proclaim their status.

In the Army, the inherent fault line between women being recruited into a gender-based corps, but often employed with trade specific corps alongside men, revealed problems in career pathways. Insistence that women could not be put at risk, or that they would simply be a nuisance in theatres of war, placed such a restriction on careers as to make progression outside of the WRAC's own hierarchy problematic. Discussed but not resolved at the highest levels of the War Office, these issues were destined to hamper career development for those women.

The Admiralty continued to be the most reluctant employer of servicewomen, as was inevitable when seagoing was not on offer. What the Directors' WRNS of the time described as consolidation was more a case of retaining a foothold.

6

A RIGHT TO BE DIFFERENT?

Reporting in 1979 on a visit to the United States' Third Armoured Division stationed on the outskirts of Frankfurt in West Germany, Angus Macpherson (the *Daily Mail's* defence correspondent) observed that 'a hell of a lot of [the soldiers] seem to be women'. Not only were they women, but some were also mothers or soon-to-be mothers. Some of these mothers were not married, a situation described as 'just another operational problem', solved by the growth of unofficial crèches. Female soldiers were trained to use M-16 rifles and automatic pistols. Macpherson concluded that America was 'in a vast experiment – social as well as military' and he quoted an unnamed British general as describing problems that arose as hideous.[1] American policy changed significantly in the 1970s as the USA reverted to all-volunteer forces and responded to challenges brought by its servicewomen using equality legislation to overturn restrictive practices. Women lost the right to leave on marriage, gained maternity leave benefits, were trained to use weapons and started to be employed in flying in all the Services, seafaring in the Coast Guard and subsequently in the US Navy.[2] Besides the actions of individual women bringing lawsuits, policy change was influenced by the Defense (sic) Advisory Committee on Women in the Services. A committee of prominent women formed in 1951 by George Marshall (Secretary for Defense), its role was to raise the prestige of military women in the public mind.[3] It was a persistent advocate for the removal of obstacles to women's careers. There was no British equivalent.

Other allied nations also made significant changes to women's roles and terms of employment. Of the NATO nations that employed servicewomen, all but the UK, Turkey and West Germany trained them to use weapons.

Only Norway had the same policy as Britain in allowing women to leave on marriage. Britain was alone in not permitting servicewomen to rent married quarters and receive associated allowances.[4] Britain was falling behind the policies of its allies, stuck in the mind-set that servicewomen represented a short-term, disposable workforce.

Meanwhile, change was also afoot in British society. Influenced by the European Economic Community and by the feminist movement in Britain, women in the civilian workforce gained more rights. Three major pieces of domestic legislation affecting employment were enacted: the Equal Pay Act (1970) which came into force in 1975, the Employment Protection Act (1975) and the Sex Discrimination Act (1975). The first required employers to pay staff equally for work of equal value. The second enshrined working women's entitlement to paid maternity leave and a return to their former jobs. The Sex Discrimination Act (SDA) had two main components: clauses concerning employment and those covering provision of education, goods, facilities, services and premises. In essence, men and women were to be treated equally in employment and in terms of access to services. Discrimination, against men or women, was deemed illegal. However, the SDA accepted that some jobs needed to be performed by a person of a specified gender.

Britain's social mores were also changing as the Labour government in the late 1960s introduced three pieces of legislation on sexual matters. Women gained more control over their reproductive capacity. The Family Planning Act (1967) allowed the contraceptive pill to be prescribed by doctors on the National Health Service and permitted local authorities to establish family planning clinics. Contraception was not only a matter for married couples. Single women were entitled to seek advice and they could be prescribed or buy the contraceptive pill. The Abortion Act (1967) legalised abortion in defined circumstances in England, Scotland and Wales, but not Northern Ireland. Finally, same-sex relationships between consenting adults were recognised under the Sexual Offences Act (1967).

Many of these developments passed by Britain's armed forces whose policymakers saw the Services as different from society. The MOD negotiated an exemption from the SDA's employment clauses, but not its other clauses, and the Employment Protection Act. A caveat in the Equal Pay Act enabled the MOD to continue to pay servicewomen less than men on the grounds that their work, being non-combatant, was not equivalent to men's. The Sexual Offences Act also did not apply to the armed forces. Homosexuality remained an offence in military law.

While allied nations widened servicewomen's employment and encouraged longer service by making it easier to combine marriage and career, Ministry of Defence policy remained rooted in what had been established as norms with the creation of regular service. After three years' work, a paper for the Principal Personnel Officers' (PPOs) Committee advised that:

> ... where the circumstances of their service are the same, men and women ... should be treated equally. To seek to do less ... might lead to a charge that MOD was sheltering behind the exemption clauses contained in recent legislation. This ... might lead to pressure for absolute equality (including the full range of military duties) which has been in evidence in other areas both at home and abroad in recent years.[5]

In approving the paper's recommendations, the PPOs agreed that publicity for any new policies would not be sought on the grounds that 'measures taken to ensure equality of treatment in conditions of service may draw attention to the restrictions placed upon the employment of women in combat and other related roles'.[6] In other words, they did not want to trumpet improvements in case that led to more questions about what was not tackled (weapons training, seagoing, flying, land warfare roles) rather than achieving credit for what had been changed.

However, social change could not be entirely ignored if the armed forces were to be seen as attractive employers. The PPOs Committee was faced with a dilemma: how to appear sympathetic to the times by abiding by the spirit of new laws despite the negotiated exemption, without surrendering the essential principle that women should not be employed in combat? What concessions could be made without actually tackling the main obstacles to servicewomen's careers, namely the non-combatant principle and the requirement to leave if pregnant?

Pregnancy

Noting that 'the permissive society is with us, or at any rate apparently more than it used to be' and that 'girls in the Services are still part of that society and conditioned by it', Mr Taylor (a senior civil servant in the MOD) questioned intended restrictions on single women's access to contraceptive advice and the birth control pill. He thought these developments had merit as they might 'lessen the incidence of pregnancy and consequentially the loss of trained servicewomen'.[7] On the issue of

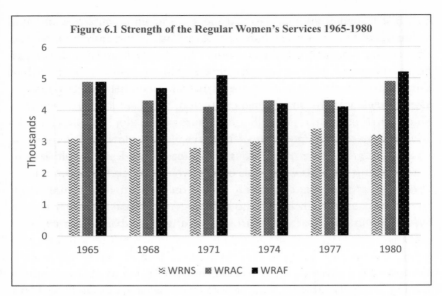

Figure 6.1 Strength of the Regular Women's Services 1965-1980

Source: *Annual Abstract of Statistics*, No.106, (London: HMSO, 1969), Table 137 and No. 117, (London: HMSO, 1981), Tables 7.4 and 7.8.

single women, he thought that publicity could go in either direction – condemnation of lax morals in allowing them the pill or, if they were denied contraceptives, a failure to safeguard young women in an environment where they might be vulnerable to pressure to have intercourse without the precaution of contraception.

Taylor certainly had a point about the impact of pregnancy in the 1960s. Exits on or after marriage and dismissal on pregnancy continued to undermine targets for the strength of the women's Services (Figure 6.1). However, the contraceptive pill presented a test of the women's Directors' moral stance. They were against a liberal approach, seeing the negative side of publicity and the potential harmful effect on recruitment rather than an opportunity to reduce wastage due to unplanned pregnancy.

Servicewomen were not excluded from the terms of the Family Planning Act. Like civilian women, they were entitled to seek advice on contraception from their doctor or, if the local authority established one, from a family planning clinic. Under the Act, doctors could prescribe the pill free of charge if it was deemed necessary for a woman's physical or mental health. It could be prescribed on social grounds for a fee. Armed forces personnel were registered with Service doctors who worked with regulations set not only by the National Health Service but also by the Ministry of Defence. The RAF medical service was the first to issue a policy letter on the subject. It instructed its doctors that they could give all women contraceptives on clinical grounds. Unmarried women could be prescribed the pill on social grounds only if they could prove intent to marry within a month.[8]

While it had been common place for condoms to be made available to servicemen, the Directors considered provision of contraceptives to unmarried servicewomen as amounting to official sanction of immoral behaviour and promiscuity. They believed parents of potential female recruits would be horrified and feared corruption of easily led young women by those of bad influence in communal accommodation. They also suggested that wives of servicemen would protest because servicewomen were perceived as a threat to marriages.[9] The Navy's senior chaplains shared these concerns.[10]

Reluctantly, the Directors agreed that women who were about to marry could be prescribed the pill and, bowing to revised medical advice, acceded to the extension of the timeframe to three months prior to marriage. Other single servicewomen could not obtain the pill through their medical officers. In 1969, the PPOs endorsed the policy. Making a distinction between methods of contraception and attitudes towards official sanction of sexual behaviour, the PPOs observed that 'there was nothing inconsistent in providing contraceptives for men as this was to contain the spread of venereal disease and not to prevent pregnancy'.[11] No moral judgement was passed on men's behaviour.

A draft policy letter was sent to Roy Hattersley (Minister for Defence Administration in the Labour government) for approval. Rejecting the idea that the Services acted *in loco parentis* for young women given that the age of legal majority was due to fall from twenty-one to eighteen in 1970, he thought undue emphasis was placed on promiscuity. Where the policy required medical officers to make decisions based on their 'knowledge and judgement of character' he questioned whether 'a girl of known bad (i.e. promiscuous) character [was] to be denied this service, or [was] it to be made available to her because of her palpable "need" for it?'[12]

Despite Hattersley's reservations, the policy letter was issued allowing prescription of contraceptives to unmarried servicewomen on social grounds if they could prove intent to marry within three months. Otherwise, such prescriptions were to be made only with 'very great discretion ...bearing in mind all the circumstances of the case.'[13] None of this prevented unmarried servicewomen from seeking contraceptives via a family planning clinic where imminent marriage was not a pre-condition.

The Abortion Act permitted abortion in authorised hospitals and patients were entitled to secrecy. On the recommendation of the PPOs' Committee, Ministerial authority was granted for Service doctors to perform abortions in approved military hospitals.[14] While the MOD acted swiftly to comply with the Act, the RAF blundered. Its own regulations allowed a woman who miscarried, a term now used to cover both actual miscarriage and abortion, before her twenty-eighth week of pregnancy to be retained in the Service. However, if she was not married, a report would be made on her character and a recommendation made as to whether or not she should continue to serve.

The view within the WRAF Directorate was that such women were promiscuous, a bad influence on other servicewomen and that the normal recommendation would be for discharge.[15] In practice, station commanders responsible for signing off the reports took a more charitable view, with more than half of such cases attracting a positive recommendation for retention.[16] Nevertheless, as the decision rested with the WRAF hierarchy, airwomen were normally discharged. In consequence, it was surmised that they sought abortions through civilian hospitals rather than risk being reported by RAF medical officers.[17]

Contradictions between patient confidentiality enshrined in the Abortion Act and RAF regulations came to light in late 1976. Air Vice-Marshal Soutar, the principal medical officer at Strike Command Headquarters, sought clarification on the regulations from the MOD. Information about an abortion could come to medical officers from civilian hospitals, so RAF doctors did not know whether they should keep the matter secret in accordance with the Act or inform MOD authorities under Queen's Regulations. Mindful that a report could lead to the woman's 'discharge without delay', Soutar complained that 'many medical officers [were] genuinely confused about their responsibilities'.[18] Staff work on his letter revealed the other two Services had properly implemented the 1969 policy letter concerning confidentiality. RAF regulations were amended to comply with the Act, thus allowing women who had abortions through a civilian hospital to maintain their privacy and hence avoid the threat of discharge.[19]

Nevertheless, there was concern that young women, away from home and living in a predominantly male environment were at risk. Efforts were made to ensure that they did not enter their new environment ignorant of sexual matters. The WRAF had a comprehensive day dedicated to sex education during recruit training. There was an expectation that airwomen would seek male company so the approach was that of the importance of forming healthy relationships, not just the biology of sex. Civilian speakers from the Central Council for Health Education were brought in to speak to officer cadets at RAF Henlow and airwomen recruits at RAF Spitalgate. Cadets were encouraged to think about how they would deal with questions that airwomen might ask them about sexual relationships, including dealing with the question 'how much reliance could be placed upon various reassurances from boyfriends?'[20] Sadly, from the historian's perspective, a model answer was not provided, but it is likely that some discussion of the sensitive subject of contraception might follow. Speakers were not supposed to introduce the topic with recruits, but were allowed to answer direct questions.

In 1968, Chief Officer Mary Talbot decided that the WRNS should adopt the WRAF system. She introduced a syllabus that included a film on human reproduction and discussion of motherhood, personal and social problems related to sex such as venereal disease, unmarried mothers, dangers of premarital sex, friendships with married men, and alcoholism. There was also a session on marriage: marital problems, early marriage and the importance to the future of the race of healthy marriage with particular stress on the part played by the mother. The WRAC was reluctant to adopt the same educational approach. It placed its efforts on training of senior NCOs and officer cadets, presumably so that they could provide guidance to the young women under their supervision. One issue on which the Directors were agreed was that chaplains should not participate in the instruction. If they wanted to take up any moral issues, they must make use of their own scheduled time with recruits.[21]

Despite the availability of contraceptives, improved sex education and regulations on dismissal, there was still room for the exceptional case. A report made to Commandant Mary Talbot in 1974 drily recorded that 'A WRNS rating unexpectedly gave birth to a child soon after going off duty one afternoon'. The report continued, '[WRNS Regulations] do not at present provide for a discharge in such a contingency'.[22] Clearly, as the Wren was no longer pregnant, the dismissal clause did not apply. Her parents wanted her to stay in the Service – presumably content to assist with the care of the baby. Medical advice was sought and it was agreed that the woman would not be emotionally fit to resume work. Meanwhile, Talbot took action to ensure that such circumstances were covered in the regulations, as apparently those for the WRAC and WRAF already did.[23]

While policies on contraception and abortion were adopted, the women's Services were left behind by workplace maternity leave schemes. For example, married and single women in the civil service could take maternity leave. Initially, an unmarried woman could only make use of the leave for a first child. A subsequent pregnancy outside of marriage resulted in dismissal – perhaps on the grounds of being a 'bad character'. Once legal abortion became possible, there was a view that it was unfair to dismiss a woman who kept her baby while a woman who had an abortion could continue to work.[24] The distinction was dropped. Paid maternity leave became a right for civilian women under the terms of the Employment Protection Act (1975), provided they had worked for the same employer for a prescribed period of time. However, the armed forces' policy was protected by an employer's right to dismiss a woman if 'at the date of termination of employment she [was] or [would have] become, because of her pregnancy, incapable of adequately doing the work which she [was] employed to do.'[25]

Generally, sentiments concerning the introduction of maternity leave failed to move senior women officers. The Directors agreed that pregnancy was incompatible with military service. There would come a point where a pregnant woman could no longer fit into her uniform. She would be unable to fulfil all of her duties. Living in shared accommodation, commonplace even for married women due to the difficulty of colocation with husbands, exposed other women to the morning sickness associated with the early weeks of pregnancy. This was deemed unfair. Worse, if the woman was not married, she would be judged adversely by other women with whom she shared barracks.[26] The Directors were equally keen to be rid of any pregnant woman, married or single. As far as the WRAF Directorate was concerned, women with children represented an administrative burden.[27]

A few servicewomen had the opportunity to observe the widening gulf in conditions of service between policies in Britain and those of allied countries. Captain Montanaro, returning from an exchange tour with the USA's army, reported to a WRAC officers' conference in 1977 that 'pregnancy [could] come and go without remark'. Sergeant Murray, having spent a few months with the Australian army, told the same conference that servicewomen could take a year's unpaid leave to have a child. Two years later, Lieutenant Rollo reported to that year's conference that New Zealand also allowed a year's unpaid leave for both married and single women, remarking that ' "solo" mothers [were] accepted as part of the way of life in New Zealand'.[28]

Noting that their conditions of service now compared unfavourably with civilian life and some allied nations' policies, young officers suggested to a WRAF conference that women should be able to have six months unpaid maternity leave. Wing Commander Mackintosh, on Director WRAF's staff, rejected the idea on the grounds that there would be no guarantee that the woman would return to work and that such a policy would have to apply to single as well as married women – a situation she clearly regarded as untenable. She reminded the conference that a married officer could apply to re-join at a later date.[29]

Indeed, there had been such an example in 1968. Tragically, a WRAF officer who left the Service to accompany her RAF husband to Singapore, gave birth to their child just seven weeks before he was killed in a flying accident. Returning to Britain, she applied to Air Commandant Felicity Hill to be permitted to resume her career on the grounds that this was the only way she knew of supporting herself. Legal arrangements were in hand to allow her parents to take care of the baby. Felicity Hill, although of the opinion that the mother/baby bond should override other considerations, was sufficiently sympathetic to send the case notes to Air Chief Marshal Sir Brian Burnett for a decision. He agreed that the officer be re-instated. She served for a further two or three years, remarried and left.[30] This was a rare instance of a new mother re-joining the Service.

Sexual Offences Act (1967)

A clause in the Sexual Offences Act re-affirmed that a homosexual act remained an offence under military law even if no civil offence was committed. The MOD claimed this exemption on the basis of the 'different conditions of Service life' summarised as the need to maintain discipline, morale and security. On discipline, its argument was that the hierarchical nature of the Services created conditions under which a man might influence his juniors and so undermine his own authority if it became known that he was a homosexual. Where men were in a closed community for protracted periods, such as at sea, men might be drawn into acts they would not otherwise engage in if there was 'an unsuspected pervert among them'. This would damage morale. Notwithstanding that homosexual acts conducted in private between men over the age of twenty-one were no longer illegal in society, the Security Committee's view was that homosexuals in the armed forces would still be vulnerable to blackmail and hence a security risk.[31]

Men suspected of homosexual acts were either court martialled or dealt with under administrative or medical procedures, which entailed examination by a psychiatrist. Prior to 1967, men were charged on the basis of an offence under civil law also being an offence under military law. After the passing of the Sexual Offences Act, servicemen were usually court martialled under catch-all clauses in Service discipline acts of 'conduct prejudicial to good order'.

Servicewomen were treated differently. As lesbianism had not been a civil offence, there was no track record of prosecuting servicewomen. The subject was seen as sensitive and complex, as reflected in a lecture given to WRAF officer cadets during their training. In a script not much changed from a 1941 version, the cadets were told that 'affectionate friendships between women are not only natural but are an essential part of a well balanced and happy life'. However, there was a need to distinguish between 'healthy affection and lesbianism'. 'Perverted physical practices' were put down to 'women of a depraved type or among the self-conscious intelligentsia who [were] probably more activated by craving for excitement than by real desire.'[32]

The speaker, a senior female Provost officer, drew attention to four forms of relationships that the trainee officers should look out for. First, there was the crush developed by a young woman on an older one – compared with adolescent feelings at school. This situation was to be managed 'with a light hand'. Second, 'the unwise expression of interest and attachment between older women and young women.' This was attributed to loneliness of the older women or her disappointment in life. This as seen as more worrying than the crush as it could lead to favouritism and jealousy. Third, there was the possibility of 'close friendships between a pair of women, often about the same age, but usually of contrasting dispositions'. This was their own business if they were discreet but was to be 'firmly discouraged' if they 'boasted that their behaviour was part of a cult'. Finally, there were women of 'very masculine characteristics' who were regarded as unfortunate as they could not develop normal relationships with men and would be lonely.[33] There were also four possible courses of action. Women against whom evidence was found could be discharged under the heading 'services no longer required'. Women could be posted to different locations. They could be offered re-mustering to a different trade with the option of discharge if they preferred. Finally, they could be given an official warning and then discreetly observed. Some women who stayed in the Service following investigation of accusations could be offered medical help from a neuropsychiatrist as though lesbianism was an ailment.[34]

'Services no longer required' was a widely used category, not confined to those with poor disciplinary records. Statistics for discharge for lesbianism were not routinely collected. Figures for the WRAC from 1973–79 showed an average of 41 dismissals per year. But figures varied significantly from a high of 64 in 1974 to a low of 14 in 1975.[35] Figures also fluctuated in the WRAF, with 21 dismissals in 1969, only 8 in 1970 and 29 in the first ten months of 1971.[36] These fluctuations are suggestive of a purge in one year and, consequently, a lack of women to pursue the next. The tone was one of rooting out ringleaders, women who were deemed a menace to easily led young women.

After 1967, although servicewomen could have been prosecuted under 'conduct prejudicial to good order' like servicemen, the custom of dealing with them administratively or medically continued.[37] Guidance letters urged against watchfulness turning into witch hunts, but it would seem that accusations could quickly build up in a unit. Speaking in 2011, Commandant Anne Spencer (Director WRNS 1991–3) recollected from the early 1960s that it was policy for a time for the WRNS to collocate suspected women for the ease of observation. She remembered:

> [lesbianism was] handled very badly... When I was at *Dauntless*, they had had a sweep of the Fleet Air Arm and put all the lesbians that were still in the Service – and wanted to be in the Service – at HMS *Dauntless* of all places – the new entry training establishment – which I thought was madness. A lot were discharged but a lot were kept in. Again, this was in Dame Marion's [Kettlewell] time. Well, she was a superintendent then. ...She did the sweep of the Navy. Every now and then there used to be a witch hunt. It was done badly. It was all horrid. They got the naval police – the SIB [special investigation branch] people – going. Seeing if they shared a bed. It was really, I thought quite unnecessary. ... they handled it very badly. Very witch hunting – unpleasant. And the girls went out. But we did have this great collection at *Dauntless*.[38]

MOD policy came under persistent attack from the Commission for Homosexual Equality. It made the point that it was the Services' own banning of homosexual acts that left personnel vulnerable to blackmail and hence a potential security risk. It also suggested that, at some future date, service personnel might take the MOD to court in pursuit of their human rights under European law.[39] It took until the late 1990s for these ideas to gain traction with policy makers.

Policy was also disparaged in the feminist publication, *Spare Rib*. This monthly magazine opposed British defence policies, taking particular issue with the basing of American cruise missiles at RAF stations and condemning aggressive actions of the Army in Northern Ireland. Rather than pressing for British servicewomen's equality, as it did for women in other predominantly masculine professions, it expressed dismay at their participation. In 1981, Lesley Merryfinch, in a four-page article under the headline 'Equality in the Army – No Way!', wrote that her reaction to British servicewomen was one of:

anger, sorrow and pity ... ang[er] at the terrible force of false promises which lured them into wanting to join up ... [sadness] to see them caught up in that most patriarchal of structures and blinded to what that [was] doing to them as women ... and pity for them because ... you [could not] automatically leave by giving notice.[40]

The following year, an article by Jan Parker highlighted the treatment of three lesbians dismissed from the Army, describing the Army as 'oppress[ing] women within its own ranks'.[41] This was not a campaigning article pressing for equality. Rather, it continued the theme of criticising the armed forces. One of the women described her experience:

Going to a new unit as a lesbian, well, you have to pretend a lot. If anyone asks, you've a boyfriend on the other side of the world. ... it was one of the other women who reported us ... As a result the SIB [Special Investigations Branch] came on camp, two women ... After our rooms were completely stripped we had a bed-check at three in the morning. They knock on the doors and get everybody up.[42]

This soldier appealed against a decision to dismiss her. She wanted to stay in the Army. But then she thought better of it, 'Why do I want to stay ... if I'm going to have to deny I'm a lesbian? ... I felt women should be able to be lesbians and still serve'.[43]

Administrative discharge remained MOD policy until the year 2000.

Service Pay and the Equal Pay Act (1970)

The Services' historic practice of paying single personnel less than married colleagues was problematic when it came to presenting the armed forces as a career choice to young people. As Denis Healey (Secretary of State) observed, pay for the single man appeared to be only half or a third of take-home pay from the local factory.[44] Figures from 1966 bear out his observation. Average earnings of manual workers were 405 shillings per week. A single soldier, starting out in the rank of private, earned about 121 shillings per week and an unmarried corporal in semi-skilled work received about 201 shillings per week.[45] The true value of emoluments, including benefits in kind such as food and accommodation, was higher but this was hard for individuals to understand and made comparison with other possible employment difficult.

As male recruitment declined in the 1960s, the Ministry of Defence[46] decided to tackle this anachronistic system. It wanted to adopt a 'military salary', meaning paying the rate for the job. New pay scales, determined by comparing armed forces' trades with civilian occupations, were devised by the National Board for Prices and Incomes and introduced in 1970. Single and married men undertaking the same work received the same pay. Food and accommodation now had to be paid for, rather than being a benefit in kind. Under this new scheme, women's pay was increased from 85 per cent to 90 per cent of men's basic pay rates.[47]

The revised pay code also introduced a supplement to basic pay called the X-factor. It 'recognise[d] those special conditions of employment which [were] peculiar to Service life, and which [could] not therefore be compared with civilian employments.'[48] It took account of potential exposure to danger and turbulence created in private life by frequent moves. It cited commitments to accept military discipline, liability for duty at all times without extra pay and inability to resign at will, change jobs or negotiate for pay. These disadvantages were weighed against the perceived advantages of adventure, travel, the chance to learn a trade, substantially longer paid leave than most civilians and greater job security.

Women were described as having a lesser commitment than men because they were excluded from combat and they could leave if they married. Accordingly, while men received an X-factor worth 5 per cent of basic pay, women's rate was set at 'a token 1 per cent'. Combining the effects of lower basic pay and X-factor, women earned about 13 per cent less than men from the 1970 pay deal.[49]

The armed forces were not exempt from the Equal Pay Act (1970) which came into effect in 1975. However, the Secretary of State for Defence was only required to avoid making or recommending:

terms and conditions of service ... [having] the effect of making a distinction, as regards pay, allowances or leave, between men and women ... not being a distinction fairly attributable to differences between the obligations undertaken by men and those undertaken by women.[50]

More simply, the MOD could differentiate between men's and women's pay on the grounds that work and commitment were not the same. This allowable differential was embodied in the X-factor. Basic pay for women was made the same as men's in April 1975 to comply with the Act. At the same time, X-factor rates were increased to 10 per cent for men and 5 per cent for women, narrowing the gap but still preserving superior pay scales for men.[51]

Differences between British policies and that of allied nations emerged at NATO's committee for women's Services, set up as a forum for developing the goals and objectives of women's Services, but mainly a means of sharing information. At these meetings, the Directors learned that other countries trained women in the use of weapons and did not give them the right to leave on marriage. These were the two fundamental points underpinning pay differentials in Britain.

As the Equal Pay Act came into force, Brigadier Sheila Heaney (Director WRAC) and her successor Eileen Nolan accepted these differences and thought it was not right to press for an equal X-factor.[52] The case for equal pay was hardest to make for the WRNS which had no liability for seagoing. Wrens' jobs and commitment were palpably different from those of naval ratings. The Air Force Department had been in the vanguard on equal pay since the 1950s. Even so, there was no re-opening of its case with the introduction of the military salary. The work of the National Board for Prices and Incomes had defined the differences and, in future, pay settlements would be determined by the newly created Armed Forces Pay Review Body.

Sex Discrimination Act (1975)

The Ministry of Defence was accustomed to exemption from legislation which might affect personnel's rights on the grounds that military work was different from civilian. It required little effort to gain exemption from the SDA. Urged on by the Home Office, which had been arguing about the impact on the police and fire services, the MOD sent a paper on the roles of servicewomen to Lord Royle, chairman of the House of Lords select committee investigating the need for legislation.[53] The paper set out the MOD's case against extending women's employment to match men's. It cited: the short period of women's service compared with men's, public opinion being against women in combat roles, the harsh nature of field conditions in the Army, women's lack of physical strength, cost inefficiency, and assumed problems in maintaining morale and discipline in combat units if women were present. The key point was that combat was men's work. A further argument was made about the inability to tie women to their initial engagement, quoting that 75 per cent served for less than the theoretical minimum period which was three years after completion of training. This arose from policy allowing exit on marriage and the practice of dismissing pregnant women. Lord Royle's committee accepted the MOD's argument and the armed forces were exempted from the employment clauses of the Act.[54]

Despite the impending exemption, the Air Force Department thought it prudent to 'look around for the loose ends of the Sex Discrimination Bill' as a journalist from the *Daily Mirror* was taking an interest in MOD policies following the introduction of maternity rights in the USA's armed forces.[55] Policy departments were urged to 'identify those areas where there [was] discrimination and satisfy [themselves] that it [was] justified'.[56] The criterion was whether a minister could reasonably be expected to defend the situation. Thus, the tone of staff work was a stock-take rather than a commitment to equality.

Work revealed differences in the treatment of men and women, sometimes in favour of women but more frequently to the advantage of men. Men were employed in more roles, were better paid, accrued better pensions and received more generous allowances. The number of women who could be recruited was strictly controlled. Those who were single on joining had the advantage in being able to leave if they subsequently married.[57] Men, women who were already married when they joined and single women who wanted to leave early had to apply for premature voluntary release – a scheme that had variable waiting times according to the role for which the person was trained and it came at a financial penalty. Unlike servicemen, women were not required to transfer to the Reserve on completion of regular service.[58]

The aspect of conditions of service that provoked most debate and uncertainty was centred on the married quarters' policy. Women were not entitled to apply for married quarters. However, did quarters come under the SDA's heading of goods and services, meaning that women should be eligible? Initial advice was to hold firm to the current policy. In the opinion of Mr Ellis of the Treasury Solicitor's department, under common law, a man was obliged to support his wife but the reverse was not the case. Accordingly, it was appropriate for men to be offered married quarters so that they could fulfil their duty as head of household to provide a home for their families. Ellis argued that, as a married woman did not have a duty to support her husband, there was no requirement to offer married quarters to women.

The Air Force Department latched onto a potentially emotive issue if women were allowed quarters, namely the practice of dismissal on pregnancy. Leaving the Service would entail giving up the quarter, so the family would be made homeless at a critical time. Such a policy would have all the potential for bad publicity and no positive benefit.[59]

Pressure for change was growing within the women's Services. Noting that the number of married servicewomen was increasing, Brigadier Nolan argued against treating them as though they were single. She wanted them to have the right to quarters, observing that it was particularly hard for those married to civilians or retired servicemen who could no longer qualify for a house.

Nolan's points were well illustrated when a female squadron leader, married to a former RAF officer, complained about the unfairness arising from her posting to West Germany. Not eligible for married accommodation, she had to go unaccompanied. She was not entitled to the separation allowance, or to free food and accommodation for living in the officers' mess, as an unaccompanied married man would receive. Such men were called 'bean stealers'. Nor could she claim for travel expenses for her husband to visit her in Germany, again a benefit available to men who could claim for their wives' travel costs. She concluded that she was being deprived of the right to a normal family life. Air Commodore Molly Allott supported her case, arguing that married women wanted to stay in the Service and the Service would benefit from keeping experienced and trained women.[60] Making married service both financially costly and personally difficult drove women to leave.

Although no change emerged from the Germany case, two years later matters came to a head in the Navy Department. A WRNS officer married to a former naval officer, now unemployed, applied to rent a married quarter on posting to the Naval Headquarters at Northwood on the outskirts of London. Although none were available at Northwood, there was unoccupied accommodation at Hendon that would suffice. As an exception to the regulations, the naval authorities proposed allowing the officer to take a quarter because her husband was 'to some measure dependant on her'.[61] They wanted to charge her the same rent as a male officer, on the understanding that if it was needed for an entitled family, she would have to vacate the house. The Air Force department was intending to go further. It wanted to make it a matter of routine to offer surplus married quarters to women at the standard rent. However, finance staff in the Army department argued that the officer should be charged either the rent levied on 'irregular' occupants or the market rent set for those MOD civilians who were permitted to take a quarter. Both of these solutions would result in her paying about 50 per cent more in rent than a married male officer.[62] Supported by naval and air authorities, she won her case.

It was clear by now that the married quarter policy needed to be addressed coherently and not changed by erosion brought about by particular cases, as Mr Stevens of the Army Department's finance staff noted. The issue went to the Principal Personnel Officers' (PPOs) Committee for a ruling as part of the review of policies brought about by the SDA. They had new advice from the Treasury Solicitor who now stated that a woman could be regarded in law as head of her household. Noting also that married women in other public services were entitled to the same allowances as male colleagues, without reference to who was head of household, the PPOs agreed that common law considerations should be set aside. Married women were to be entitled to the same allowances as men, including 'bean stealer' rights when obliged to live in single accommodation. For those married to civilians, they would in future be able to rent married quarters and receive the associated allowances.[63]

Staff Sergeant Barton was one such servicewoman. The vicar told her that married life would be an uphill struggle but she had not anticipated that the battle would be with Army bureaucracy. Her husband being a civilian, the first hurdle was to obtain a married quarter in West Germany in her name. Once that was achieved, the next problem was the issuing of a dependant's identity card, so that Mr Barton could come and go at the base. The application came back stamped with the word 'Rejected' – how could a husband be a dependant of his wife? Not in Army regulations. A solution was found. He was issued with a special chitty. At least he had a sense of humour about his invitation to join the Wives' Club. Apparently, it might be renamed Wives and Husbands Club in his honour.[64]

Conclusion

Britain led the way in 1946 when it announced that women would have a place in the regular armed forces. By the late 1970s, it had fallen well behind policies of allied nations. In America, change was brought about by need when it ended the draft and reverted to all-volunteer forces in the aftermath of an unpopular war in Vietnam, by equality legislation, through an influential government-backed committee and via legal challenges brought by servicewomen themselves. The American situation was different from Britain's.

Senior female officers had the opportunity to learn from the experience of their counterparts through a NATO committee. However, what they saw was the costs of a programme of maternity leave, not the benefits of longer service that it brought. It was a deeply held view that motherhood and service in the armed forces were incompatible and it would take more than American feminists to change their minds. Nor were they willing to surrender the right to leave on marriage which they believed to be an essential part of the deal in persuading young women to join the armed forces.

Through annual MOD budget rounds, with the constant questioning of the value for money of women's Services, the Directors were sensitive to anything that suggested women were not a good economic bet. The circular nature of the British situation was summed up by a civil servant:

> ... the failure to mitigate the difficulties of combining marriage and a service career [for women] has a direct bearing on individual decisions to leave on the grounds of marriage, the prime course [cause?] of premature exit, thus contributing to short service which is one of the limiting factors on the employment of women.[65]

The Directors did nothing to break this cycle. If women were not prepared to lead, then male policymakers were under no pressure to change the regulations. It was only the question of married quarters on which the Directors offered their support to individual women seeking help. The concession of quarters for married women was a useful step along the way to making married service easier both practically and economically.

If individual servicewomen felt aggrieved, there was no mechanism by which to challenge the rules as MOD had gained exemption from key legislation. Nor was there any external pressure. The Equal Opportunities Commission, established under the Sex Discrimination Act, had no remit on employment matters due to the exemption. Nor did the feminist movement seek to champion greater rights for servicewomen. However, servicewomen's own choices began to change. Like women throughout British society, access to the pill and family planning advice enable them to take better control over their fertility. Along with trends of marrying at a later age compared with the immediate post-war period, so women's length of service increased. Women's behaviour undermined the argument that they were not cost-effective.

The Ministry of Defence staked its claim to a right to be different from social change most clearly in response to the Sexual Offences Act in 1967 and again in the 1970s as the Sex Discrimination Act was drafted. The case was based on the unique nature of combat and the demands that placed on servicemen's commitment, compared to all other types of employment. But something significant had changed within the Ministry. The armed forces needed to be seen as modern employers if they were to recruit successfully. Despite the exemption from legislation, the MOD wanted to abide by the spirit of female equality. In future, discriminatory practice had to be identified and defended, not simply assumed to be normal as had been the case to this point. The unthinking stance of 'why would we employ women in this role?' became instead a need to justify 'why not employ women?'

7

COMBATANT STATUS

Captain Gael Hammond (later Brigadier Gael Ramsey, the last Director WRAC) was stationed in Cyprus when the Turkish army invaded in 1974. She organised the evacuation of tourists and then the families of British servicemen. Emotions ran high when she refused to include a Cypriot without documentation. Hammond recalled:

> ... I was attacked and held up against a wall with a knife against my throat. Fortunately, Colonel Leo Macy, the paymaster, walked in at that moment and from then on I had an armed guard with me all the time. ... Had I been trained in arms I could have looked after myself.[1]

But servicewomen were not combatants and could not be armed, even for self-defence. In potentially hazardous situations they had to be protected by men diverted from other duties.

In the first twenty-five years of regular service, not much had changed as far as servicewomen were concerned. They were non-combatants and they could not be employed in combat roles. As had been the case in the Second World War, these terms were open to interpretation. The effect was to limit the number of women who could be recruited, roles they could train for, postings, promotions, pay and pensions, and status. For the Services, the non-combatant principle created a cohort that could not be employed as fully as men. Such inefficient use of people was possible during the period of men's national service. It became more problematic after Britain reverted to all-volunteer armed forces in the early 1960s and with subsequent budget cuts leading to further reductions in establishments.

The RAF appeared to be treating airwomen equally to airmen in ground-based trades. But commanding officers, reluctant to have more non-combatant women, manipulated establishments in favour of men by claiming not to have accommodation for women. Barriers to women's employment were greater and more overt in the Navy and the Army. In the mid-1970s, both commissioned studies on their employment of servicewomen. Together with external pressures, these were to begin the process of dismantling the barriers.

Combatant Status

By the early 1970s, the authorised size of the WRNS had reduced from 2,875 to 2,500 because of closure of bases in east Asia and cuts to the Fleet Air Arm. Further job losses were expected: 40 at Naples, 50 from Malta, 30 from other overseas bases, 58 from the cinema operator trade due to modernisation of equipment, and 45 steward posts as work transferred to civilians. More unquantified reductions were expected. Meanwhile, the WRNS was becoming less cost-effective. A third of officers were employed simply to run it, as were 10 per cent of ratings. This overhead would worsen as more posts were lost.[2]

It was proving difficult to identify more jobs ashore for women as posts needed to be preserved for men as respite from seagoing. In August 1973, a brief for Second Sea Lord Admiral Sir Derek Empson concluded that:

> WRNS ratings would become more cost-effective if they could become direct substitutes for male ratings. The ultimate would be Wrens at sea. Unfortunately, trends in the [radio operator] world indicate disintegration rather than the reverse.[3]

This encapsulated the problem: would a decision to send Wrens to sea be made before the need for them ashore disappeared? Without seagoing the only way to improve value for money would be to achieve greater integration, allowing a reduction in overheads. Admiral Empson informed the new Director WRNS – Commandant Mary Talbot – that she must request a study into the future employment of Wrens. She duly complied. Work started at the beginning of 1974, under the chairmanship of Alan Pritchard, the Assistant Under-Secretary for Naval Personnel.[4] The WRNS still inhabited the ill-defined position of uniformed civilians operating under a voluntary code of conduct.

Pritchard was told that he could address this point if he saw the need, but he was reminded that the current arrangements were popular. That may have been the case, but in Pritchard's view bringing the WRNS under the Naval Discipline Act (NDA) was only a matter of time – so why not now?

Different disciplinary systems for men and women caused problems when they conducted offences jointly but faced different disciplinary processes. For issues such as drug offences, women should be tried in the civilian courts as the naval authorities had no jurisdiction without the NDA. Bringing women under the NDA would enhance the status of officers as they would exercise their authority by right. Pritchard concluded that it would 'stretch the goodwill of the RN' to extend women's employment if the degree of separateness indicated by different disciplinary codes remained. He advised that the timing was good. The legal basis for the armed forces' disciplinary codes was due for its quinquennial Parliamentary review. It would be a simple matter for the NDA to be extended to cover the WRNS while the Armed Forces Bill passed through the Parliamentary processes.[5]

Admiral Sir David Williams (successor to Empson) described Pritchard's proposal as contentious.[6] Indeed, there was considerable reluctance to go down this route. Male and female senior officers alike described the voluntary code as the 'basis of [the] special relationship' between the WRNS and the RN. It was linked with 'the widely held view that the WRNS [had] remained a "feminine" organisation'.[7] Commandant Mary Talbot had been against the NDA, preferring the voluntary code. However, invited to give her views at the Board meeting, she accepted the need to regularise the situation. Objecting to a formal civilian code as it would erode Wrens' status if sanctions amounted to no more than could be applied to the civil service, she preferred the NDA.[8] The Board agreed. The WRNS came under the NDA on 1 July 1977.

Rather than a ringing endorsement, Talbot told her annual conference of senior WRNS officers that the Board decision must be 'accepted and supported'.[9] In doing so, she echoed Commandant Jocelyn Woollcombe's words of 1947 decrying the failure to introduce the NDA. However, bringing the WRNS under NDA authority was a genuine increase in its status. Although not universally welcomed, fears of mass resignations by offended Wrens proved groundless. Protest apparently amounted to female cadets under training at Dartmouth wearing black armbands for the day.[10]

With female officers now holding the Queen's commission, saluting them became mandatory for junior men rather than courtesy as previously. Jackie Mulholland, at the time a junior officer, recollected:

> We were walking down the road in Yeovilton and sailors would be diving into bushes – anywhere to avoid saluting these awful women, you see. But after a few months it all became the norm. And things eased down. But that was a bit of a culture shock for everybody to get used to. [11]

More importantly, the incidence of walking out of the WRNS declined as it was now desertion. Under the voluntary code, women could not be held to their employment and some did walk out of their jobs. Statistics from Naval Home Command recorded 100 female 'deserters' in 1974 (before the NDA), 31 in the financial year ending 31 March 1978 (the year it came in) and 9 cases from 1 April to 20 November 1978.[12]

The Admiralty Board accepted the change to improve the disciplinary situation but the decision brought a wider consequence. The issue of combatant status was being clarified in international law in negotiation of additional protocols to the Geneva Conventions. The new text stated that, with the exception of medical personnel and chaplains, all members of armed forces were combatants, defined for the first time as having the right to take part in hostilities.[13] Britain signed the Protocols in December 1977.[14] As the WRNS were now, in law, part of the armed forces, so Wrens acquired combatant status as did other servicewomen.

This revision to the Geneva Conventions was given as a reason for a change in status for the WRAC. Until this point it was described as a non-combatant corps, limiting the powers of command of its officers. Referencing the imminent Protocols, the fact that nothing in UK military law prevented women from having combatant status, and the work of the wartime ATS, a 1976 report on women in the army recommended that the WRAC should be listed as a combatant corps.[15] Although this implied women could command men by right, described in Army Board minutes in 1977 as an emotive issue, the Board accepted the recommendation.[16] Given that the Service Chiefs agreed the new Protocols to the Geneva Conventions and internal legal advice that nothing in law prevented the change, it is hard to see how the Army Board could do otherwise.

While making this change, the Army Board took the opportunity to revise the formal statement of the role of the WRAC. In 1949 it was described as 'provid[ing] replacements for male officers and men in such employments as may be specified by the Army Board of the Defence Council from time to time.'[17] The updated text stated that the WRAC was:

> ... organised and trained, as an integral part of the Army, to carry out those tasks for which its members are best suited and qualified, so that it will contribute to the maximum efficiency of the Army as a whole.[18]

This new definition moved away from the idea that women were only employed when manpower was deficient. It did not define 'best suited and qualified'.

Airwomen's status was not constrained in the same way as the WRNS and WRAC because the WRAF was not an entity in its own right. However, like other servicewomen, airwomen had been described as non-combatants. This was manifested in regulations that barred them from using small arms. Arming was the first test of servicewomen's new standing as combatants in the late 1970s.

Arming

Although there were occasional exceptions such as for female close protection officers in the Royal Military Police, the policy of all three Services was that women should not be trained to use small arms – rifles, pistols, sub-machine guns. This was increasingly difficult to sustain as defence cuts continued. The 1974 defence review planned a 10 per cent cut in numbers by April 1979, with the RAF taking the greatest share both numerically and as a percentage (18 per cent). As a consequence, the number of men available to undertake armed guarding fell.

The threat from Irish Republican terrorists, particularly to army barracks in Britain, made such duty a real issue, not a theoretical shortfall that would be solved by the call up of reserves in the event of war. For example, bomb attacks were carried out on an officers' mess in Aldershot in February 1972, at Claro Barracks near Ripon in March 1974 and at the Green Howards camp at Strensall near York in June 1974.[19]

Air Commodore Joy Tamblin (Director WRAF) was frustrated by women's exclusion from weapons' training. She believed that:

> RAF officers – the women they knew in their lives were wives and daughters – they couldn't see *them* doing lots of the things that women in the Services did. But it wasn't the same thing at all. Women who come into the Service and trained in the Service knew exactly how they

ought to behave and what they needed to do and how strong in purpose they ought to be. ... Men were not really comparing like with like when they were saying that women as a whole couldn't do this – probably women as a whole couldn't – but *servicewomen* could.[20]

Tamblin recollected that some station commanders believed guard duties 'fell very heavily on the men because the women couldn't do armed duties'.[21] During visits to RAF stations Coltishall, Waddington and Boulmer, she encouraged commanders to raise the matter through their chains of command.

Change was in commanders' interest. Stations were tested against their war roles and the career prospects of commanding officers depended on the outcome of such evaluations. However, requirements for peacetime establishments were lower than those planned for war. Operating below war establishment, flexibility was further hindered by airwomen not being available for armed duties.

RAF Boulmer, a UK air defence station, exposed anomalies in women's participation in hostilities. Women were employed in fighter control work and so were responsible for 'fighting the tactical air defence battle and for ordering fighters to shoot at and destroy enemy aircraft'.[22] Supporting arming, senior male officers at Boulmer thought that:

> There appear[ed] to be little moral difference between giving an order to kill and carrying out the killing ... the effect of a female Sector Controller ordering a wing of fighter [aircraft] or a [surface to air missile] section to engage [the enemy was] infinitely greater than the damage that [could] be done by the same individual using a sub-machine gun.[23]

This work was not new. Regular servicewomen were admitted to fighter control roles from 1950, without any discussion as to the extent that women contributed to hostile action.[24]

In April 1978, taking up the arming issue 'as part of our general review of "sex-equality" questions ...', the Air Member for Personnel's department sought the views of policy areas.[25] In response, Air Commodore Reed-Purvis (Director of Security) defined three categories of combat: offensive action in which personnel would seek and destroy the enemy; defensive action where weapons would be used from prepared positions near the place of work; and self-defence in which the individual would react to being confronted by an enemy. Of these, he accepted that women could undertake the third task but not the first two. He thought

'... it was unrealistic to imagine that all airwomen could be expected to react as combatants when under fire. To plan otherwise in peace would be to court disaster in war.'[26] Clearly, he thought women would not be up to the job.

Meanwhile, Air Commodore Parkinson (Director of Training) refuted a description of armed guards as non-combatants. He argued that 'armed women [would] be combatants in the same way that all male RAF personnel ... already [were]'.[27] Parkinson was right. The liability to take up small arms was *the* duty which distinguished airmen's responsibilities from those of airwomen as had been argued in post-war policy discussions.

In November 1978, Air Marshal Sir John Gingell (Air Member for Personnel) took his recommendation in favour of arming women to the Air Force Board. He cited shortages of personnel, a difficult recruiting climate and attitudes towards sex discrimination. He thought commanders would be willing to accept more airwomen if they could be armed. He quoted the new Protocols to the Geneva Conventions and he produced evidence that arming servicewomen was commonplace in NATO and Commonwealth forces. Agreeing his recommendation, the Air Force Board saw the proposal 'not [as] a matter of "women's lib" but of practical advantage'. Although concerned about possible adverse public opinion, it agreed women should be armed to '[defend] themselves, others and Service property' on a trial basis.[28]

A proposed change in women's employment of that magnitude required Ministerial approval and for the other Services to be informed through the Principal Personnel Officers' Committee. The Navy was opposed, its official position was that as sailors rarely needed to be armed, there was no need to extend arming to women. Vice Admiral Sir Gordon Tait (Second Sea Lord) more vehemently expressed fears that the decision would 'give rise to vociferous demands from vocal minorities for other and wider changes in the employment of servicewomen'.[29] His remarks were made in the context of an ongoing study into whether women should serve at sea, an idea firmly resisted at the time (*see* below).

General Sir Robert Ford (Adjutant General) was more supportive because the Army was also considering arming women. With echoes of Air Commodore Reed-Purvis' view that women could undertake armed duty but not be regarded as employed in combat, Army authorities proposed describing women as 'combatant but non-belligerent'. Female soldiers would use 'defensive weapons' for self-defence purposes only.[30] Four months later, he took his proposal to the Army Board. His main argument centred on the efficient use of personnel. He hoped that arming them would enable more jobs to be opened to women and so have the dual benefit of easing the shortage of men and improving women's career opportunities. In March 1979, the Army Board agreed that women could be armed for self-defence.[31]

Service Chiefs then had to convince the politicians. Frances Pym (Secretary of State in the Conservative government) feared 'strong and vociferous opposition' from the public.[32] However, such evidence as there was of general opinion pointed more towards indifference or surprise that women were not already armed. As an article in the *Daily Mail* pointed out, in the Second World War women 'helped to blast German planes out of the sky' and now Britain 'lagged behind other Western countries, including France and the United States in moves towards arming women.'[33] The issue apparently generated only ten letters to the Prime Minister and these were of divided opinion.[34] Public relations officer Ian McDonald believed 'the Press regard[ed] the issue as stale and the public never seem to have caught on at all'.[35]

Following successful trials in 1981, RAF policy was rolled out, though it was voluntary for women already serving. Its introduction was hindered in the RAF's operational command because of the outbreak of the Falklands War in April 1982. Resources could not be easily diverted to the initial weapons' training of airwomen.[36] In addition, because they were unclear about the implications for their conditions of service, fewer women volunteered than anticipated. Following this stuttering start, compulsory training for all female recruits was introduced from 1 April 1984.

Army implementation was initially more limited than the RAF's. Women were not to be employed to guard bases, but only to be armed for self-defence.[37] In order to avoid wasting weapons, ammunition and instructors' time, commanders of units were to make their own decision on whether or not women were to be trained, based on their assessment of the requirement.[38] Thus arming was initially only permitted, not necessarily open to all women who might volunteer, and not compulsory. Policy was quickly extended to allow guard duty, though Brigadier Anne Field (Director WRAC) complained that she did not want her Corps to become 'americanized'. She had a more salient point about the attempt to widen arming without provision of the necessary resources, including extending the length of the recruit training course for women.[39] Arming was introduced into basic training for women in July 1988.[40]

As usual, naval policy lagged behind these developments but they could not be ignored. The tri-Service environment of the garrison installed in the Falklands Islands following the 1982 war with Argentina provided the impetus for change. In 1986, the commander of British forces complained that, with his bases constantly operating at a heightened state of alert, Wrens were the only servicewomen unable to make a full contribution. He intended training them to use weapons which would only be issued in the event of an emergency. His stance was supported by Commandant Marjorie Fletcher (Director WRNS 1986–8) who thought that Wrens should take their fair share of the tasks. Later that year, the commander at Faslane submarine base also requested arming of Wrens to cope with additional guard force tasks generated in response to protests staged at this nuclear base. The argument rumbled on for two years before the decision was made in 1988. Arming of the WRNS was introduced on 1 April 1989.[41]

One immediate consequence of arming women in 1982 was an increase in the military pay supplement (X-factor) for all servicewomen, whether or not they took up weapons training. A key factor in men receiving a higher X-factor than women was their liability to take up arms if the need arose. This could now apply to servicewomen. A civil servant's objection that arms training would not have 'any radical effect on the day-to-day duties of those WRAF who [were] trained' and that bearing weapons would be a 'minor rather than a major change in role' was rejected.[42] The MOD put forward a case to the Armed Force Pay Review Body (AFPRB) and servicewomen's X-factor was increased from 5 per cent to 7.5 per cent of basic pay in 1982. Men's rate remained 10 per cent.[43]

In acceding, the AFPRB was careful to avoid overstating women's new responsibilities, saying that women were 'not trained to undertake a combat role' and they did not serve as pilots in the RAF or go to sea in the Navy.[44] There was an obvious, but overlooked, implication of that definition of combat for the RAF, namely the majority of men also did not fly. However, they were still regarded as having combat roles as was apparent in the post-war negotiations on pay. The Pay Review Body reflected the position of the Service Chiefs who needed some servicewomen to be armed in limited circumstances but wanted to play down the significance to avoid more demanding questions about limits to servicewomen's employment.

'Never at Sea'

In the 1974 review of the WRNS, Alan Pritchard was asked to redefine the role of the WRNS for the following ten years. Although invited to take account of the national tendency towards the wider employment of women, his scope was limited by direction from Vice Admiral David Williams (Director General of Naval Manpower and Training) that women would not be serving at sea in the near future.[45]

Commandant Mary Talbot described the WRNS as being at its worst crisis point since the late 1950s. She feared it would disappear by default. Good quality officers were underemployed or misemployed and she decried the failure to build up experience outside of WRNS administration. Although she acknowledged that some women were joining ships in the United States Navy, she was not asking for Wrens to go to sea. If it was required, she would not object.[46]

Allaying Talbot's fears, Pritchard's report in November 1974 made a strong case for the WRNS. First, well-qualified female recruits were available and filled roles for which male recruitment was difficult or, if there was no seagoing equivalent, not required. Second, they were cheaper than sailors and likely to remain so even after the introduction of equal pay in 1975. This came about because of the X-factor and because men with seagoing liability were in a higher pay band than women. Third, in isolated locations, civilians were not available. Fourth, Wrens were a loyal workforce whereas 'growing militancy of trades unions and even staff associations [had] cast doubt on the unquestioned dependability of both industrial and non-industrial civilian support.'[47] Wrens were also described as contributing to 'the social cohesiveness of otherwise male establishments, especially in isolated areas.' This was an interesting observation. Whenever seagoing was discussed, the presence of women was usually presumed to be disruptive.[48]

Pritchard was surprised by women's 'general lack of desire for change'.[49] Apart from bringing the WRNS under the NDA, the main changes that flowed from his work were the dismantling of the WRNS administrative posts on units and the relocation of women's recruit training and initial officer training. Although Mary Talbot objected on the grounds of the 'disparity in educational level and social class between the WRNS and the [male] ratings under training', Vonla McBride (her successor) agreed the move of recruit training from the dilapidated HMS *Dauntless* (near Reading) to HMS *Raleigh* (Plymouth).[50] This was only collocation. McBride drew the line at combined training.[51]

Likewise, officer training moved from its prestigious home at the Royal Naval College, Greenwich, to Dartmouth where new entrant male officers trained. Again, this was collocation rather than joint training. There was some reluctance. Being at Greenwich enabled female cadets and staff to socialise with senior men's courses. The WRNS course included visits to galleries, museums, Parliament and the Courts of Justice.[52] A modernised twelve-week programme at Dartmouth gave less time to WRNS matters, allowing more for Royal Navy organisation and functions, Britain's role in the world and leadership training. Two places per annum for staff training were also reserved for female officers. In a separate development, the MOD's National Defence College was opened to women of all three Services. These advanced training opportunities were intended to open up more staff jobs at headquarters and MOD.[53]

Unhappy that seagoing had not been considered, Frank Judd (Under Secretary of State for the Navy) commissioned more work. Despite his intentions that it be 'thorough and open-minded', there was a caveat that only non-combatant roles would be considered.[54] An assertion that neither public opinion nor the Royal Navy was ready for women in combat roles, together with points concerning physical strength, operational requirements and the consequential reduction in seagoing jobs for men, were sufficient grounds for limiting the scope.[55] With warships ruled out, two questions needed to be answered: what jobs could women do at sea and what vessels were non-combatant?

Roles identified as suitable included radio operators, writers (i.e. clerks), cooks and stewards. But Wrens in these categories were described as 'unfortunately ... drawn from the lower intelligence level and [in need of] more guidance and supervision than others, [having] a greater tendency to get into trouble over disciplinary matters.'[56] Junior Wrens at sea should therefore be accompanied by a senior woman – officer or petty officer – for welfare duties. Various other difficulties were foreseen: divisiveness between sea-goers and shore-based women; lack of interest in sea service; seagoing might attract a different sort of female recruit; and wives' suspicion of Wrens with whom their husbands worked.[57] Or perhaps they meant doubts over husbands' fidelity?

The list of possible ships comprised four survey vessels controlled by the Hydrographer (responsible for provision of maritime charts and navigational information), three trials ships (used for test firing of weapons) and the Royal Yacht. However, the future of Rear Admiral Haslam's (the Hydrographer) ships was uncertain as their mapping function was being considered for transfer to the civilian sector.[58] Haslam expressed 'grave misgivings about the adverse effects on morale, operational ability and discipline' if women served in his ships. He cited: the loss of efficiency in duties where strength was required; his ships were combatant in war; the expense of modifications 'at a time of national monetary crisis'; opposition from 'younger officers and men'; opposition from wives 'to having ladies cooped up at sea for long periods with traditional sailors'; and disciplinary problems arising from having a mixed crew.

Haslam was 'opposed to being the front-runner in any experiments of such a controversial nature'.[59] By now he was not just the front-runner, he was the only runner. The Royal Yacht had no difficulty in being excused. The Duke of Edinburgh was said to be against the idea on grounds of the cost of creating accommodation for Wrens.[60] Trials ships also dropped out because they were due out of service and costs could not be justified.[61] Admiral Sir David Williams (now promoted to Second Sea Lord) agreed with Haslam's objections, suggesting that hydrographic ships were 'peculiarly <u>un</u>suitable [original emphasis] for women' as they spent so long at sea. In a telling phrase, Williams concluded that now (1976) was not a good time to 'burden the [ships] with women.'[62] The matter was deferred.

In 1977, a revised paper set out the case for seagoing: the public relations benefits of 'acting in the spirit of the Sex Discrimination Act', benefits for morale and recruiting in the WRNS by showing 'that they [were] capable of making a worthwhile contribution in what [was] traditionally a man's world', sea experience for women that would provide 'valuable background for a wider range of shore jobs', providing personnel in categories short of men, and giving the Navy experience of women at sea before predicted shortages of men for the 1980s and 1990s materialised.[63]

From this positive introduction a reader might suppose that a robust proposal was to follow. Given the list of supposed benefits, the recommendation was absurd. The paper settled on employing just eight women aboard the Seabed Operations Vessel – a ship not yet built and only due into service in 1982. An argument made in favour was that this would be a dull posting. Men would be bored and might leave the Navy but, as Wrens tended to leave after short service anyway, it would not matter if they were bored. The case against was that only eight jobs were proposed and just two of these were in trades which were short of men.[64] Patrick Duffy (Judd's successor as the Minister) was told by a senior civil servant that 'Politically the move might merely be seen as a gimmick'. He was persuaded to put off the idea.[65]

Imbued with the Wrens' motto 'Never at Sea', leaders of the WRNS lacked enthusiasm for seagoing. Mary Talbot expressed this view to the Admiralty Board in 1975.[66] Her successor Vonla McBride wanted to be convinced that there was a 'real and continued requirement' for seagoing.[67] There was some merit in her point as limited seagoing for a small number of Wrens would not enhance women's career prospects. However, McBride was strongly opposed to women in combatant roles. She feared that the feminine image of the WRNS would be lost if it attracted women who sought the tough conditions of life aboard ship, with limited privacy, lack of individual space, noise, dirt, and the need for physical endurance. She '[didn't] want to know the butch girls' who could pass such physical tests.[68]

Commandant Elizabeth Craig-McFeely (McBride's replacement in July 1979) encapsulated these views in addressing her senior officers, saying:

> ... if the RN has a requirement for the WRNS to undertake particular tasks then we must do it. ... It is important that [women's] careers are safeguarded, that we retain our femininity, the rights of the individual and the reputation of the WRNS. ... it is vital ... that the WRNS remain a separate corps. Our infiltration into the male world must be gradual. If we are to go to sea, fly or be armed then it must be in selected jobs where needed, and NOT [original emphasis] undertaken as a publicity stunt.[69]

Mary Talbot was more enthusiastic about the possibility of flying roles. In 1975, she told her conference of senior WRNS officers that five women would be asked to attend aircrew selection with the intention of choosing three in order to fill two posts. A year later her successor reported the initiative had been shelved. As the Navy was not short of pilots, the cost of training women could not be justified.[70]

Growing demand for helicopter pilots from the North Sea oil industry changed the picture. By 1980, the Navy was unable to meet NATO standards of aircrew availability, being short of about 130 pilots out of a requirement for about 600. Male recruitment was meeting targets but the Service struggled to retain trained pilots.[71] Recollecting that the main obstacle for WRNS pilots had been their exclusion from combat roles, a senior civil servant wondered whether 'under pressure of a serious shortage we might manage to persuade ourselves to take a different view of that problem?'[72]

Admiral Cassidi (Second Sea Lord from September 1979) saw female officers as part of the solution to the Navy's shortage of aircrew. To increase the number of possible postings, he included anti-submarine warfare (ASW) helicopters. He thought that:

> if the UK is now ready to envisage [armed] Servicewomen in eyeball to eyeball confrontation with an armed enemy in emergency or war there is unlikely to be strong objection to WRNS officers being trained ... for anti-submarine helicopter operations.[73]

Including ASW helicopters, the Navy could employ at least sixteen female pilots. To ensure a reasonable return on training costs, Cassidi proposed that female pilots should not be able to leave on marriage. But he sounded a note of caution. He reminded his Admiralty Board colleagues that exclusion from combat 'was the main reason for exempting the Armed Services from ... the Sex Discrimination Act'. Accordingly, the Board 'would need to consider very carefully indeed any move that left the Service vulnerable to all the demands of the sex equality movement'.

Avoiding calling anti-submarine warfare combat, Cassidi suggested that ASW could be described as 'operational roles short of actual combat.' This failed to convince Captain Briggs of the naval warfare department who wrote:

> The merry souls in a Charlie Class SSN [a Soviet submarine] may well feel they have been involved in combat if Jenny Wren drops a [depth bomb] on their heads.[74]

Cassidi's Board colleagues also rejected the idea that anti-submarine helicopter operations were not combat roles. They concluded that female pilots could 'compromise the Services' position with regard to the Sex Discrimination Act'. They doubted the ability to hold women to long contracts and thought commercial employers were just as likely to poach female as male pilots. Summarising, Admiral Sir Henry Leach (First Sea Lord) observed that an experiment 'would attract a lot of attention and would be difficult to abandon'.[75] Cassidi was invited to keep the idea to hand in case it was needed in the future.

After so much staff work in the 1970s, the WRNS had progressed to legal status as part of the armed forces, officers holding the Queen's commission and collocation of initial training. Despite the effort expended on studies into seagoing and flying, both ideas were rejected by the admirals. Elizabeth Craig-McFeely remarked:

> It is unrealistic to suppose that we can go on attracting high calibre young women unless the Service offers them the widest range of interesting and challenging employment.[76]

Army Careers

Lieutenant Colonel Fisher, responsible for postings, reported to a WRAC conference that half of the non-commissioned ranks left in 1971. Wastage was so high that deficiencies built up at corporal and sergeant ranks. As she so aptly put it: 'the simple reason [is] that the time taken to earn chevrons [rank insignia of a corporal] equals time taken to find husband.'[77] As numbers dipped in the early 1970s, so a new report on the future of the WRAC was commissioned.

After three years of staff work, the paper that went to the Army Board in 1977 recognised that women did not have worthwhile careers. They were constrained in the roles they could undertake and the locations in which they were permitted to serve. High levels of wastage due to women leaving on marriage or pregnancy meant that women were an unpredictable component of the overall strength of the Army. General Sir Jack Harman (Adjutant General) observed that the WRAC had no difficulty in attracting bright women with good degrees to become officers, but they left if they could not see proper career opportunities.[78]

Non-commissioned women were trained in 23 career employment groups (CEGs), meaning groups of trades, of which 14 were identical to or similar to those of men. However, women's opportunities were limited by truncated rank structures. For example, with the Royal Signals only those female soldiers who worked as data telegraphists had an opportunity to hold warrant officer (class 1) posts.[79] Harman proposed making appropriate CEGs combined so that women could compete with men equally for appointments and promotions.

For those women who stayed with mainstream WRAC employment, prospects were bright. Early promotion within the WRAC beckoned as they filled gaps left by departing colleagues. For example, the average time to reach corporal rank was 2.8 years in the WRAC against an average for men of 6.2 years. Promotion to sergeant took 4.9 years for women and 10.2 for men. It was only promotion to the highest Senior NCO rank (warrant officer class 1) that took longer for women – 20.2 years compared with 18.5 for men.[80]

As with earlier studies, organisational factors were considered. Looking at NATO allies, the report assessed that armies who only employed women in a corps of their own suffered from insularity, underutilising women's talents. Those countries that dispersed women into employing corps experienced unacceptable problems in training, control of numbers and in social contexts.[81] General Harman advised keeping the current practice of recruitment into the WRAC but with opportunity for employment with men's corps. To improve prospects, he suggested two employment paths: one for those who worked solely in the WRAC and another for those primarily employed in other parts of the army where women would compete with men for jobs and promotion.[82]

Harman undermined his own ideas in the limitations placed on Commanders-in-Chief as they reviewed their establishments. Women were not to be in jobs where they could come into direct contact with the enemy. They could not fill a role if its primary purpose was to kill the enemy. They were to be at limited risk of capture. Women were not to be trained in peacetime for a job that they could not also undertake in war. Nor were they to do jobs that required demanding physical work.[83]

Two years after the Army Board approved Harman's paper, progress amounted to identification of 45 additional posts that officers could fill and 527 for non-commissioned ranks.[84] The key stumbling block was British Army of the Rhine (BAOR) policy that women could not be deployed forward of divisional headquarters. BAOR complained that employing more women would seriously degrade defence plans. As an example, if there were more female data telegraphists at headquarters, then there would not be enough men to send forward to operational formations in the event of war.[85]

The geographic restriction was significant as one-third of the Army was stationed in West Germany. The effect was amplified as units in the UK with a war role in West Germany also restricted women's employment. These limitations undermined combined CEGs and the competition with men for promotion, as many trades required 'field force' experience as a prerequisite for more senior jobs.[86]

There was an exception to exclusion from an operational area. Members of the WRAC were employed in Northern Ireland from September 1972 as part of the army's deployment in that troubled part of the United Kingdom. Some participated in intelligence duties. Others were more visible as searchers, drivers or used to interrogate female suspects.[87] However, female civilian participation in terrorist incidents was thought to be increasing. A 1972 report suggested that women were involved in 308 out of 924 armed robberies, in 451 out of 1,317 bombings and there were 23 instances of women firing weapons.[88] Hard pressed to provide sufficient female personnel to cope with searching and interrogating female suspects, the government decided to allow women to join the Ulster Defence Regiment (UDR) in August 1973.

The UDR was an unusual departure from the normal policy for the employment of women. First, women joined the Regiment directly. Brigadier Sheila Heaney (Director WRAC 1970–73) refused to accept them as part of the WRAC, declining to be held responsible for women over whom she had no actual authority. She was also steadfast in rejecting the use of WRAC uniforms, claiming a shortage of the lovat green uniform.[89]

UDR women would mostly be part-time and would live in their own homes. They were to be used as searchers, clerks and radio operators, with lower entry standards than applied in either the Royal Ulster Constabulary or the WRAC, in order to attract the 700 women needed. Married women would be accepted provided their husbands agreed and their duties did not conflict with their domestic responsibilities. They would not be armed, the view being that if they carried weapons they would be more likely to be seen as targets to be attacked. However, they could apply to the civil authorities for a firearms certificate if they considered themselves to be at risk.[90]

The Territorial Army (TA) also provided interesting opportunities for women intent, like men, on taking part in a challenging activity in their spare time. TA units were integrated. Women joined a local unit and identified with its function rather than with the WRAC. TA commanders, who had to find their own solutions to shortfalls of personnel, took a more relaxed view of who could do a job than the regular Army. This became apparent in connection with the infantry.

As he was leaving office in 1973, Major General Charles Dunbar (the regular Army's Director of Infantry) proposed allowing women to serve with infantry battalions in support roles. His idea was rejected by his successor Major General David House, who thought women would be a burden to commanders of field force battalions.[91] But the TA embraced the concept. Women were accepted for General Reserve Infantry Battalions from May 1975. Initially, up to 20 women could serve in a headquarters' company. However, unlike some male-only TA infantry battalions, the ones open to women were earmarked for roles in home defence in the event of a general war. By 1977, 250 women were serving with TA infantry battalions.[92]

The majority of TA women served in signals units, about 1,100 out of 2,130 women in statistics for 1977.[93] Major Jean Blackwood, commanding a signals squadron, explained to a conference of WRAC officers that she recruited and trained personnel and organised exercises for her soldiers (male and female). About 20 per cent of her squadron were women, though they were confined to jobs as data telegraphists, clerks and cooks. Speaking in 1979 at the annual WRAC conference she said:

> ... one has an enormous sense of achievement after a successful exercise when 200 soldiers, 130 items of [motor transport] and all the technical equipment have been moved from our home base to a field location, sited, plugged together, camouflaged, weapons' pits sited and shift working commenced. The whole thing running like a well-oiled machine.[94]

She clearly did her job well. Promoted to lieutenant colonel, she went on to command 37 Signals Regiment in March 1982, becoming the first woman to command a TA unit.[95]

By 1982, a further review of regular Army jobs had been completed. It identified 500 officer jobs and 3,500 non-commissioned jobs that could be filled by either men or women. Cautious about units becoming too 'diluted', not more than 50 officer posts and 300 non-commissioned jobs were permitted to be given to women at any one time. Employing corps were to take over career management, with a requirement only to consult the WRAC hierarchy. Promotion boards with women competing with male colleagues were to be tried for drivers with the Royal Corps of Transport, and data telegraphists and switchboard operators with the Royal Signals. There was an important cultural limit to this integration – all women were to retain the WRAC cap badge.[96]

Reviving Major General Dunbar's stalled initiative from 1973, two trials of women working with field force units were set in train. Ten women joined 49 Field Regiment Royal Artillery and fourteen went to the 1st battalion of the Gloucestershire Regiment, an infantry battalion stationed at Münster in West Germany. Working on the personal staff of the Adjutant General in the late 1970s, Lieutenant Colonel Robin Grist (later Major General) knew of this aspiration to test the concept of women working with field units. As he was about to take command of the Glosters, he offered to run the trial. The battalion's role was to escort nuclear weapons in support of 1 British Corps. As escort for convoys, it was exempt from the normal rotation of infantry battalions to Northern Ireland and so provided a stable environment in which to test the employment of female soldiers. The first WRAC component of clerks, drivers and medical orderlies arrived in February 1980. They worked with the headquarters' company. Speaking in 2015, Robin Grist recollected the scheme as being a great success despite the fears of contemporaries that he would be running a brothel.[97]

This period saw important developments for women in the Army. The WRAC was no longer described as simply making up for deficiencies of manpower. It had combatant status and its members could be trained to use small arms. Although there was some success in identifying more jobs for women, this expansion was still constrained by geographic principles governing postings. Importantly, with the introduction of career management within some employing trades, the Director of the WRAC was beginning to lose control over members of her Corps.

Female Aircrew

Like the other Services, the Air Force department of the MOD dabbled with the idea of employing women more widely. For the RAF, this was to compensate for shortfalls of men of the required quality rather than to improve careers for the majority of its servicewomen. In the late 1970s, the RAF experienced one of its periodic crises of pilot and navigator recruitment and retention.

> Recruiting [was] well down, quality of those accepted ... [had] reduced; wastage in training [was] higher than predicted; there was a bottleneck [in training]; retention [was] below expectations and premature voluntary release applications [were] well up on previous years.[98]

Failure to recruit was attributed to uncertainty created by the 1974 defence review cuts, which led to a redundancy programme. Retention problems were blamed on poor pay and conditions of service. The backlog of men wanting early release from the RAF was such that junior officer pilots were expected to wait until the mid-1980s for an exit date, causing 'a serious morale problem'.[99]

One potential solution was to recruit women as pilots and navigators for roles described as non-combatant, as was happening in America.[100] However, Air Marshal Sir John Gingell (Air Member for Personnel) was against it.[101] All RAF pilots were recruited on their potential to fly fast jet aircraft, an avenue that would be denied to women on the grounds that they could not take up combat roles. Those trainees who did not make the grade for fast jets could train for multi-engine or rotary wing aircraft. In terms familiar from the 1940s, Gingell argued that non-combatant women would take training places needed for men. Furthermore, women tended not to serve as long as men and so it would not be economic to train them. Finally, he doubted that the idea would receive support.[102] The suggestion was dropped.

By the late 1970s, the RAF relied heavily on a training scheme which it ran at universities. These University Air Squadrons (UASs), as they were known, were a key source of pilots and were expected to be 'the primary source of the future leadership of ... the RAF'.[103] Cadetships were awarded to selected male undergraduates. These young men trained as pilots and were obliged to serve in the RAF after graduation. Other male undergraduates were selected by UAS commanding officers as volunteer reserves. They were given fewer flying hours than cadets. Those of acceptable standard were encouraged, but not obliged, to join the RAF.

The UASs also experienced a crisis of recruitment. In 1977, only 91 of 183 available cadetships were awarded. The aptitude for flying training of men accepted as volunteer reserves declined. Air Vice-Marshal Harcourt-Smith (Commandant of RAF College Cranwell and responsible for UASs) put local difficulties down to 'the sex discrimination problem'.[104] In addition to anti-military views on campuses, he observed a worsening situation due to the growth in women's rights movements. The RAF was seen in a bad light compared with the Army and the Royal Navy which both admitted women to university units. Consequently, some Students' Unions hindered recruitment to UASs by preventing them from attending freshers' fairs.

Harcourt-Smith proposed volunteer reserve membership for women, with some flying training, on the grounds that it would 'remove a major source of complaint and [UASs] would therefore have direct access to a larger pool of potential male recruits'.[105] In 1979, a draft Air Force Board paper recommended up to 10 per cent of Volunteer Reserve places be open to women as a way of overcoming complaints. Women would replace men at the lower end of the quality spectrum who were unlikely to be offered commissions.[106]

The paper was criticised by the finance department which argued that as women could not join as pilots, it was inappropriate to train them to fly at public expense.[107] Another respondent was concerned about explaining in public why women could fly with UASs but not in the RAF. Air Vice-Marshal Bailey (Director General of Personnel Services) doubted that a 10 per cent quota would 'mollify the women's rights firebrands at the universities'.[108] He hinted that the Air Member for Personnel was against women pilots. As predicted, Air Marshal Gingell decreed the proposal 'should be put on ice'.[109]

Ideas emerging from within the Service, but rejected at the top, recurred when it came to rear crew roles. New work emerged in the form of the airborne early warning (AEW) role. Shackleton aircraft, crewed by pilots, navigators, air electronics officers and air electronic operators, were employed on this task.[110] In the 1970s, planning was underway to replace the Shackleton fleet with more capable Nimrod aircraft, fitted with a new radar, surveillance systems and data processing equipment. The necessary skills of detection, tracking, recognition and reporting of airborne traffic were akin to those of fighter control officers and the non-commissioned trade of aerospace operators in ground-based air defence control centres. Although these specialisations were short of personnel, it was decided to earmark up to a third of the posts on the AEW Nimrod for them. The remainder would initially come from existing Shackleton crews.[111]

As women formed a significant proportion of fighter control personnel, the question arose as to whether they would be eligible for AEW Nimrod. Trying to make a case to include women, but seeking a way to conform to their exclusion from combat, Wing Commander Borrett (an air defence staff officer) sought advice as to the definition of a combat aircraft. He thought AEW Nimrod could be described as non-combatant as it did not entail 'bring[ing] weapons to bear directly on the enemy'.[112] He also thought that the risk to which women would be exposed was certainly no more than, and possibly less than, when they did similar work in UK control centres. In war, women might be safer when airborne than working at ground radar stations.

Yet again, it was pointed out that there was no international or domestic legal prohibition on employing women in combat. It was a matter of MOD policy, and political and public acceptance.[113] However, the idea of employing women in AEW Nimrod was rejected by Air Force Board members. Air Chief Marshal Sir Rex Roe (Air Member for Supply and Organisation) offered 'to field it, presumably into touch?'[114] Air Chief Marshal Sir Michael Beetham (Chief of the Air Staff) agreed and ruled that women would not fly in Nimrod aircraft.[115]

Air Vice-Marshal Hayr (Assistant Chief of Air Staff – Operations) also championed a new role. He wanted airwomen, who as qualified linguists on 26 Signals Unit in Berlin monitored Warsaw Pact military communications, to be considered for Nimrod reconnaissance aircraft in an air signals specialisation. This career pattern was open to airmen. Hayr set out three particular considerations: whether this constituted combatant work; terms of service; and the potential for unnecessary publicity for this normally secret work. He argued that the reconnaissance role was 'not [regarded as] a combat aircraft in the strictest sense' as it operated at a distance behind the front line. The work would not place women 'in any greater danger than girls currently serving in Operations Centres in RAF Germany'. However, he cautioned that 'unwanted publicity' for the Squadron would need to be carefully handled.[116] This seemed to give his superiors a reason for rejecting the initiative. Consistent with his stance on AEW Nimrod, Air Chief Marshal Beetham asked Air Marshal Sir David Craig to 'pour cold water on this – and drown it'.[117]

The one flying role that was open to women came close to being abandoned in the late 1970s. This was the modest encroachment of women into the world of the Air Quartermaster, renamed Air Loadmaster (ALM) in 1970 to achieve NATO standardisation of terminology. By then, female ALMs worked on passenger-cum-freight flights.[118] Women were not employed on the Tactical Transport Force for what Air Chief Marshal Sir John Aiken (Gingell's predecessor as Air Member for Personnel) described, without spelling out, as 'obvious reasons'.[119] The Force's task was listed as: moving heavy freight; conducting air drops; and carrying troops, potentially to forward airfields. The reader was left to deduce why women were not employed, presumably lack of physical strength, geographic issues of having women close to conflict zones, dealing with soldiers and women's non-combatant status.

Women's employment on the Strategic Force's VC10 aircraft, used in place of Britannia and Comet aircraft of earlier years, was now also questioned by Aiken. Withdrawal from overseas bases (as Britain relinquished its empire) had reduced the need for passenger flights on which women worked. He also observed that female ALMs were physically unable to handle the aircraft's emergency evacuation chutes and dinghies, so male ALMs always had to be on board, thus creating financial inefficiency. In war, VC10s would be used for troop movements and ammunition supply, tasks from which women were excluded.[120]

Writing to James Wellbeloved (Under Secretary of State for Air) in January 1978, Aiken proposed disestablishing female ALM posts. However, aware that this could be politically sensitive just three years after the passing of the Sex Discrimination Act, he sought ministerial approval.[121] Air Marshal Sir John Nicholls (Air Member for Supply and Organisation) opposed disestablishment. He thought the principle of female aircrew was 'important and we should not walk back from it'.[122] Wellbeloved agreed, deciding that the 'opportunity for women to become aircrew [was] highly important, both psychologically and presentationally'.[123] The ALM trade remained open to women. What had started as a need in the late 1950s was preserved as a token in the new climate of workplace equality.

Conclusion

The principle that servicewomen were non-combatants had not needed any definition when regular service was introduced. Initially there were anomalies left over from the elastic interpretation from the Second World War, but the general principle was simple. Women could not be employed in ships, fly aircraft or be employed in land warfare. Nor could they train in the use of small arms. Exclusion from the employment clauses of the Sex Discrimination Act was achieved on the premise that combat was men's work.

These certainties were overtaken by developments in the mid-1970s when new Protocols to the Geneva Conventions made clear that members of the armed forces had combatant status and this entitled them to take part in hostilities. Accepting that servicewomen were combatants, the debate in the MOD shifted from the status of an individual to roles acceptable for women. What constituted hostilities and to what extent should women participate?

The immediate answer appeared to be that not much changed in terms of roles. Women were still excluded from ships. They could not fly aircraft. Geographic restrictions in the Army still constrained women's postings even in work they were permitted to undertake in the UK. But it was possible to place a wider interpretation on the idea of participation, as senior staff at RAF Boulmer argued. If a woman could direct the air battle, then why not also train her to use a personal weapon?

The decision in the RAF and the Army to train women to use weapons was pragmatic. Reductions in personnel meant that the self-inflicted inefficiency of excluding women from armed duty was a luxury that could no longer be afforded. The new description of women as combatants and the example of allied nations contributed to a climate for change. But the language used was carefully chosen to maintain a distinction between servicewomen's liability to take up arms and that of men. Men could be employed in offensive combat, seeking out and killing the enemy. Women could be armed to defend themselves or perhaps guard a base. But that was as far as the concession was to go.

The Services' responses to legal and policy changes mirrored their organisational and operational differences. The Navy department initially remained aloof to the arming initiative. However, the status of women in the WRNS ceased to be the previously ambiguous civilians-in-uniform. Wrens came under the Naval Discipline Act. But without seagoing, careers remained limited. While Labour ministers in the late 1970s seemed open to the idea, senior admirals were opposed. Until the Navy signalled it was ready, successive Directors of the WRNS refused to press the case for sea service. They recognised the precarious state of their Service in a shrinking naval organisation – base closures and transfer of work to civilians put Wrens' jobs at risk. But the WRNS had cultivated a sense of being an elite, with the emphasis on femininity. Seagoing would be a fundamental challenge to this ethos. The Directors would go along with seagoing if the Navy said it was needed, but they would not lobby for the change.

By permitting rather than mandating arming, employment policy in the Army was inconsistent. Still constrained by geographic rules, there remained considerable opposition to widening women's roles. While there was a growth in opportunities for permanent employment within some support corps, jobs within the WRAC were still described as women's mainstream employment. Rather than mainstream, women in the WRAC remained marginal to the operational Army. Meanwhile, where it suited the Army, more roles were opened: in the TA to compensate for shortages of men; in the UDR as a need for women to meet operational circumstances. With the introduction of some career management of women working with other Corps, the Director of the WRAC began to lose control over the careers of female soldiers.

In the RAF, women could now fill war appointments associated with career-enhancing postings. In ground-based work (the majority of the RAF), airwomen became fully interchangeable with airmen as had been intended since 1949. Flying remained almost exclusively the prerogative of men. However, women's skills in fighter control work and as linguists encouraged some senior men to champion flying roles. The question 'why not women?' was being asked.

Combatant status and arming resulted in a greater percentage of women being employed, more roles being opened, more postings becoming available, better pay, and from that, better pensions. These developments were a necessary step along the way to narrowing career differences between men and women.

Individuals mattered, even if they did not always win their arguments. Major General Dunbar was ahead of his colleagues in wanting to employ the WRAC in support roles with infantry battalions. Six years later, his ideas had taken root and Lieutenant Colonel Robin Grist volunteered his battalion as a proving ground. Air Commodore Joy Tamblin successfully used her influence to bring about small arms training. However, the Air Force Board of the late 1970s was resolute in rebuffing the ideas of men such as Air Vice-Marshal Hayr who wanted to exploit the talents of airwomen in new aircrew roles. Alan Pritchard fulfilled wartime Director Vera Laughton Mathews' aspiration to bring the WRNS under the Naval Discipline Act. But the Admiralty Board ran rings round government ministers when it came to sea service. This edifice was about to crumble.

8

COMBAT ROLES

Use servicewomen or lose them – that was the essence of a National Audit Office (NAO – the watchdog for government expenditure) message to the Army and the Navy in a 1989 report. 'The tasks on which [service]women were currently employed in many cases had a very low military content ... some 3,300 posts ... could be occupied by civilians or contracted out.'[1] This was a quarter of the strength of the women's Services. Below this overall figure, the analysis illustrated divergence between the Services. The NAO identified 47 per cent of WRNS jobs, 36 per cent of the WRAC but just 4 per cent of WRAF work that could be done by cheaper means. The WRAF was not vulnerable like the WRNS or WRAC because it was not an entity in its own right. Now armed, airwomen were fully interchangeable with airmen within integrated trades.

Anthea Larken (Director WRNS) took the report seriously, fearing it could lead to the demise of her Service if seagoing was not introduced.[2] Its shore-based support role was insufficient to sustain the Wrens. Brigadier Shirley Nield (Director WRAC) worried that the report could lead to women directly joining Army support corps.[3] If women wore the cap-badge of employing corps rather than that of the WRAC, her Corps would be by-passed and weakened. Cap-badging was very emotive in the Army; the badge worn on a soldier's headdress proclaimed identity.

Personnel issues featured high on the agenda at the MOD. There was anxiety about recruiting prospects due to a significant decline in the birth rate. This was compounded by difficulties in retaining experienced personnel. A rise in home ownership implied a reluctance to accept postings and separation from families. A home represented family stability, to the benefit of children's education and the ability of the spouse to hold a job. Recruitment targets had to be increased to compensate for the failure to retain existing personnel.

In response to these pressures, the Army Board and the Navy Board commissioned studies which were to change how servicewomen were employed. The RAF's problem was different. It was not one of quantity – to compensate for the reduced supply of young men, it simply increased the quota for female recruits. Its issue was quality. Aptitude for flying training was worsening among the young men who sought flying careers.

If servicewomen's employment was to become more military, to counter the NAO's criticisms, then the ban on combat roles needed to be tackled. Which of air, sea or land warfare roles would be acceptable militarily and politically? An unlikely champion of women's wider military participation was about to emerge – the determined Minister for the Armed Forces, Archie Hamilton (Conservative, Epsom and Ewell).

Army Policy

By the late 1980s, the WRAC had lost control over a significant proportion of its members' careers. From 1979 female officers could be permanently employed by another corps. They remained WRAC and wore the cap badge, but they could make their careers elsewhere, as they had long been able to do in the Royal Army Education Corps. Seven more corps (Royal Engineers, Royal Signals, Royal Corps of Transport, Royal Army Ordnance Corps, Royal Electrical and Mechanical Engineers, Royal Army Pay Corps and the Army Catering Corps) offered careers up to lieutenant colonel (Figure 8.1). The Intelligence Corps joined the scheme in 1987. Women not opting to be permanently employed elsewhere were described as mainstream WRAC.

The policy was not necessarily enthusiastically pursued, as Major General John Drewienkiewicz (a former Royal Engineer) recollected from his time as the recruiter for engineer officers:

> the Engineer-in-Chief – a major general – rang me up and said ... 'Of course, there is a new Army Board ruling saying that we can take women.' I said 'I've got that, General.' He said, 'You don't need to try too hard, you know.' I said 'General, if you are saying that to me, I really do need it in writing.' He said 'Don't be so silly.' ... I said, 'My impression is that there are some very good women out there and they are rather better than some of the guys we are taking – because we are taking non-graduates and we are taking history graduates. I can get you

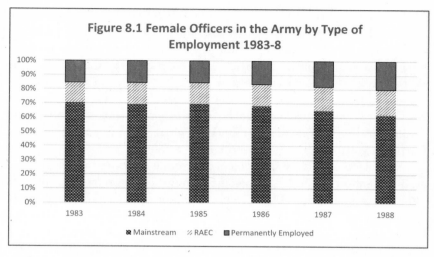

Figure 8.1 Female Officers in the Army by Type of Employment 1983-8

Excludes professionally qualified officers (medical, dental, legal, veterinary). Source: NAM: 1998-11-38, *The Corps Today*, issues 1983–88.

women engineering graduates who are good engineers and who are going to fill a gap we seem unable to fill with men.' … at my level – at the sort of senior major, junior lieutenant colonel level – by that stage in the mid '80s – there was a view that we could use and employ gainfully the best of the women. And we didn't need to take the worst [of the men].[4]

A solitary female officer was permanently employed with the Royal Engineers in 1982. By September 1988, in part due to Drewienkiewicz's efforts, there were nine.[5]

In non-commissioned ranks, careers to warrant officer class 1 were offered in some jointly managed trades – meaning the manning and records office for that trade became responsible for women's postings, specialist training and promotions. The WRAC lost its primacy, though it remained responsible for recruitment and basic training. Women wore the WRAC cap badge, but many also sported insignia of their employing corps. Joint management was trialled for drivers in 1983 followed by: movement controllers, operation intelligence and security, analysts, linguists, accountants, supply specialists, supply controllers, cooks and postal and courier operators. By October 1985, about a quarter of women were in jointly managed trades.[6]

Some women remained in WRAC appointments, running the women's Corps and its companies that provided a workforce to large garrisons.

There was a third group, who moved between various employing corps and back to the WRAC. These women suffered from a lack of career progression, doing the same basic job in successive tours with different organisations. Employers had no incentive to develop their skills. Specialist training was seen as wasted on a woman who might be reassigned to a different corps at short notice. Whichever corps women worked for, their postings, and hence prospects, were constrained by regulations that prevented them working where it mattered – in 1 British Corps' forward areas in West Germany.

The WRAC could have a problem in meeting the expectations of some graduate entrants who had experienced more relaxed rules in University Officer Training Corps (UOTC). These young women trained alongside the men. They did the same activities, including live firing of weapons on the ranges, section attacks with dummy ammunition, assault courses, and fitness training. Having rejected University Air Squadron (UAS) membership because the RAF would not let women fly, Wendy Nichols (née Smith) joined St Andrews' UOTC and found that 'there didn't appear to be anything I couldn't do with them'. She decided to make the Army her career and joined an early intake of female cadets at Sandhurst.[7] Not understanding that there was a difference between UOTC practice and regular service policy, she recollected:

> I got right towards the end of my training. ... [I had] even done the practice graduation parade. ... Then there was the careers [interview] – what do [you] want to do? ... I still naively thought I could do what I want ... I wanted to go into intelligence. ... There was this snort of derision. 'You can't do that. You're a woman.' I thought I've heard all this before from the UAS ... I couldn't believe I was hearing it again. ... They said, 'You can join the WRAC.' So I said, 'Well, what do they do?' They said, 'They're kind of secretarial stuff.' I said, 'If I wanted to do that I could be a PA to an executive in a company and earn twice as much in civvy street. Why on earth would I want to do that in the military?' 'Well, you joined.' I thought, well OK – you've got me there by the short and curlies.[8]

She left. For her, regular service did not match up to what university experience appeared to promise. Still attracted to a career in the armed forces, she subsequently joined the RAF.

In the late 1980s, the Army needed 20,000 recruits a year. The critical age group was sixteen to nineteen-year olds, from which about 80 per cent

1. Members of the Auxiliary Territorial Service training on predictor equipment tracking enemy aircraft. Although members of anti-aircraft artillery batteries, these women were said to be non-combatants. © Crown Copyright Imperial War Museum. (IWM H14972).

2. *Above left*: Air Commandant Dame Felicity Hanbury, Director of the WAAF/WRAF (1946-50) during the transition from wartime auxiliary to peacetime regular service. By kind permission of Mr Andrew Peake.

3. *Above right*: Brigadier Mary Tyrwhitt, Director of the ATS/WRAC (1946-51) during the transition from wartime auxiliary to peacetime regular service. Courtesy of the Council of the National Army Museum, London. (NAM 9407-345-8).

1958

4. *Above left*: Air Quartermaster Celia Watkins, one of the first women to wear a flying badge in the regular RAF. By kind permission.

5. *Above right*: Air Commodore Joy Tamblin, Director of the WRAF (1976–80), who was influential in the policy on small arms training for servicewomen. By kind permission of the Battle of Britain Bunker Museum, Hillingdon. © MOD/Crown Copyright 1976.

6. Female members of the Territorial Army undertaking weapons training. Courtesy of the Council of the National Army Museum, London. (NAM 1994-07-335-55).

7. *Above left*: Commandant Anthea Larken who was the Director of the WRNS during policy discussions on women serving in warships. By kind permission. © MOD/Crown Copyright 1988.

8. *Above middle*: Captain Alan West, who led the study that opened the way for seagoing for women. By kind permission.

9. *Above right*: Admiral Sir Brian Brown was Second Sea Lord during policy discussions on women serving in warships. By kind permission. © MOD/Crown Copyright 1988.

10. *Above left*: Admiral Sir Julian Oswald was First Sea Lord during policy discussions on women serving in warships. By kind permission. © MOD/Crown Copyright 1989.

11. *Above right*: Archie Hamilton with Anthea Larken (left) and Rosie Wilson (right) celebrating the 100th anniversary of the Women's Royal Naval Service, Speaker's House, Palace of Westminster. © MOD/Crown Copyright 2017.

12. *Above*: Flight Lieutenant Wendy Nichols, navigator on 30 Squadron. Photographer Geoff Clark. By kind permission.

13. *Left*: Flight Lieutenant Julie Gibson, the first woman to complete all phases of RAF pilot training in regular service, shown with a Hercules transport aircraft of LXX Squadron. By kind permission. © MOD/Crown Copyright.

14. *Right*: Flight
Lieutenant Jo Salter, the
first woman to qualify
as a fast jet pilot,
shown here in front of
a Tornado aircraft of
617 Squadron. By kind
permission. © MOD/
Crown Copyright.

14a. *Below*: A Tornado
GR4 aircraft over
RAF Lossiemouth.
Photographer SAC
Kay-Marie Bingham.
© MOD/Crown
Copyright 2009.
Defence Images
reference 45150789.

15. *Left*: Disbandment Parade of the WRAC – Guildford, 1992. By kind permission of Major Dot Ryder and the WRAC Association.

16a. *Below left*: Reverse of the Operational Service Medal for Afghanistan (Operation HERRICK) awarded to service and civilian personnel who completed at least thirty days deployed to the country. Photographer Petty Officer Terry Seward © Crown Copyright 2012. Defence Images reference 45154416.

16b. *Below right*: Reverse of the Operation TELIC campaign medal for service in Iraq. The medal depicts an ancient Assyrian Lamassu sculpture. Photographer Steve Dock LBIPP. © Crown Copyright 2005. Defence Images reference 45150672.

16. Sergeant
Chantelle
Taylor (right),
combat medic in
Afghanistan (2008).

16c. *Above left*: The Military Cross awarded in recognition of exemplary gallantry during active operations against the enemy on land. © Crown Copyright 2007. Defence Images reference 45147519. The first woman to be awarded the MC was combat medic Lance Corporal Michelle Norris for action in Iraq.

16d. *Above right*: The Distinguished Flying Cross awarded in recognition of exemplary gallantry during active operations against the enemy in the air. © Crown Copyright 2007. Defence Images reference 45147523. The first woman to be awarded the DFC was helicopter pilot Flight Lieutenant Michelle Goodman for action in Iraq.

17. *Left*: Captain Catherine Jordan, commanding officer HMS Collingwood (2019). By kind permission. Photographer Keith Woodland. © MOD/ Crown Copyright 2019.

17a. *Below*: The frigate HMS *St Albans* commanded by Catherine Jordan (December 2013–April 2015). Photographer L(Phot) Dave Jenkins. © MOD/Crown Copyright. Defence Images reference 45161945 (2017).

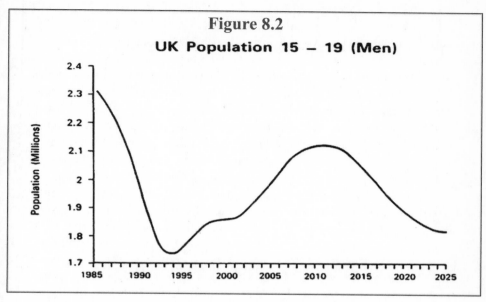

Figure 8.2

UK Population 15 – 19 (Men)

Actual and projected male population figures (millions). Source: FOI MOD: MARILYN Report, 1988.

of its recruits were drawn. Falling birth rates meant there was a 30 per cent decline in this cohort (Figure 8.2). This was known as the demographic trough. In addition, more young people were staying in education beyond the school leaving age of sixteen and so entered the work force later than earlier generations. A brighter economic outlook was making the job market more competitive. Youth unemployment was reducing, in part because school leavers were expected to join a government-sponsored programme called the Youth Training Scheme as a route into jobs. A 1989 report for the MOD noted that 75 per cent of school leavers took this route into work. While the armed forces participated, only the RAF's offer was working well. The Army's was the worst because infantry experience did not provide a path to qualifications or a civilian job.[9]

Concerns about the demographic trough masked more unwelcome truths about recruitment. As the authors of a 1988 report noted, recruitment was poor in the 1970s, when the pool of potential recruits was increasing as the young population grew towards a peak in 1982. However, the Army then could more readily accept ill-qualified young men. Equipment was less technically based and so training was not as demanding as it became by the late 1980s. Establishments were more generous, giving more leeway to make allowance for less effective soldiers.

The Army of the late 1980s had to be more selective. Only 25 per cent of applicants became trained soldiers. Of the rest, 27 per cent were rejected at the careers office, 40 per cent withdrew from the process and 8 per cent failed to complete training. The recruitment problem of the late 1970s had been solved by pay rises brought in by the Conservative government, which came into office in 1979. In the late 1980s, although pay had again fallen behind civilian norms, this was not seen as a likely solution. Perhaps most worryingly, 'the dilution of Service experience within society and greater expectations and aspirations among the young [had] led to a diminution in the attraction of Army careers.'[10]

Meanwhile, the MOD's control and use of manpower (meaning women as well as men) came under NAO scrutiny. It was not impressed by Army support functions. There were nineteen support corps, each with its own headquarters, administration and personnel organisation. Women's careers were badly managed. In the opinion of the NAO, these areas were ripe for savings.[11] The MOD put up a stout defence of its use of servicewomen arguing that 'factors such as mobility, geographical location, unsocial hours, discipline and flexibility or expertise mitigated against the employment of civilians.' It also claimed that in some locations civilian staff with the necessary skills were not available or that they 'commanded salary levels above the Service rates of pay' – not an argument that particularly convinced the NAO.[12]

Fearing that the NAO's work was leading towards cap-badging women into support corps and civilianisation of other jobs, Brigadier Shirley Nield proposed a study into the employment of the WRAC. She sought to protect her Corps by finding a role that mainstream WRAC could call their own. She achieved her objective of a study, but not in the terms that she wanted. Nield thought the terms of reference (TORs), prepared in the Director General Army Manning and Recruitment department, anticipated the outcome by stating that mainstream WRAC were unhappy with being employed as 'expediency manning'. In other words, women covered gaps when men could not be found and were dispensed with when no longer needed. The TORS suggested that there was scope for more corps to employ women permanently and that officers aspired to full integration, cutting ties with the WRAC and wearing a cap-badge that proclaimed their role not their gender. Above all, Shirley Nield complained that the study's title referred to the 'long term role and employment of women in the Army' rather than in the WRAC.[13] Her objections were overruled. A team under the leadership of Brigadier Tony Crawford (late of the

Intelligence Corps), with Colonel Gael Ramsey (née Hammond) as deputy, started work in August 1988.

Brigadier Nield set aside her reservations about how the study had been defined and wrote to Tony Crawford setting out her views on policy as it stood in 1988. She complained that rules concerning deployment of women and arming were too complex. As they left room for interpretation, so local commanders changed policies as they saw fit. She urged Crawford to introduce unequivocal rules. She agreed with his definition of direct combat as meaning a role with the primary purpose of engaging and destroying the enemy. But she had little time for 'extensive and heated discussion on speculative theories about the physical/emotional capacities of women, the chivalry/gallantry of men or the current state of public opinion'. She described these as 'at best marginal, certainly not proven and without doubt irrelevant'.[14] Although not calling for direct combat roles to be opened, she wanted an easing of geographic restrictions so that women could gain career-enhancing field force experience.

Crawford examined, but dismissed, the possibility of the WRAC taking over a role in its entirety as suggested by Shirley Nield. For functions such as postal services, welfare, movement control and command and control systems, the WRAC did not have sufficient expertise or skilled senior women to take over all the jobs and would be unlikely to develop the capacity in the near future. Taking over all clerical jobs would discriminate against men. Crawford favoured more permanent employment with other corps, including allowing women to join them directly rather than via the WRAC, to fully integrate and wear the appropriate cap badge. This was the view of men and women alike, including many 'mainstream' WRAC. Crawford wrote:

> Women wanted to be recognised for their talents and felt that by being denied integration within employing Corps, they were being discriminated against. Many felt that the WRAC had served its purpose as an all-female Corps. The WRAC structure and WRAC Chain of Command [had] gradually been eroded both in terms of quality and in the number of posts offering command [jobs].[15]

Crawford concluded that the USA and Canada had integrated women under pressure from equality legislation and had implemented changes too quickly. He preferred a slower process – evolution not revolution. First, permanently employed officers would re-badge to their corps in 1990, from which date new officers were to commission directly into those corps. Second, the proposed increase in women's jobs, estimated between 2,700 and 6,200, was to be worked out in detail. The third stage would involve non-commissioned ranks transferring to employing corps. The fourth phase would determine the number of women officers needed in the chain of command and in initial training schools. Once all this was achieved (in a 10–15-year time span), the future of mainstream WRAC as a corps would be re-examined. At some point the Director's title would become Director of Women (Army) as the role would be a focus for women across many corps.[16] Crawford signalled the demise of the WRAC, but it was to be a protracted affair. He stopped well short of suggesting that women be employed in combat roles.

Crawford made 105 recommendations from which three major policy issues needed Army Board approval. First, deployment rules needed to be eased. Corps would be directed to determine which jobs could be opened. The guiding principle was that women could not be in direct combat, defined as jobs with a 'primary role to engage and destroy the enemy'. Women should not be employed in brigade areas of 1 British Corps in West Germany or in jobs that would deploy there in the event of war. But Corps were encouraged to be 'as imaginative as possible' and 'not to restrict deployment unnecessarily'. Second, joint management of trades was deemed a success and was to be extended over a 10–15-year period. Reassurance was given that no currently serving woman would be obliged to change her cap badge. Third, the WRAC was to be retained for the foreseeable future, but it would be reviewed again.[17]

Approved in July 1989, public announcement was delayed until October due to the Parliamentary recess. The junior minister – Lord Arran – told Parliament that up to 6,000 more jobs could be opened to women, deployment rules would be relaxed, women would be more integrated but the WRAC would continue as a corps. Brigadier Nield wrote in re-assuring terms to her senior officers, emphasising that the Corps would continue but acknowledging that women might prefer to join other corps.[18]

The Army expanded women's opportunities without the need to consider direct combat roles. Able to recruit more women, men could be channelled into roles from which women remained excluded. General Sir Robert Pascoe (Adjutant General) warned his opposite number Admiral Sir Brian Brown (Second Sea Lord) that the Army was opening thousands of jobs, but not combat roles. Speaking in 2015, he said:

I can remember going down to see the Second Sea Lord to tip him off that we had made this decision and were going to go public with it. ... I said, 'The reason I have come down Brian is that the Army has decided to have women all over the Army except the infantry and the cavalry.' He said, 'Bob, thank you very much for telling me. But the Navy will not be going down the same route.' Six weeks later, Archie Hamilton sent for him and said, 'Why aren't the Navy doing this?'[19]

Navy Policy

The answer to Archie Hamilton's question was that the Navy Board could not make eye-catching changes to women's employment without abandoning the exclusion from combat roles – a step it tried to avoid by all possible means.

The Navy Board shared Army Board concerns about the personnel situation. Too many experienced men were leaving, increasing time at sea for the rest, which led to more men leaving. This put a strain on recruitment targets. The Navy would not have been short of male recruits if the usual assumption that high unemployment aided recruitment had held good. However, unemployment was most prevalent among school leavers with poor qualifications. In 1988, 40 per cent of the unemployed aged sixteen to twenty-four had no qualifications. A further 17 per cent had a top attainment at Certificate of Secondary Education level below grade 1.[20] Vice Admiral Sir Neville (Ned) Purvis (Director General Naval Manpower and Training) explained that in the 1950s he had 'people who could barely read and write' working for him, but in the 1980s the Navy was 'looking for people with technical qualifications, with good GCEs (O levels) and A levels because those were the things which we needed to be able to train them'.[21]

There was a fundamental dilemma in recruitment policy that the Navy could not resolve. It wanted sixteen to nineteen-year olds to accustom them to seafaring before they settled into a more sedentary lifestyle, but it needed them well-qualified in order to meet the demands of the work.[22] Those with necessary aptitudes delayed entry to the job market to gain qualifications. The Navy accepted youths of lower quality than it needed in order to meet targets.[23]

While the Board lacked a clear idea on how to make better use of Wrens, it agreed that treating them as a manpower make-weight would not suffice. It was aware that allied nations made greater use of women's talents. Limited seagoing was open to women in the USA, Australia and New Zealand. Canada was conducting a trial of women in warships. Denmark and the Netherlands had women serving in warships; Norway also allowed service in submarines.[24] The Board believed these policies had been imposed on their counterparts through pressure from equality legislation and political directives, a fate it wanted to avoid. It commissioned a study in order 'to pre-empt imposed tasks ... [or] a worse fate – a withering on the vine' for the WRNS.[25]

Captain Alan West, decorated in the Falklands War and earmarked for high rank, was appointed to lead the study. West had spent most of his career at sea and had little experience of working with Wrens. He recalled that his instinctive reaction would have been against women at sea, an opinion he thought was shared by 'most people in the Navy'. Looking back, he remarked 'some people who picked me thought "get West to do that because he will [say] it is totally impossible and we can forget it"... A lot of senior officers just thought it would be a complete disaster'.[26] Among these opponents was a Navy Board member whom he would not name.

Alan West characterised the traditional view of Wrens as a 'decorative uniformed corps of secretaries'. Many male officers were 'unconsciously patronising' in their support, senior ratings were 'least likely to be aware of the quality of professionalism' of Wrens, and junior ratings thought they blocked shore jobs. The feminine image used to encourage recruiting 'inhibit[ed] understanding of the fact that the WRNS [was] closely involved in highly technical and operational work'.[27] Seagoing was thought likely to attract a different sort of woman that would be detrimental to this customary view of a feminine Service. West took pains to say that women in other navies were no less feminine even though they served at sea.

Worries about femininity could be seen as code for sexuality. Alan West was briefed to consider the potential for sexual liaisons and also the assumed poor work performance of women during menstruation.[28] The latter he dismissed after consulting the Navy's medical authorities. Having examined experience in the US and Dutch navies, he acknowledged, but played down, problems arising from heterosexual relationships. Lesbianism was a more sensitive subject. Homosexual practices were banned under military law, a situation that continued until the year 2000. West sought to allay fears, noting 'evidence [did] not suggest that the incidence of lesbianism [rose] with the introduction of sea service.'[29] Nevertheless, there was recognition that seagoing would appeal to a cohort of women prepared for the rigours of life at sea and thus there would be a divergence from the former image of the WRNS.

Alan West recommended that women should go to sea from April 1990 and the WRNS should merge with the RN on 1 April 1991. This was intended to give women full career opportunities, solve both quality and quantity issues in the Royal Navy and, by reducing the strains caused by shortages of personnel, improve retention.

But what ships would be opened to women? Concentrating on minor vessels, Captain West proposed a limit of 10–15 per cent of posts in any one ship. This was to take account of suggestions that women were not strong enough to carry out communal duties such as loading ships' stores and damage control tasks. The potential female complement was also affected by accommodation. Junior ratings lived in communal mess decks. West recommended that these should be single sex, thus constraining the number of bunks for women according to the configuration of each ship. He identified five possible ships as a starting point: HMS *Hecla* and HMS *Roebuck* (survey ships); HMS *Shetland* (an offshore patrol vessel); HMS *Challenger* (the seabed operations vessel); and HMS *Juno* (a former frigate then used as a navigation training ship).[30] Applying his upper limit of 15 per cent to these ships' complements, about 80 billets would be open to women. This figure could increase to about 250 if all ships in these classes were subsequently opened.

Alan West saw this as a critical moment as many Wrens felt they were 'poised for a big breakthrough ... Failure to grasp the opportunity would be a major disappointment, leading to frustration and demotivation.'[31] He believed he was safeguarding women's roles from the 'predatory gaze of the NAO'. Speaking in 2007, he described his report as pusillanimous.[32] He knew the issue was deeply unpopular in many quarters of both the RN and the WRNS. Although he had supporters, he received abusive telephone calls from contemporaries who were not convinced of the need for women to serve in ships. However, detractors had no viable alternative to offer to personnel shortages. Alan West thought he had 'kick[ed] open the door' with a seagoing recommendation which he described as 'what the market would bear'.[33]

The key men determining the future of the WRNS were Admiral Sir Brian Brown (Second Sea Lord), Admiral Sir Julian Oswald (First Sea Lord) and Archie Hamilton. Brian Brown, a supply and secretariat specialist who had also served as a pilot in the Fleet Air Arm, described himself as the Navy Board member with most reservations about seagoing as it would be his responsibility to make the policy work. He also appears to have doubted the morality of employing women in combat roles while men might be in safe jobs ashore. Remembering media coverage of the

Falklands War, he recoiled from the thought of female burns victims appearing on television.[34] Admiral Oswald, who took over as First Sea Lord in May 1989, was also reluctant to have Wrens at sea.[35]

In contrast to the Adjutant General's handling of the Crawford study (from receipt in March 1989 to Army Board approval in July), the unwelcome West report languished with the Second Sea Lord. Brian Brown was not persuaded that women's career prospects were inadequate. Rather, he thought there was no evidence that women were leaving, there was a plentiful supply of replacements, and it would not necessarily be a disadvantage if new recruits were of lesser quality than hitherto. He dismissed NAO criticism. He was 'not firmly [author's emphasis] opposed to women at sea' but he thought Wrens did not want seagoing.[36]

Brian Brown sought comments on the report. Naval Home Command argued that women at sea could worsen the situation if unhappy wives persuaded their husbands to leave. A staff officer working in naval discipline wanted clarity on fraternisation rules in ships and feared that changes could 'endanger our line on homosexuality'. Fleet Headquarters suggested that, if a reduction in men's early leaving from the prevailing 8 per cent down to 7.4 per cent could be achieved, it would cover the shortfall. Rear Admiral White (Assistant Chief of the Naval Staff) thought better pay for men to improve retention would be better than women's limited seagoing.[37] However, aspirations to improve retention had been unfulfilled for decades. Better pay, even if it could be negotiated, was only likely to be a short-term palliative before patterns of behaviour based on family and career factors were reasserted.

Ideas for extending women's seagoing included Royal Fleet Auxiliary ships, warships during periods when they were only doing sea trials, providing skeleton crews needed when ships were undergoing refit, warships until war was in the offing then replacing women with men.[38] The latter was a persistent idea which Brown saw as the worst possible solution, undermining the credibility of women who would be seen as 'fair weather sailors'.[39] It would undermine the work-up concept, during which ships' complements trained together in a variety of scenarios and simulated emergencies. Further, if an operation was mounted in haste, there could be insufficient time to replace women. Indeed, there might not be men available. Fundamentally, it would weaken operational effectiveness, a key fear of policy-makers. In these efforts to increase billets, nobody recommended full service in warships.

Alan West's other key recommendation, that women should be integrated into the Royal Navy by April 1991, attracted little support.

There would be too few women gaining experience at sea to make integration meaningful. However, there was willingness to offer outward signs of convergence by adopting RN rank titles, and gold lace to replace the blue lace of the WRNS for rank and badges on uniforms.[40] Mr Brack (Assistant under Secretary for Naval Personnel), observing that the other Services were making changes in women's employment, agreed. As these measures were completed in the Army in 1950 and the RAF in 1968, this hardly seemed to meet his own test of making 'one or a few distinct and high-profile changes' to keep pace with the other Services.[41]

Meanwhile, opinion in the WRNS hierarchy was hardening against the limited nature of changes being suggested. Anthea Larken, the Director of the WRNS, knew that women could not compete equally with men of the Royal Navy for jobs ashore without seagoing experience. She characterised lack of sea experience, not as a glass ceiling, but as a brick wall that blocked women's potential.[42] Encouraged by her new deputy Chief Officer Rosie Wilson, she argued that the WRNS could not survive as a shore-based service.[43] Opening only five support ships would mean 'too few opportunities to permit a balanced development of female seagoing expertise and experience', undermining the idea of integrating women into the RN.[44] She described a draft Navy Board paper based on West's recommendations as 'timorous and negative'.[45]

However, Larken also knew that Wrens were divided on seagoing, a view confirmed in a survey conducted for West's study. Of 298 ratings who responded, 147 replied that they would go to sea, 113 would not and 38 were undecided. Officers were similarly split: 26 replied 'yes', 24 opted for 'no' and 5 were 'undecided'. As Wrens were women who had joined a shore-based organisation, it was not surprising that many would not volunteer for seagoing. Some would already be too senior in rank to make a successful transition. More important was the attitude of potential recruits. Evidence presented to Alan West suggested interest.[46]

Anthea Larken asked to see Archie Hamilton and told him that more extensive seagoing was needed.[47] She was not in a position to overturn opposition on the Navy Board, but Archie Hamilton was. Having read West's report, he was unimpressed by the 'toe in the water' approach compared with bolder moves by the RAF and Army. At the suggestion of Commander Roy Clare, his military assistant, he visited the Netherlands Navy whose Fleet Commander arranged for him to go to see a frigate. This experience was a turning point for Hamilton and his ability to argue the case for wider opportunities for women.[48] The Dutch Navy had had women at sea in warships for about ten years. It had ocean-going capability and its mixed-crew ships performed well in operational training, which was run by the Royal Navy from Portland. The gap between Dutch experience and West's recommendations was apparent to Hamilton.[49] He could not understand why the Royal Navy accepted 'substandard men' while turning away 'good women'.[50]

With Brian Brown resistant to wider seagoing, Admiral Oswald was in a difficult position. Maintenance of good relations with Ministers was important to Service chiefs. Rightly or wrongly, it was perceived as influential in the share of resources allocated to the Services in annual budget negotiations.[51] He was unlikely to also want to lose ground with Archie Hamilton, compared with RAF and Army counterparts. Meanwhile, he was encouraged to open warships to women by the two captains who worked on his personal staff. Captain Lippiett, who accompanied him on visits to naval establishments, took him to visit female reservists who already went to sea for training weekends.[52] Having sounded out officers in the Naval staff, Captain Wilkinson told Admiral Oswald that:

> There were very severe shortages in certain branches – radio operators in particular – also stewards – where the women were very strong ... and radar operators, too – we all knew that women were very good at sitting in front of a radar screen or listening for long periods – much better than young men. ... Basically, people thought that if we were going to do it, do it properly and get on with it.[53]

The radio operator category was a key example, having about 70 vacancies in ships for able seaman. Overall, by January 1990, the Navy was short of 300 men at sea and a further 600 men were filling posts in ships for which they had insufficient experience.[54]

Government policy which prevented women from serving in combat roles was cited as the obstacle. Some respondents to the West report thought the time had come to seek political guidance on what <u>was</u> acceptable. Was the defining characteristic the use of weapons, the risk of becoming a casualty or some geographic reference to a 'combat zone'?[55] In November 1989, Archie Hamilton challenged the existence of a formal policy that excluded women from combat roles.[56] The reply on 1st December said that no such policy paper, endorsed by government, could be found in the Services' historical records. The oft quoted position was now described as a precept, not a policy.[57]

Roy Clare suggested that Admiral Oswald could 'see which way the political wind was blowing', but he had to manage the Navy Board to bring about agreement.[58] But first, he had to clear his own mind. Nick Wilkinson suggested that the absence of a political policy objection was important to Oswald's own sense of the moral and legal position. Oswald held a number of meetings with individual officers in December 1989, including a discussion with Alan West who re-assured him that seagoing would work despite areas of entrenched opposition such as senior ratings.[59] Visits, during which he discussed the proposals with young male and female officers, also helped him to reach a judgement. By the time he returned from leave at the beginning of January 1990, he was ready to support the bolder policy of women serving in warships. This was despite opposition from his head of personnel, Brian Brown, and the nervousness of the Chief of the General Staff and Chief of the Air Staff who had introduced wider employment for women while maintaining elite combat roles for men.[60]

However, Brian Brown's views were not keeping pace; he and Admiral Oswald argued over the extent of seagoing to be introduced.[61] In mid-December, Brown had added warships while undertaking sea trials and Royal Fleet Auxiliary ships with naval detachments.[62] On 8 January, he briefed Archie Hamilton that he was now including aircraft carriers and Landing Platform Dock ships to the list.[63] The latter ships were used to carry Royal Marine forces into combat areas. At the meeting, Hamilton re-affirmed 'his strong personal support for a more relaxed policy towards women in combat' and that 'definitions of combat and non-combat ships [were] not relevant to the work in hand.'[64]

Meeting General Robert Pascoe and Air Marshal David Parry-Evans at the Principal Personnel Officers' Committee on 10 January 1990, Brian Brown told them that the Navy Board had recommended non-combat ships, but that Archie Hamilton and Tom King (Secretary of State) wanted to go further. He emphasised that while Wrens might serve in aircraft carriers, the Navy had no intention of putting women in ships that would seek out danger.[65] Just a day after re-assuring his army and RAF counterparts on the limited nature of seagoing being proposed, Brian Brown found himself in a minority of one at a meeting of the Navy Board.[66] The concept of any distinction as to degrees of combat was abandoned, deployment in destroyers and frigates was contemplated. Moreover, women were to be at sea during the course of 1990.[67]

Bowing to the majority against him, Brian Brown produced a Navy Board paper which presented a cogent case for seagoing, with integration of women into the Royal Navy to follow in the medium term. He based sea service predominantly on the Navy's needs, with brief reference to equality of opportunity for women. He described demographic trends as 'adverse' but 'not of themselves disabling'. He referred to 'economic and social conditions inhibit[ing] recruiting and encouraging restiveness among serving personnel.' He observed that 'Greater risks in male recruiting quality [were] being contemplated at a time when there [was] no shortage of women of high quality who wish[ed] to join.' Thus, he argued, women would improve both quantity and quality, representing 'a real improvement for manning'.[68] In approving the paper, the Navy Board decided on two co-equal aims: 'to meet manning needs, and to improve the prospects for equal opportunities for the WRNS'.[69] The Navy Board was persuaded to support the policy unanimously.

The precept that women should not serve in combat was set aside in a letter from Archie Hamilton to Margaret Thatcher and a short reply from her secretary saying that she was content.[70] The Queen's approval for use of naval rank titles for women was also sought.[71] Hamilton regarded his approach as pragmatic. He did not claim to advocate equality of opportunity. Indeed, he thought he was perfectly capable of resisting any such pressure. He feared reactionary Conservative MPs would cause trouble, but anticipated less difficulty with the Labour opposition who would be obliged to accept the equal opportunities case.[72] He announced the decision in the House of Commons on 5 February 1990, saying that he was 'sure that the service [would] rise to meet the challenge' – a phrase he regretted, as it prompted ribald remarks.[73] It was hardly surprising that a largely male House of Commons perceived a sexual connotation to Hamilton's words.

Flying

Developments in the Army and the RAF contributed to pressure on the Navy Board. The Air Force Board of the mid-1980s overturned decisions on flying roles taken a few years earlier. One such was the issue of mission crew for airborne early warning (AEW) aircraft. The fighter control specialisation had a high failure rate in training so an ability to master the skills was more important than limiting the number of women. In 1983, women filled more than 20 per cent of fighter control officer posts.[74] In the related non-commissioned trade of aerospace operator, of 378 recruits accepted between April 1976 and March 1978, 128 were female.[75] Air Marshal Sir Peter Harding (Vice Chief of the Air Staff) revived the proposal to employ these women in the Nimrod AEW. Repeating the 1981 case, Harding added that exclusion would be bad for women's morale and could have an adverse impact on fighter control recruitment. Air Force Board members endorsed his proposal unanimously, expressing surprise that their predecessors had been opposed.[76]

To present the decision as compliant with women's exclusion from combat, Nimrod AEW was described as 'an airborne radar unit directly comparable to a ground radar unit', with women 'placed at very little more risk through being airborne' than in ground-based facilities where they already worked.[77] Delay ensued because conversion of Nimrod to the AEW role was a procurement fiasco. The programme was cancelled in 1986 and the MOD bought the USA's aircraft, the Sentry. The first woman entered training for the role in 1989.[78]

Overturning exclusion from UASs had more immediate impact. University authorities and student bodies kept up their complaints about membership rules. Some female undergraduates who wanted to fly wrote to their Members of Parliament, the Secretary of State or the Prime Minister. While Chief of the Air Staff Sir Keith Williamson's staff briefed him on the perceived detrimental impact of admitting women, Under Secretary for the Armed Forces Lord Trefgarne was more enthusiastic. This seems to have been a battle that the Chief decided not to fight. Following a meeting with the Minister, Williamson directed his staff to write a paper in favour of offering UAS flying training to women. As they could not join the RAF as aircrew, they would have to be offered ground branch (rather than flying branch) membership.[79] Approved in 1985, the policy gave male and female ground branch members a new entitlement to some flying training, with a quota for women of up to 10 per cent of the membership.[80]

Meanwhile, in common with NATO allies, the RAF faced a shortage of aircrew. Although targets for pilots were met, quality was declining and failure rates increasing. One in three men failed training at this time. Retention of experienced men was problematic. The percentage opting to leave at break points in their terms of service rose from 28 per cent to 38 per cent between 1987 and 1989. In addition, applications to leave the RAF early (premature voluntary release) reached a five-year high in 1989. The situation with navigators was worse. This specialisation was mainly populated by men who failed selection for pilot or did not make the grade in pilot training. Only 10 per cent of navigators made the role their first choice. The RAF missed its target for newly qualified navigators in all but one year in the 1980s.[81]

Worsening the shortfalls, squadron establishments were due to rise from 1991 to meet new NATO requirements. Means of increasing aircrew numbers were discussed at a NATO conference in 1988. Ideas included improving terms and conditions of service to aid retention, bonuses for longer service, reducing overall requirement by cutting office jobs, and increasing recruiting targets.[82] Female pilots were not discussed. However, the RAF could not compete on pay and conditions with civilian airlines and North Sea oil operators. Increasing recruiting targets would exacerbate the already evident problem of the quality of entrants.

Lacking sufficient men of the necessary standard, the Air Secretary's department considered opening cockpit roles to women to increase the recruiting base. However, the 'no combat roles' policy was assumed to prevent any such initiative because all potential pilots were selected on their aptitude to fly combat jets. Those not making the grade were then offered multi-engine or rotary wing aircraft roles. If women were to be employed, either the restriction on women's employment or the RAF's approach to recruitment of pilots would have to be abandoned. It was the assumption that all pilots should demonstrate aptitude for combat jet flying that was set aside.

The new Chief of the Air Staff gave staff a strong public hint. In an interview for the *RAF News* in January 1989, Air Chief Marshal Sir Peter Harding praised women flying with UASs, lamented that they could not join as pilots, and promised it would be considered.[83] A few weeks later, a draft paper was produced. It noted that the USA, Canada, Australia, New Zealand and the Netherlands all had female pilots. Female undergraduates were proving their aptitude at universities and the RAF already employed women in some rear crew roles. There was growing pressure for change from external bodies such as the National Audit Office and the Equal Opportunities Commission. Air Vice-Marshal Bob Honey (Air Secretary, responsible for career management) suggested that aircrew roles for women would enhance 'the Service's reputation as an equal-opportunities employer'. He recommended women be employed as pilots and navigators in unarmed aircraft and as flying instructors.[84]

Not alone in objecting, Air Vice-Marshal Roger Austin (Director General Aircraft) expressed his opposition in emotive terms, saying that he had tried but probably failed to set aside male chauvinism. He rejected claims which might be made for equal opportunities, arguing that '[our] requirements are special (hence ... we are still allowed to reject homosexuals even though most other occupations cannot).'[85] He advocated improving men's terms of service. He thought that women aircrew would be a reality sooner or later, but he would be retired by then and could rest content that 'my air force [was] awake and alert – and powdering its nose as it admire[d] Robert Redford and Tom Jones on the Flight Safety calendar'.[86]

Some of those in favour thought the recommendation did not go far enough. Having presented the top prize for flying to a female member of Cambridge's University Air Squadron, Air Commodore Tim Garden foresaw problems if a woman came top in Basic Flying Training but was assigned a lesser role than men. He wanted women to fly fast jets. Air Vice-Marshal Eric Macey (Director General Training) suggested women could fly air defence combat jets and reconnaissance aircraft, drawing his line short of offensive action. Air Commodore Farrer, Director of Air Defence, could not understand why women should be '[confined] to roles in which they [could] be shot at but [could] not themselves shoot back.' Air Vice-Marshal Mills, Director General Medical Services, argued to exchange 'excluded' and 'included' aircraft types. He thought that as 'size for size and weight for weight women have less strength than men', they might be more suited to fast jets than to 'larger and heavier aircraft with a potential for asymmetric and other problems of control'.[87]

Bob Honey's paper glossed over women's potential short period of service compared with men, which even those in favour of its recommendation observed. The key concern was that women would leave early as the policy of compulsory discharge on pregnancy was to be retained. He proposed that female aircrew could be 'allowed to complete at least their obligatory service sometime after childbirth'.[88] This was not a maternity leave proposal, only a restatement of the little-invoked policy that allowed mothers to apply to rejoin. Mills thought pregnancy was 'unlikely to be a notable factor with the highly motivated young women' who would initially volunteer to train as aircrew.[89] Rather than pressing a perspective as the adviser on women's terms of service, Air Commodore Shirley Jones (Director WRAF) was a passive observer, remarking only that she would be 'interested to know how best these [matters could] be resolved'.[90]

Air Vice-Marshal John Thomson (Assistant Chief of the Air Staff) was an important critic. A highly regarded officer, tipped to be a future Chief of the Air Staff, his particular concern was the fast jet squadrons. Men who performed best in training were selected for fast jet roles or 'creamed off' to become instructors for a tour of duty, later transferring to an operational squadron. High-quality female candidates would not be eligible for fast jet squadrons, though the intention was that the best could be instructors. Thomson observed that these rules implied that the quality of pilots for the fast jet force would not be improved, as only the occasional selection of a woman for flying instructor duties would replace a man of fast jet standard. However, he was not in favour of a bolder policy. He felt 'an underlying unease at the anthropological and psychological factors concerning women and combat and the further effects on male colleagues and the civilian population of placing them at risk.' He urged the need to 'differentiate between women's ability to fly high performance aircraft in peace ... and the appropriateness of commanding them to kill and be killed in action.'[91]

Despite John Thomson's complaints about inconsistencies, the paper that went to the Air Force Board Standing Committee in June 1989 was substantially unchanged.[92] The minutes of the meeting focussed on the acceptable list of aircraft, the status of support helicopters being contentious. As Chinook and Puma helicopters were used in support of land forces, they were deemed to operate too close to potential action for women to be involved. They were deleted from the list. The meeting approved women to serve in non-weapon carrying aircraft. A quota was set of up to 10 per cent of annual intakes for pilots and navigators, starting from 1 April 1990. New terms of service were to be agreed with the Treasury.[93] As one of his last actions before handing over to Tom King, George Younger gave approval on 19 July. From circulation of the draft paper to approval by Ministers took under five months.

The Air Force Board had found a way of opening more roles to women but stopping short of the elite roles of fast-jet flying. It successfully designated some aircraft as 'non-combat' and hence suitable for women. The position was untenable once the Navy Board overturned exclusion from combat roles and turned its attention to its own policy on flying. Like the RAF, the Fleet Air Arm was short of pilots, being 16 per cent below its complement. Admiral Brian Brown was keen to have 'consistent criteria throughout the Naval Service on the extent to which women should be involved in combat', but he did not want to 'prejudice the achievement of tri-Service agreement on combat in non-seagoing contexts.'[94] Conforming to the RAF's policy of exclusion from fast-jets, he suggested that Sea Harrier squadrons remain for men only. These were the Navy's fighter aircraft which operated from carriers. In December 1990, the Navy Board approved plans for female naval aviators to be employed in anti-submarine warfare.[95]

Women were to join the Army Air Corps as ground crew from 1991.[96] As the army selected its non-commissioned pilots from ground crew, this opened the way for women. It was also agreed in principle that women were to be eligible to join directly as officer aircrew. However, this was deferred because such entrants were obliged to undertake a six-month attachment with an infantry regiment or the armoured corps in order to gain experience of the environment which they would support as pilots.[97] However, infantry and armoured operational roles were still closed to women. Nevertheless, due to a shortage of male aircrew, the army was expected to have women flying Gazelle and subsequently Lynx support helicopters. The plan was endorsed by Ministers.

Under pressure from Navy and Army developments, the RAF had to review its stance on female aircrew before a non-combat flying policy had time to take full effect.[98] Air Marshal Sir Roger Palin (Air Member for Personnel) put a further paper on women aircrew to Air Force Board Standing Committee colleagues in July 1991. He recorded two legal grounds for continuing to exclude women from a role. The first was that they would have an adverse impact on military operations. The second was statutory health and safety reasons. However, the Navy now had Ministerial approval to employ women in all its aircraft, including Sea Harrier combat jets. Consequently, he recommended immediate opening of support helicopter roles and maritime patrol aircraft. He stopped short of combat jets, suggesting instead that the experience of other countries should be investigated. He described this move as 'put[ting] our own house in order before find[ing] ourselves forced down possibly less welcome routes'.[99] This latter remark seemed to imply a desire to maintain exclusion from combat jets. It was the only additional route not yet proposed.

Roger Palin's line was recognised as indefensible in all but one reply to his paper. Remarking that it would be seen as 'too little, too late', Air Marshal Sir Michael Simmons (Deputy Controller Aircraft) speculated that the policy would fall to the first Parliamentary Question on the subject. Tim Garden, now Assistant Chief of the Air Staff, opposed the step-by-step approach, claiming that it 'promote[d] the idea that we are entrenched male chauvinists – hardly ideal for the Service that should be most forward thinking.' He thought that 'Ministers have moved rather more quickly than the military in their acceptance of women on combat duties'. Moray Stewart (Second Parliamentary Under-Secretary) urged the opening of all roles to 'widen the recruiting base' and to remove 'this contentious subject from the sex discrimination arena'.[100]

The decision to open all flying roles to women was taken in principle by the Board in September 1991. As an immediate step, support helicopter roles and maritime patrol aircraft were approved and Air Marshal Palin was asked to produce a paper on fast jet roles, 'taking into account the legal position'.[101]

Palin circulated his final paper in November 1991. He included an annex assessing women's effectiveness as combatants, starting from the historical figure of Boadicea. He mentioned female Soviet fighter pilots in the Second World War but dismissed them as 'few and far between'. He went on to say that Israel excluded women from combat because previously their presence had prevented men from 'operat[ing] with the necessary ruthlessness'. He observed that Britain now had armed policewomen but thought there was a difference between 'confronting a criminal and an enemy'. He tried to draw a distinction between the types of combat, claiming that fast jet action 'involv[ed] a more intimate contact with the enemy than is the case ... [in] dropping torpedoes or depth bombs against an unseen submarine'. He concluded with two risks. The first was uncertainty over how women would react in combat. The second was whether women would have a 'deleterious effect on their male counterparts'.[102]

Having presented arguments against women flying fast jets in his Annex, Palin argued in the main text that it would be difficult to make a legal case for excluding women from combat jets in the absence of firm evidence that they could not do the job. Also, such a stance had been undermined by 'our own and our sister Services' decisions to open other combat roles to women.'[103] He concluded that fast jet roles should be opened.

Roger Palin's paper attracted criticism for its ambivalence. Air Commodore Barnes, Director of Public Relations, would have 'preferred a more positive approach, "why we should do it" rather than "are there sufficient reasons not to?"'[104] Palin defended his paper, remarking that he had to 'cover the concerns that we know some senior officers feel and indeed, have voiced.'[105] He appears to have been attempting to accommodate the views of Air Marshal Sir John Thomson (now Commander-in-Chief of Support Command) who saw the annex as a 'relevant starting point'.[106] Thomson wanted time for the first female aircrew to reach operational service before extending their employment to fast jet aircraft.

Far from seeing the annex as a starting point, Air Chief Marshal Sir Peter Harding asked for it to be withdrawn.[107] Palin agreed, saying he was now 'persuaded that some of the more negative views expressed have their foundation in myth rather than in reality.'[108]

Conclusion

In the forty years since start of regular service, the armed forces conducted frequent investigations into the employment of women but Navy and Army studies of the late 1980s were different in scale from those previously undertaken. Their scope included wide-ranging assessments of social issues, pressures on male recruitment and retention, and employment policies in the armed forces of other countries. Factors such as demography, home ownership, children's education, and employment opportunities for spouses created conditions in which servicemen demanded more stability and were less likely to pursue long-term careers than previous generations. Servicewomen, well-qualified, ambitious, willing and able to defer family responsibilities, expected fulfilling careers.

Combat exclusion was critical to perceptions of servicewomen but there were important differences in how the armed forces understood participation in combat. In the RAF, the key question was whether women would press home an attack and kill enemies. This emphasis on belligerent action allowed a simple classification of aircraft. Combat aircraft carried weapons, those which did not could be described as non-combat. The existing hierarchy of male aircrew's status, implied by selection of the best in training for fast jets and the remainder for multi-engine or helicopter roles, made it simple to extend women's employment to pilot and navigator duties in a limited list of aircraft. RAF policymakers took a step-by-step approach, without adequately addressing the pressing problem of the quality of crews for fast jet squadrons. Until the decision to send women to sea, the RAF was able to stay ahead of the Navy and Army without ending exclusion from its elite combat roles.

The Army had considerable opportunity for widening women's employment, offering an eye-catching number of new jobs, without needing to consider infantry or armoured corps roles. Integration was already underway as officers opted for permanent employment outside of the WRAC and non-commissioned ranks served under joint management with a variety of support Corps. However, career progression was hampered by restrictions on postings. Geography and risk were at the heart of the issue. Following the Crawford report, the Army Board permitted Corps to make their own judgements about where women could serve, as long as they were not in jobs with the primary purpose of killing the enemy. The Board was not under pressure to go beyond recommendations made by Brigadier Crawford. It seemed self-evident that women lacked the physical strength and stamina to undertake direct combat roles.

The RAF defined some aircraft types as non-combat and the Army could offer thousands more jobs to women without raising the prospect of land warfare jobs. However, with all ships equipped with some weapons and difficulty in delineating risk on a geographic basis, it proved impossible for the Navy to follow suit. Nor did its structure allow it to open thousands more jobs to women to counter its shortfall of men unless meaningful numbers could go to sea. Rational analysis of the demands of jobs at sea, skills of women, quality of male recruits, poor retention of experienced men, examples from allied navies, and fears for the future of a shore-based WRNS, all pointed to widening women's employment.

Even had there been a convincing definition of non-combat ships, sending women to sea in a few ships was not a solution to the scale of naval personnel problems. Nevertheless, this was the proposal pushed by Admirals Brown and Oswald, reluctant as they were to have women serve in warships. In different political times, their suggested policy may well have been accepted. However, unlike his Labour government predecessor of the late 1970s, Archie Hamilton had the luxury of serving in a long-term government with a comfortable majority in Parliament. In wanting evidence that government had ever explicitly approved a policy paper that barred women from combat roles, he asked the question that eluded his predecessors. The Royal Navy found itself at the forefront of policy on women in combat roles because it could not match the steps taken by the other Services in extending women's employment piecemeal. But in Admiral Oswald, it also had a leader who was prepared to listen to those around him who urged the bolder policy – to younger officers who were more open to change.

The RAF's evolutionary approach fell victim to the Navy's revolution as naval aviation opened to women. Taking a critical view of the development of RAF policy, successive incumbents as Air Member for Personnel were reluctant to show leadership to remove barriers to female aircrew. Attempting to placate those who objected, Air Marshal Palin was isolated much as Brian Brown was on the Navy Board. Air Force Board colleagues and the rising generation of air commodores and air vice-marshals were ready to make the change. With proof emerging from University Air Squadrons and early female aircrew candidates that some women met the criteria for fast jet flying, the Board conceded the need to match the Navy's policy.

Women's influence on these policy developments varied between the Services. The WRAF Directorate was peripheral to the work. It was periodically informed, but it was not important in deciding the outcome. In contrast, Commandant Anthea Larken took an active part in pressing for seagoing. While she knew Wrens were divided, she voiced the need for change. She could act because she still had standing as the Head of Service in a way that the Director WRAF did not. Meanwhile, like any senior army officer whose organisation was under threat, Brigadier Shirley Nield fought for the future of the WRAC. However, she was also an advocate of easing of geographic restrictions on women's employment.

It would be a mistake to suppose that the armed forces had now embraced equality as a principle to replace the 'no combat roles' one that had hitherto governed women's careers. The RAF had arrived at this point through issues of quality – declining ability to recruit men of the necessary aptitude for critical roles and the skills of women seeking RAF careers. Army policy was still hedged with uncertainty. New jobs for women were permitted, but Corps were left with the freedom to implement policy as they interpreted it. The Navy Board claimed equality of opportunity for women as a co-equal aim of its policy of seagoing in warships as a means of rationalising and explaining the decision to the naval community. But this had not driven the deliberations. Without the persistence of Archie Hamilton, the Navy Board could have adopted a more cautious approach – one that would have satisfied neither the RN's manpower crisis or provided a future for women in naval service.

Hamilton claimed quality of recruits as his imperative rather than equality.[109] But the importance of proclaiming equality as a justification was to emerge quickly as integration of women proceeded in parallel with significant defence cuts associated with the post-Cold War climate.

9

INTEGRATION

Watching television one evening in July 1989, Flight Lieutenant Julie Gibson heard a news item that transformed her career. The MOD announced that women could become pilots and navigators in the RAF. Gibson was one of the few female aircraft engineering officers but her ambition was to be a pilot. In the early 1980s as an engineering student at City University, London, she lobbied London University Air Squadron (UAS) for flying membership rather than the social membership offered to women at the time. She was rebuffed on the MOD's usual grounds of women's 'exclusion from combat roles and because of the improbability of amortizing [flying] training costs before marriage or motherhood'. An appeal through her MP was rejected in the same terms.[1] She recollected that 'Although [in 1989] I knew that female aircrew might be coming in, no one said exactly when. It was on the news one evening ... I put my application in the next morning.'[2] She fulfilled her ambition, becoming the first woman to complete all phases of pilot training and join a squadron in the regular RAF.

The following year, with the Navy Board agreeing seagoing throughout the surface fleet, it became compulsory for Wrens joining from 1 September to accept a liability to serve in ships. 'Why would I want to join the Navy if I didn't want to go to sea?'[3] Such was the response of a female applicant when a naval recruiter explained the commitment. For this young woman the decades of women's shore-based support to the male RN was history. She expected to go to sea – it was why she had gone to the careers' office.

RAF flying policy was for the few women who had the necessary aptitude and motivation to become aircrew. For future Wrens, seagoing was for all recruits. Changes for Army women sat between these two extremes – they could now choose between an employing Corps or the WRAC. As Fiona Walthall recollected:

> I approached the Intelligence Corps ... and said that I would like to join them. Even though they had agreed to take just nine officers, one captain and the rest subalterns, they agreed to take me as a major... This was a remarkable act of faith by the Corps.[4]

She was far from alone in opting out of the WRAC, the future of which was to be shaken by the haemorrhage of women from its ranks.

Servicewomen's careers were transformed in the 1990s. However, implementation of new policies took place in a different defence climate from that of the late 1980s. Concerns about recruitment and retention of experienced personnel were overtaken by the ramifications of the collapse of the Warsaw Pact, symbolised by the breach of the Berlin Wall in November 1989. The government immediately sought substantial cuts to the defence budget – the so-called peace dividend associated with what was heralded as the end of the Cold War. In 1991, the MOD was planning to cut the armed forces' strength by 18 per cent by 1996.[5] Recruiting targets were reduced and thousands of service personnel were made redundant. Implementation of plans to increase women's roles took place in a period of retrenchment – not an ideal circumstance.

Seagoing

In January 1990, the Navy Board agreed two aims for its policy on the future employment of women. The first was to cut the manpower deficit (meant literally) which then stood at 2,000 posts ashore and 300 at sea.[6] The second was to 'improve the prospects for equal opportunities for the WRNS'.[7] Captain Tim England, and subsequently Captain John Marshall, led an implementation team to introduce seagoing for women and to revise career paths for existing Wrens. He had a long list of tasks: terms and conditions of service; calling for and training volunteers; planning career patterns; merger of men and women's branches; promotion regulations; uniforms, protective clothing and equipment; selection of ships for modification of accommodation and ablutions;

revision of ships' complements; and rules of behaviour for ships' companies.[8] Internal communications and public relations campaigns were to complement his efforts.

Initial publicity misfired, with Commandant Larken describing the Navy as being 'hoist in [sic] our own petard'. Playing to the stereotypical glamourous image of the WRNS, photogenic young Wrens were chosen for a media day aboard HMS *Gloucester* in the Pool of London. To Larken's regret the newspapers printed 'a lot of sexy images' rather than concentrating on the Navy's preferred line of the new career opportunities.[9] Some sailors' wives reacted angrily. Demonstrations were staged in Portsmouth and Plymouth amid protests that marriages would be put at risk.[10] One woman wrote to Archie Hamilton saying that it would be 'like dangling carrots before donkeys'.[11] The national press soon lost interest, but local papers in areas with major naval bases persisted with articles about wives' objections.

The *Navy News* gave the issues extensive coverage. In the following months, the paper published pages of letters for and against women at sea from serving men and women, retired personnel and wives of sailors. Its postbag was dominated by the subject with letters described variously as 'critical, welcoming, acidic, witty – and unprintable.'[12] A majority of printed letters emphasised problems concerning men and women living together in ships rather than whether women should take on combat roles.

Early feedback to Tim England showed that more credence was given to solving manpower deficits than to equal career opportunities for women. In a letter to commanding officers for use in briefing their subordinates, England reinforced the belief that the decision had been political. Citing well-established experience in other navies, he explained that there was no need for a trial period although many sailors thought there should be. He countered the rumour that women would be withdrawn from ships in the event of hostilities.[13] One idea mooted as a means of avoiding mixed-crew ships was to give women their own ships. Alan West and Brian Brown had both dismissed this concept. A ship's complement needed experienced personnel and where were such women to be found unless they had been to sea already in mixed-crew ships?[14] Nevertheless, women-only ships retained some currency in the early 1990s among those who thought men and women serving together at sea would be a disaster.[15]

Admiral Oswald knew that small-scale implementation of seagoing would encourage opponents to hinder the new policy. It had to be undertaken on a scale that would overcome resistance within the Navy. In essence, he issued a 'make it so' order. Oswald wanted 300–400 women at sea by the end of 1990, with the first contingent aboard ship by 1 October 1990.[16]

This was an ambitious timescale, giving staff just eight months to implement a policy which Board members had spent nearly ten months considering. As new recruits would not be ready for sea jobs until 1991, serving Wrens were needed to meet these targets. The first call went out two days after the announcement.[17] Initially, the objective was to choose women whose training for their trade most closely matched men's. Already competent in their trades, they would only require seagoing training: safety at sea, firefighting, and in nuclear, chemical and biological warfare defence.

Priority was given to radio operators, radar operators, photographers, stores accountants, cooks, physical training specialists, writers (i.e. clerks), regulators (disciplinary staff), aircraft mechanics, meteorological observers and stewards.[18]

Commandant Larken was disappointed by the initial response. She blamed the slow uptake on adverse reporting and 'some lack of welcome from men'. She urged commanding officers to 'personally do [their] utmost to counter gloomy and unhelpful counsel, and put the positive and forward-looking view'.[19] But at this early stage, Wrens were being asked to make a commitment without being told under what terms and conditions they would serve, the work on these details having only just started. Perhaps the surprise should be the enthusiasm with which many Wrens stepped forward, particularly in light of sometimes hostile reactions from men.

Admiral Oswald's target for volunteers was achieved by June.[20] However, his aspiration that they should all join ships by the end of 1990 proved unrealistic as training and ship modifications could not be scheduled so quickly. Nevertheless, 16 ratings and 3 officers joined the frigate HMS *Brilliant* in October 1990. By the end of the year, a further 71 joined the aircraft carrier HMS *Invincible* and 11 were serving in the training ship HMS *Juno*. The Navy was critically short of radio operators, needing 70 more at sea. By mid-January 1991, when women joined HMS *Battleaxe*, 32 female radio operators had been drafted to sea, nearly halving this problem within a year of the policy announcement. Planned ship modifications allowed for 567 berths, rising to over 1,300 in 1994. The impact on female recruitment was positive. Intakes increased both in absolute terms and as a percentage of the total intake. The WRNS recruited its first engine room mechanics, sonar operators and seamen (sic).[21]

The most intractable issue was the shortage of female officers and senior ratings willing to go to sea, with about 8 per cent of the latter volunteering.[22] Senior women aboard ship were regarded as important for two reasons: young female ratings would have someone to turn to if they needed advice and senior women would be available to assist male supervisors or managers who might encounter difficulties in integrating Wrens into their departments.[23] This issue was foreseen by Alan West's observations of the Dutch Navy. He predicted that women without sea experience early in their careers would be unable to step into supervisory posts. Lack of basic seamanship would undermine their authority with subordinates.[24]

Well advanced in her career working in radar and intelligence duties, Lieutenant Commander Elaine Smith's account illustrated the difficulties. Not being qualified for other branches, she became a seaman officer – the executive branch of the Royal Navy, providing the route to the command of ships. She was assigned to HMS *Fearless* for three months as an officer-under-training, a status normally associated with the junior officer ranks of midshipman or sub-lieutenant. She worked in the various departments in the ship for about a week each to learn about their organisation and roles.

Smith explained the difficulties she faced by drawing on her experience of shadowing the work of officers on the bridge. She held the same rank as the senior navigation officer, but although accustomed to working with charts, she had no experience of taking fixes to establish the position of a ship or of the calculations necessary to navigate a ship safely. The junior navigation officer assigned to instruct her had difficulty in coping with an officer senior to himself in rank, but deficient in skills and knowledge associated with her seaman officer status. This experience proved to her that she was not employable at sea as a lieutenant commander. Although the senior officers aboard *Fearless* encouraged her, Smith decided that there was too much to absorb and too many training courses that she would need to complete. She believed that, without sea experience accumulated as a more junior officer, she lacked the necessary expertise to take charge of a department in a ship. She curtailed her career, opting for redundancy.[25]

The concept of women in combat was almost immediately tested when HMS *Brilliant* deployed to the Gulf War in January 1991. Its commanding officer in 1990, Captain (later Rear Admiral) Richard Cobbold, volunteered to take the first Wrens to sea. He thought it would be an interesting challenge for his final months in command. The ship was already scheduled for a minor refit, so adjustments necessary for female crew members were added to the work. It was programmed for duty in UK waters but the crisis in the Gulf led to a change of orders. Cobbold reflected that 'as it turned out, it was a very good thing – it stopped people messing about, and they had to get on with it.'[26]

The media took no interest in women at sea during a war in which air and land operations dominated. However, *Brilliant's* crew made news when sex was the story. After hostilities had ended and while the ship was still in the Gulf, a married male officer and a more junior single female officer were found naked together in his cabin. This contravention of strict rules about socialising aboard ship was made more unacceptable by his marital status. It played into the fears expressed by wives. The officers were sent for court martial and, as *The Times* recorded it, were found guilty of being naked together 'without reasonable excuse'.[27] Each was fined £750. *The Sun* provided the headline 'Nude romp', describing the female law graduate as a 'randy Wren' while the man was more flatteringly called a 'dashing lieutenant'.[28]

The second story concerned a female radio operator who became pregnant. Unlike the officers, she and her able seaman boyfriend had not contravened rules because they conducted their relationship while on shore leave. The Wren co-operated with the *Daily Mirror*, which reported her story sympathetically. Apparently, she concealed her pregnancy while aboard ship because she did not want to be sent home. The doctor thought she was putting on weight due to overeating and the stress of war.[29]

The Navy Board commissioned an evaluation of seagoing from Plymouth University. Research, based on questionnaire surveys and interviews in mixed ships and men-only ships between 1993 and 1995, revealed problems created by haste in sending women to sea.[30] The reports exposed harsh realities of life aboard ship for women trying to break into previously male domains. Volunteers had limited training and were not confident in fulfilling general duties aboard ship, particularly emergency roles. Uniforms appropriate to seagoing were not finalised until 1994. Protective clothes and equipment were not initially available in female sizes.

Ratings complained of unfairness in how supervisors allocated tasks. Men thought they were given the heavy or dangerous work; women felt they were used too much for cleaning jobs. In some ships, the best accommodation for ratings had been given up to women. This led to rumours that women received preferential treatment. Men thought themselves vulnerable to unjustified complaints while women worried about making an accusation in case they were subsequently bullied. Male managers had no training in dealing with harassment complaints. But more positively, Plymouth University noted that the Navy was doing more to aid implementation of equality policies than most employers.[31]

Fleet Headquarters staff, who visited ships as a matter of routine, also observed progress with implementation. In addition, Commandant Anne Spencer (Anthea Larken's successor) visited ships and passed information on to Headquarters staff. It was a commonly held view that the spirit aboard ship could be assessed within minutes of the start of a visit.[32] Anne Spencer recollected:

> It was atmosphere – you know. Commanders there [to meet you], smiling – take you to the captain. Captain smiling 'We're doing terribly well. We're enjoying it. The Wrens we've got are superb ... Got a few problems here – a few problems there. But it's wonderful.' ... others – surly, rude – not 'we didn't want it' sort of thing. Not outright – but you just knew. [On one ship] they had let the [male] ratings paint the whole mess deck black before the [Wrens] arrived ... just unkind things.[33]

Where a ship's company was not integrating, responsibility was placed on the ship's senior officers. It was seen as a failure of leadership and commanding officers were to be held to account.[34] Training on equality issues was introduced for officers and NCOs in an effort to improve management and leadership.[35]

Meanwhile defence cuts led to 530 officers and over 1,000 non-commissioned personnel leaving on redundancy terms by 1993.[36] To minimise redundancy, recruitment to all the armed forces was severely curtailed from 1992. With reductions in recruitment, there were insufficient new women to replace those coming to the end of their first assignment at sea. In 1994 women were consolidated in fewer ships; between six and eight ships reverted to male manning.[37] This fuelled belief that sending women to sea was an unsuccessful experiment that could be reversed.[38]

It is difficult to gauge the extent to which the Navy wished it had not made its decision just as post-Cold War planning started. A lone officer, writing for the *Naval Review*, suggested the policy should be abandoned. He thought it was being judged successful because opinion was being suppressed. He called for a 'frank and honest debate'.[39] Admiral Bathurst, Commander-in-Chief of the Fleet in 1990, subsequently said 'we would rather at the time – we would rather we hadn't had to go down this route. But we couldn't man the Navy with men only.'[40]

Flying

In 1989, the Air Force Board set a recruiting target of 25 female pilots and 10 female navigators each year, 10 per cent of the planned intake. The figures related to the number of male candidates at the lower end of the aptitude scale that it wanted to replace rather than being an assessment of how many women could realistically be recruited. Allowing for training failures, it was anticipated that there would be 100 female pilots and 45 navigators within five years.[41] Reality fell well short – in April 1994 about 10 female pilots and 10 navigators had reached squadrons.

Three main reasons are apparent. First, the 1989 policy paper set unrealistic targets through inadequate assessment of physical criteria which were determined by cockpit layouts designed for men. Sitting height was the most important as it determined the clearance for the pilot wearing a helmet and his or her fields of vision. If sitting height was short, then 'functional reach' became important. This was the ability to operate aircraft controls. For ejection seat aircraft, there was an upper limit for leg measurement from buttock to knee. This factor, supplemented by the measurement between buttock and heel, also had a minimum limit so that the pilot could reach controls operated by the feet. Criteria varied between aircraft and candidates accepted for training could have restrictions placed on them as to which aircraft they could fly.[42]

Air Vice-Marshal Mills, Director General of Medical Services, warned that perhaps 50 per cent of women would not meet the physical criteria.[43] The Institute of Aviation Medicine compared data on sitting height, buttock to knee length and reach for women in the United States Air Force with the RAF's standards. Assessed against RAF aircraft, 55 per cent of women would not meet the requirements for the Jet Provost training aircraft and 60 per cent would fail those for Hawk aircraft used to train fast jet pilots.

Ejection seat parameters were another critical factor. Some women were too light, increasing risk of serious injury if they had to eject.[44] Flight Lieutenant Dawn Hadlow, the first woman to qualify as a flying instructor, thought that a woman would not have dared to withdraw because of increased risk of injury through being too light. She recalled flying with flight reference books in her pockets to increase her weight.[45] The paper for the Air Force Board simply said that women who did not meet the criteria would be weeded out during the selection process as happened to male candidates.[46]

The second issue glossed over in the 1989 proposal was experience in Canada and the USA. Canada opened some aircrew roles from 1978, with unrestricted employment from 1986. By 1989 there were 18 female pilots from a total of 2,053 and 8 navigators out of 783. In the previous two years, 9 women had been recruited to these roles compared with 410 men. Canada attributed the low numbers to two reasons: lack of interest and rejection of female candidates on the grounds of stature or weight. The United States Air Force set targets for women as a proportion of the available squadron jobs. Each year 40 places were available to female pilots on squadrons, compared with 1,700 for men. Its target for female recruits was just over 2 per cent of its male intake.[47] The Air Force Board paper included this information but failed to explain how the RAF was to do so much better in attracting women who met the criteria.

The third factor could not have been foreseen by the Air Force Board in July 1989 – the changed strategic environment brought about by the collapse of the Warsaw Pact. Defence cuts of the early 1990s overturned plans for numbers of personnel and severely interrupted training. The RAF's 50 operational squadrons of 1989 reduced to 42 by 1995.[48] With experienced pilots redeployed from disbanding squadrons, considerably fewer places were available for junior pilots (male or female) emerging from training. New intakes were substantially reduced and trainees' progress through the sequence of courses was interrupted. Waiting times for courses could exceed a year.

Dawn Hadlow, selected for ground attack Tornado aircraft, recollected being told she would have to wait 18 months for her course because training had also been affected by the diversion of resources to the Gulf War in 1991.[49] Helen Gardiner waited 18 months for her operational conversion unit course for the fighter variant of Tornado (this was the final course before joining a squadron – see Figure 9.1 for the training pattern).[50] It took until financial year 2002/03 before the initial target of 45 navigators was surpassed. By 2007 there were about 50 female pilots, half of the target set for 1994.[51]

Figure 9.1 Pattern of RAF Pilot Training 1989

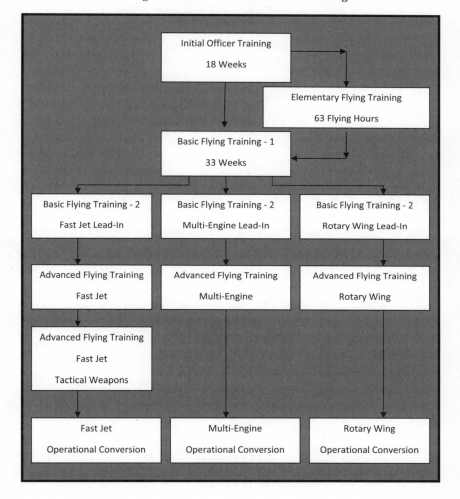

Like female sea-goers, women experienced practical problems. The RAF could have handled the issue better having already encountered problems with flying equipment and clothing with the introduction of female air loadmasters into the Hercules transport aircraft fleet in the early 1980s. Coveralls were designed for men of minimum height 5 feet 6 inches; flying boots were a minimum size 6. Even with women of the requisite height, other dimensions did not match up to men's. Feet, hand and neck sizes all tended to be smaller in women than in men of the same height. In consequence, boots, gloves, helmets and aircrew respirators were too large for some women. Some could not achieve a neck seal with the respirator, which was necessary for safeguarding against the threat of chemical or biological agents.[52]

If possible, women made do with the nearest men's size. Julie Gibson recollected:

> My hands were a lot smaller. And I'm not necessarily a small woman. In flying training, they tried to sew some gloves for me but it was never really satisfactory and the flying suit was always too big.[53]

Flight Lieutenant Keren Watkins remembered having her hands and feet drawn around so that gloves and boots could be made for her.[54] Former Army cadet Flight Lieutenant Wendy Nichols, one of the first trainee navigators, also remembered that nothing fitted. Only 5 feet 3 inches, her flying suit was too big. With long sleeves getting in the way of plotting positions on maps, she 'took matters into [her] own hands and got the stuff better tailored'.[55]

Fast jets provided a challenging twist to the usual dilemma of toilet facilities for women. Men could urinate into a tube containing absorbent sponges. A different solution was needed for women. The USA's National Aeronautics and Space Administration introduced incontinence pads for crew use during the launch and entry to orbit phase of space shuttle missions in the early 1980s.[56] The Institute of Aviation Medicine worked on the same idea. Incontinence pads were provided to women but they were not popular.

As all RAF pilots and navigators were officers, there was substantial delay before recruits completed selection processes and officer training (at the time an 18-week course). In order to make an early impact with the new policy, the RAF sought volunteers from within its ranks. There were 47 applicants within 10 days of the announcement: 5 were civilians and the remainder were already in the Services.[57] Eleven candidates attended the selection centre at Biggin Hill on 14 August 1989.[58] Some women were accepted although they were too short according to the limits set. This waiver of the normal rules had been applied previously to male candidates who were judged to have excellent potential.[59]

Julie Gibson was among the first accepted. She was working towards a private pilot's licence, intending to pursue a career in civil aviation after leaving the RAF. Attempting to fast-track her because of her 30 hours of civil flying, she was exempted from Elementary Flying Training and sent directly to Basic Flying Training. Her male colleagues had at least the 63 hours of elementary training or possibly more than 90 hours at a UAS. Not surprisingly, she found her limited experience, spread as it was over a number of years, left her ill-prepared for the intensity of RAF training. She needed, and was given, extra hours of flying to come up to standard.[60] This was no small matter. Flying training syllabuses defined the number of hours (a proxy for cost) available to each student. There was a small margin of additional hours which were used at the discretion of training staff.[61] The allocation of extra hours was contentious. Men who were struggling could complain that women were treated more favourably. Overcoming initial difficulties, Julie Gibson was awarded 'wings' in June 1991. She flew Andover communications aircraft with 32 Squadron before moving to the Hercules transport fleet. Starting as a co-pilot in 1994, she was the first woman to become a captain on Hercules aircraft in 1998.[62]

Intent on claiming credit in the arena of equal opportunities, the RAF sought to capitalise by publicising the progress of female aircrew. However, publicity proved to be a source of friction. Julie Gibson described dealing with publicity as 'horrible ... [it] created jealousy because people were jealous of the attention, jealous of the opportunity that was coming. It created stress'.[63] Keren Watkins thought women could be seen as seeking the limelight and not serious about a career in military flying. It damaged their professional standing with male colleagues.[64] Flight Lieutenant Jo Salter, the first woman to qualify to fly fast jets, avoided the glare of press interest until she became a combat pilot with 617 Squadron. She dealt with subsequent fan mail by enlisting the help of male colleagues to reply.[65]

The RAF Public Relations staff wanted to emphasise that female aircrew retained their femininity. Dawn Hadlow recollected:

> They sent down this [female officer] to try and sweet talk us into doing publicity. ... they were on about making a television programme which is so naff I can't believe it. Getting us to shop in Dorothy Perkins [a retail chain] for frilly underwear and the next shot is us flying jets. Fairly nauseating stuff. ... I said 'No' to that. ... this course is pressure enough. You don't need to be doing this to us. It's ridiculous. But I got the message later on – they said when you are on a squadron you are ours! There's no getting out of that publicity. I resented that greatly.[66]

Sally Cox, the first woman to progress to tactical weapons training, failed her course. Her unsuccessful attempt to become a combat pilot was mostly handled sympathetically by the press. Reference was made to the difficulty of the training, the earlier failure of a male colleague and the fact that 20 per cent of candidates usually did not make the grade.[67] Exceptionally, the London *Evening Standard* used her failure as an opportunity to run an editorial piece questioning the morality of allowing women to serve in combat roles. The paper asked whether the country wanted 'our Sally Coxes dropping bombs?'[68] It subsequently published two letters, one from a man and one from a woman. Neither agreed with the editorial line. Rather, both correspondents argued that excluding women was discriminatory, that the expectation of willingness to fight should not be a burden borne only by men and that if women were willing and able, then combat roles should be open to them.[69]

Initial volunteers for pilot training suffered higher failure rates than the planned figure. This prompted Air Marshal Thomson to complain about the quality of candidates. However, he thought that better candidates were coming through the system.[70] Thomson's better candidates included women who had benefitted from membership of UASs or the Air Training Corps (a cadet organisation for children from age thirteen). Helen Gardiner had 100 hours in her logbook and Keren Watkins 140 hours before embarking on Basic Flying Training.[71] This was a substantially better platform than Julie Gibson's level of experience at the start of training. Both were successful. Gardiner was the first air defence pilot, flying Tornado F3 fighter aircraft. Watkins, initially becoming an instructor, went on to be the first woman to fly the single seat Jaguar aircraft.[72] Kath Bennett, the third woman on their basic course and a former member of the Air Training Corps, qualified as a helicopter pilot.[73]

The 1989 policy paper claimed that women could usefully add to the quality of navigators and so it proved. With navigator training being shorter than that for pilots, these were the first to reach operational squadrons.[74] As with pilots, initially they were employed only on non-combat aircraft. However, early successful candidates showed up a limitation of this policy. Some women were outperforming men at the Air Navigation School, but they could only be assigned to air transport or air-to-air refuelling aircraft. This meant that 'an undue proportion of their less capable male colleagues [were being] posted to Nimrod [aircraft], where they [would] either fail training or the present standard [would] have to be reduced.'[75] According to Anne-Marie Houghton (née Dawe), the first woman to qualify as a navigator, some men feared that women would take the available jobs in multi-engine aircraft. Men would miss out if they could not qualify for more demanding roles. She recollected that this created some animosity.[76] The Air Force Board's decision in December 1991 to extend women's employment to all types of aircraft prevented this problem from persisting.

Female volunteers for aircrew roles faced a different challenge from that of Wrens opting for seagoing. The latter faced a new environment which tested their professional skills and, perhaps more demanding, required that they integrate socially into ships' companies. But they were assigned to ships as groups, with some mutual support and knowing that Director WRNS was taking an active interest. Aircrew training was a more individualistic experience, as was subsequent posting to a squadron. Air Commodore Ruth Montague (Director WRAF) was side-lined both by her limited advisory role and by inclination. She thought it best that work was carried out by specialists within existing committees and policy areas.[77] Women struggling with inadequate clothing and equipment and burdened by unwelcome publicity had to find their own solutions.

Choosing Integration – the Demise of the WRAC

Army self-satisfaction in the wake of the Crawford report (1989) on extending women's employment was shaken by the seagoing decision and Ministerial endorsement of women's combat roles in the Navy and the RAF. After attempting initially to convince themselves that women serving in warships did not constitute a combat role, Army staff at the MOD conceded the need to refine the justification for excluding women from the infantry and armoured corps.[78]

The Army Board had no intention of making further concessions on employment of female soldiers. The unsurprising list of factors that it claimed prevented women from joining all elements of the Army included an assertion that the public would object, lack of physical strength, potential for disciplinary problems and implications for male bonding if women were introduced. The latter was considered essential in developing fighting spirit. Overall, women would be excluded if their presence could be detrimental to operational effectiveness, meaning the ability to successfully prosecute military operations. As there was no objective evidence on the issue of operational effectiveness, it came down to a matter of professional judgement – and that judgement was an assertion that women would be detrimental to the fighting capacity of units in contact with an enemy.[79]

Meanwhile, a team of staff officers at MOD was appointed in January 1990 to start the detailed work on opening more jobs to female soldiers as agreed by the Army Board in July 1989. First, they instructed Army Command Headquarters to review any geographical restrictions they placed on women's postings. Second, ignoring such geographical aspects, all posts (other than those explicitly excluded – infantry and armoured corps) were to be assessed for suitability and reasons were to be given if women could not be accepted. The third issue was to determine an acceptable level of dilution – the number of women that could be employed in a role without detriment to operational effectiveness. This brought back language central to policy in the Second World War, with servicewomen assumed to weaken (dilute) performance. Once these first three phases were concluded, the team would plan career structures to give men and women equivalent (note – not 'equal') opportunities. Finally, establishment records would be amended to indicate which posts were for men only and which could be either for men or for women.[80]

In July 1990, the Army Board was told that 70,000 jobs in the regular Army could be categorised as suitable for either men or women and 45,000 in the Territorial Army (TA). To control dilution, limits would be applied (15 per cent in the regular Army and 20 per cent for the TA), giving a maximum of about 21,400 and 18,000 women respectively. However, based on recruitment and retention trends, the actual number of women was predicted to be 10,000 regulars and 12,000 in the TA by the end of the decade. Women would be permitted to serve in support of fighting units in what was called the A2 echelon, going forward to the combat zone if their duties demanded. They might become involved in combat, but they would not be permanently based with fighting units. The proposals were approved in January 1991. However, the idea of setting allowable percentages of women was abandoned on legal advice.[81]

To support the opening of more roles, the Army Board commissioned research into gender-free testing for use in selection and training. Copied from the USA and Canada, the intention was to set test tasks essential to particular roles to both male and female candidates. Attempts to devise such tests continued for years, as it had in other countries. The work was hindered by inadequate funding.[82]

The apparent neutrality of the tests was undermined by Corps choosing the most extreme, rather than commonplace, tasks and was plagued by fears that weaker male soldiers would be rejected while strong female candidates would pass. As John Drewienkiewicz (then Director of Manning) recollected:

It became laughable. ...The particular lot I remember – the Royal Signals – [they] were very worried that they were being 'overrun' with women. There is probably a better way of describing that – but that would be the sort of conversation one was having. ... they devised this test where a group had to pick up a portable generator, put it on [their] shoulders and manoeuvre it on to the top of an armoured personnel carrier. The view at my level and of my colonels was [that] it was just daft. They were just looking for the most difficult, awkward thing you could ever be expected to do and say because [women] can't do that ... we said 'You're just going to be a laughing stock.' ... we called in the various work study and analysis people. ... Within about six weeks the Signals found that by the addition of a very small bit of metal [a sky hook] on the top of the armoured personnel carrier, instead of needing four soldiers to do it, you could do it with two.[83]

While this work on future employment and deployment progressed, the crucial Crawford recommendations on permitting women to join corps other than the WRAC hastened the demise of the women's Corps. Newly commissioning officers could join employing corps from April 1991. By 30 May 1991, 209 of the 241 permanently employed female officers had rebadged to their employing corps.[84] Hitherto mainstream WRAC officers also sought out new Corps to join. Non-commissioned ranks could take employers' cap badges from 1 October 1991. By April 1992, only 1,360 women remained in the WRAC.[85] The Corps, which had numbered about 4,900 in April 1989 (as Crawford's report was being considered) had swiftly dispersed, its members choosing to integrate into the Army.

Fiona Walthall was one of the many mainstream WRAC officers who sought a new Corps. Holding a commission in the TA while at university, after graduating she joined the WRAC in 1977. Bored by routine WRAC appointments, she stayed in the Army because she was given jobs outside of the Corps. By the late 1980s she had undertaken security officer duties, intelligence work in Northern Ireland, staff college and an exchange tour in the USA. Believing her experience and inclination pointed towards the Intelligence Corps, she applied for a transfer. She joined her new Corps already holding the rank of major and within two years she was selected for promotion to lieutenant colonel. On later reflection, she said:

My first job in the Intelligence Corps was commanding 4 Security Company in Germany. The Company was already mixed male and female non-commissioned ranks. I went with both intelligence and security experience and I honestly don't think it ever occurred to me that I wouldn't be accepted. ... At no time did I feel uncomfortable or out of my depth ... the Intelligence Corps accepted that professional competence was what mattered, and being female was not an issue. That continued throughout my career with the Intelligence Corps.[86]

Fiona Walthall's success in transferring to a new role was based on relevant experience gained in earlier appointments – a very different case from Elaine Smith's brush with seagoing which she attempted at the equivalent naval rank of lieutenant commander.

While the Director WRAC's attention was focussed on the Crawford outcome, perhaps insufficient attention was paid to another report, this one written by Brigadier Pett. In May 1989, he produced a review that bemoaned the state of clerical work in the Army. Male regimental clerks lacked career opportunities that those in the Royal Army Pay Corps or Royal Army Ordnance Corps enjoyed. Regimental clerks' problems were strikingly similar to those of female soldiers – career progression was ill-defined. A follow-up report, produced in May 1990, recommended the creation of the Adjutant General's Corps to consolidate clerking, including that provided by the WRAC.[87] Adjutant General Sir Robert Pascoe accepted the proposal enthusiastically, not only for improvements it would bring to administration and career paths, but also as a means of achieving much needed savings.[88] Army Board approval was given in May 1990.[89] The new Corps came into being on 6 April 1992, absorbing those members of the WRAC who had not already transferred elsewhere.

As with other Corps or regiments facing the axe or amalgamation, retired senior officers entered the fray in an attempt to preserve the past. The WRAC was no exception, with retired former Director Brigadier Anne Field embarking on protracted correspondence with Adjutant General Ramsbotham (Pascoe's successor) and his staff. In her capacity as Deputy Controller Commandant WRAC, an honorary appointment, she lobbied for senior female officers to have more prominence in the embryonic AG Corps. She claimed that the new Corps was regarded as a male take-over.

General Ramsbotham's patience came to an end in February 1992 when he wrote:

Quite frankly you have the reputation of being a bar to progress ... your advice, provided it is constructive and helpful, is always welcome. Your interventions, if they are negative, interfering or unhelpful, are not. ... I do find it intensely irritating when I have to divert my effort to read letters ... which amount to yet another lobby to people like me to look backwards instead of forwards. ... in the politest but firmest way that I can muster, can I ask you to shut up, and let us get on with what we have to do.[90]

Despite Brigadier Field's interventions, formation of the AG Corps went ahead and the WRAC was disbanded with great ceremony. More than 500 serving and retired officers and guests attended the final regimental dinner held at the Guildhall, City of London. The evening was a great success. As General Ramsbotham recollected:

The Remembrancer [the City of London's Ceremonial Officer] was a great friend of mine. He rang up and said 'Will you tell the women that they can certainly come back and have their dinner here next year ... when they played the Lass of Richmond Hill [the regimental quick march], the girls got up on their chairs and danced. Their stiletto heels ripped up half the chairs and there was a huge bill. So, could they please come back next year and do the other half!'[91]

More sedately, the last concert given by the WRAC band attracted former bandswomen from around the world and included some members from the original band formed in 1949. The main send-off was a parade of more than 1,000 servicewomen in the presence of Queen Elizabeth, the Queen Mother, on 25 March at Guildford, the home of the WRAC.[92] With that, the Army's long struggle of women's dual identity as WRAC and employing Corps was over. Female soldiers would take their chances in integrated units.

The WRNS and WRAF

Rather than the haste which had accompanied implementing the seagoing policy, time was allowed to complete the necessary planning to integrate women into the Royal Navy. The first day of November 1993 was chosen as the date for disbanding the WRNS to coincide with the last day in office of Anne Spencer, the retiring Commandant.[93] As an early symbol of women's new standing, Royal Navy rank titles for officers were introduced on 1 December 1990.[94] As female officers' titles, such as first officer, chief officer and superintendent, had been a mystery to those not closely involved, the change was welcomed. Equivalent ranks of lieutenant commander, commander and captain needed no explanation of an officer's authority. The term 'Wren' was retained in rank titles for junior ratings. Commandant Spencer described this as the most emotive subject and she announced the outcome of deliberations with some satisfaction in *The Wren*.[95]

Anne Spencer might equally have applied this emotive approach to the braid used for rank insignia and badges. Blue braid had been symbolic of the WRNS since it first formed in 1917. For many Wrens changing from blue to gold represented a real loss of identity. Yet gold braid was also seen as a further necessary step 'to reinforce the *esprit* engendered by full integration' if women at sea were to be recognised as having the same authority of rank as men.[96] Due to the need to budget for gold braid, this change was not implemented until 1 April 1992.

The policy implementation team had a major task in planning career structures for sea-goers, women who chose not to volunteer and those in roles with no jobs at sea. Possible career paths were mapped out for each individual officer. For ratings, the work was tackled at the level of the branch in which they were employed. Separate rosters for promotion were retained for non-seagoing women while those who did go to sea were merged over a period of time into the RN's system.[97] Early volunteers had the option to revert to shore-based service if they found it too hard to adjust to ship-board work. This privilege was not extended to later volunteers or new recruits. The WRNS fragmented into recent recruits obliged to go to sea, volunteers for sea, early volunteers who reverted to shore work only, non-volunteers in branches that could go to sea and women who worked in roles with no equivalent aboard ship. The latter, about 20 per cent of non-commissioned Wrens, were identified by Anne Spencer as casualties of the policy change.[98] Over a period of years, many of these roles were disestablished.

Anne Spencer identified a second group of casualties: those women too senior to go to sea. This was true to an extent. Some left voluntarily under the 1990s' redundancy programmes. However, there are striking examples of success among those who stayed despite not going to sea. Annette Picton and Carolyn Stait, lieutenant commanders in 1990, subsequently achieved promotions to commodore.[99] After their retirement, there was a demographic hiatus while those who served in ships gained sufficient experience to compete for high rank. Excluding medical services, by 2018 the most senior female was logistician Commodore Ellie Ablett. At 1 April 2018, 3.2% (32) of warrant officers were female.[100]

The WRAC having disbanded in 1992 and the WRNS in 1993, only women in the Air Force used a distinctive designation. The term WRAF was an anomaly as women had joined the RAF rather than a women's

Corps or Service from 1949. The Air Force Board decided to address the image of separateness which did not represent airwomen's actual status.

Air Chief Marshal Sir Andrew (Sandy) Wilson (Air Member for Personnel) dismissed Air Commodore Ruth Montague's plea to retain the role of Director. She argued that she carried out useful representational duties.[101] However, Wilson believed that senior women officers did not want to be promoted artificially into the role, preferring to make their careers within their specialisation. He cited Air Commodore Joan Hopkins' career.[102]

In 1982, as a group captain, Hopkins was appointed to command of RAF Neatishead, Strike Command's control centre for the air space of southern Britain and its sea approaches.[103] She was the first female officer to command a Strike Command unit. Promoted to air commodore in competition with men, she took charge of a major equipment project. Being the only female air commodore, she was sounded out to take over as Director of the WRAF to replace Shirley Jones who was retiring. But she had never seen the role as a goal, remarking in later years 'Emulate [Director WRAF]? There was no challenge there.'[104] Certainly the Director's job paled in comparison with the multi-million-pound project that Joan Hopkins was running in the late 1980s. She fended off the appointment and Ruth Montague was promoted to fill the vacancy.

The date of a planned re-organisation of the RAF Command structure, 1 April 1994, was chosen as the moment when reference to WRAF would cease.[105] This was convenient also for Ruth Montague's retirement date. For women in the Air Force, dropping the suffix WRAF was hardly noticed.

Terms of Service

Brigadier Crawford proposed equal pay for women in his 1989 report, but to no avail. By then the differential was 1 percentage point of the pay supplement known as the X-factor, justified by the Armed Forces Pay Review Body on the basis that women were 'not generally liable to combat duties'. Seagoing brought women the same liability for naval combat as men so the Navy Department wanted to recommend equal X-factor for Wrens. However, with the pay rise for 1990 about to be finalised, the seagoing announcement made in February came too late for the Army and the RAF to be consulted on this tri-Service issue. The matter was held over until the following year. Full X-factor, and so equal pay, for all servicewomen was agreed in 1991.[106]

There was a further aspect to naval pay. Male ratings received extra money for seagoing, paid in recognition of extensive communal duties aboard ship. These 'all of one company' rates, as they were known, were paid as long as the man remained available for sea duty. This seagoing pay for women was agreed as a matter of 'natural justice' and following legal advice that under both domestic and European law a pay differential could not be justified.[107] Nor could it be deferred like the X-factor if Wrens were to be encouraged to volunteer for seagoing. Treasury agreement was sought in February 1990, an approach made to the Chairman of the Armed Forces Pay Review Body in March and the Prime Minister approved his recommendation in April.[108] The pay rise for a junior Wren going to sea was estimated as just over £1,000 per annum (1990 value).[109] This was a substantial pay rise. The pay of able seamen in 1989 was in the order of £9,200.

The second key inequality in terms of service favoured women who married while in the armed forces. These women had the right to leave on or after marriage at shorter notice than men or single women. Needing to protect the investment in training, in 1989 the RAF made volunteers for pilot and navigator roles surrender the right to leave on marriage until they had amortized costs. This was set at six years after completion of the final stage of training – an Operational Conversion Unit course – conforming to the period set for male aircrew who wanted to apply for premature release. Treasury officials asked why the policy change should not apply throughout the women's Services.[110] However, flying policy was intended to affect only a few women. For the vast majority who worked in ground-based roles, the Air Force Board reaffirmed that the right to leave on marriage was 'seen as fundamental to women's terms of service'.[111] The Air Force eventually changed its rules in 1994, shortly after reference to the WRAF ceased.[112] The situation for the Navy was different. From September 1990, all WRNS recruits had to go to sea and so were given longer and more expensive training. To protect that investment, they lost the right to leave on marriage.[113] The Army also abandoned the policy.

Pay and the right to leave on marriage were easy to address. Pregnancy and motherhood were far more difficult in the culture of the armed forces. Junior women had questioned the lack of maternity leave for some years.[114] However, senior women tended to oppose its introduction. Group Captain Cynthia Fowler (Deputy Director WRAF 1989–91) feared that periods of absence could call into question the employment of women as costs would be increased.[115] Commandant Larken was against mothers being employed in the Service, believing that the responsibilities of motherhood were incompatible with the demands of a naval career.[116] In addition, if maternity leave was available, it would also have to be granted to single women. This official sanction of behaviour which went against the social code of conduct was anathema.[117]

Servicewomen were normally discharged in the sixteenth week of pregnancy, though practice varied. For example, Wrens could work in civilian maternity clothes beyond that point.[118] The timing of dismissal was made more flexible in 1990 to allow servicewomen to claim statutory maternity pay in place of the less generous State benefit known as maternity allowance. Mothers could apply to re-join provided that they undertook to fulfil their military commitments and made adequate child care arrangements. However, there was no right of return. Applications could be rejected.[119] This provision to re-apply was not well known and seems to have been rarely invoked.

Archie Hamilton believed that dismissal on pregnancy might put career-minded women off the armed forces because they would have more employment rights in civilian occupations. He wanted a study to be undertaken with the intention of achieving greater equality.[120] Terms of reference issued in March 1990 described the aim of the work as to develop policy on re-employment of women after childbirth. Options to be studied included making application to re-join easier, paid or unpaid maternity leave, and the implications of guaranteeing a right to return to work.[121] By the end of June, the RAF and RN positions were to hold the line on dismissal, though not at a fixed point in the pregnancy, and to welcome re-enlistment. The Army intended offering special unpaid maternity leave but reserving the right not to re-employ mothers on 'manning grounds'. That phrase would seem to give the Army authorities plenty of leeway.[122]

Policymakers' hopes of giving the Minister the minimum possible result from the study he had commissioned were overtaken by external events. In June 1990, the Equal Opportunities Commission (EOC) lodged a judicial review of the Queen's Regulations for the armed forces on behalf of Mrs Julie Lane, a former Army nurse, and former RAF nurse Mrs Lesley Leale.[123] The working group was advised it should bring forward a maternity leave scheme as soon as possible to avoid the embarrassment of the MOD being taken to court. It would be difficult to persuade Archie Hamilton to make a stand against the EOC on the issue, not least because MOD was likely to lose.[124] The MOD conceded. From October 1990, women became entitled to a maximum of 29 weeks unpaid maternity leave.[125] In December 1991, following further legal processes, MOD announced that women could apply for 14 weeks paid maternity leave and 48 weeks total leave.[126]

With the MOD acknowledging that it had been in contravention of EU and domestic law since August 1978, women who had been dismissed on pregnancy sought compensation for unfair treatment. Cases were brought by 5,038 women.[127] Initially many settled for the maximum payment available under industrial tribunal rules. The compensation limit of £11,000 was successfully challenged at the European Court of Justice and a few payments, reaching hundreds of thousands of pounds, hit the headlines in the national and specialist press. There were few defenders of the sums, with both men and women arguing that 'they knew the rules, so they should not be claiming this money'.[128] Payments were in marked contrast to the limited sums awarded to personnel (the vast majority men) injured in the First Gulf War. The *Sun* expressed the situation succinctly with the headline 'Barmy Army' concerning a £300,000 award to a former major. It went on (original emphasis):

> She knew the rules. SHE decided to marry; SHE got herself pregnant. YOU are paying the bill. But injured personnel get just a few grand.[129]

By 1999 all maternity claims were settled at a cost of £60.3 million.[130] These cases divided opinion in the Services and generated some ill feeling towards women at a time when morale was strained by post-Cold War redundancy programmes. This was not simply a divide on the basis of gender. Childless women could be as vehemently opposed to these pay-outs as men.[131]

Conclusion

Timing was crucial in the widening of servicewomen's roles. With the defence cuts of the early 1990s, the armed forces were no longer short of men. There was a surplus which was reduced by curtailing recruitment and offering redundancy. But the plans to widen employment of servicewomen, agreed in 1989–90, proceeded. The decision to open the surface fleet was approved by the Prime Minister and announced by Archie Hamilton on the basis of equality not just as a solution to a shortage of sailors. Likewise, the other two Services used the language of equality to explain new policies. While there may have been some regret in the armed forces about decisions made, it would have been difficult to persuade politicians to abandon the plans so soon after the fanfare of announcements simply because the need for service personnel was unexpectedly declining.

Admiral Oswald forced the pace on seagoing by setting ambitious targets. His initial objective of between 300 and 400 women at sea was met in 1991. Subsequent plans for expansion and ability to sustain the number of women at sea were affected by defence cuts. The failure of RAF policy to meet targets for numbers of female pilots and navigators was critically affected by defence cuts. However, it also occurred because they were ill-founded in the light of experience in other countries and insufficient attention to expert advice about physical criteria. As suggested when the policy was adopted, women were proving to be competent navigators. Numbers qualifying as pilots were consistent with experience in other countries.

Central direction from the Navy Board and the Air Force Board gave impetus to new policies. The same claim could not be made when it came to the Army where implementation became bogged down in the detail and different interpretations within the various Corps. But new opportunities were accepted enthusiastically by the majority of the WRAC who chose to switch to their employing Corps or sought a transfer to new Corps. As far back as the Second World War, where badges of the Royal Artillery were worn as well as those of the Auxiliary Territorial Service, women wanted to identify with their work and their male colleagues. Now they could set aside the WRAC badges that proclaimed gender rather than professional expertise. Conflicts arising from dual control of women's careers were in the past. Despite the other Services opening their main combat roles, the Army Board was not under pressure to put women into the infantry or armoured corps. Women's opportunities were still subject to limitations arising from a desire to keep them out of the fighting.

While women's job opportunities expanded, the MOD's interpretation of equality stopped short of meaning that women were to be treated in accordance with civilian employment law. While Archie Hamilton wanted to bring about a change in regulations on pregnancy, policy-makers resisted the introduction of maternity leave, not least because of opposition from senior female officers who perceived the obligations of motherhood as incompatible with military duties. It took a combination of action by aggrieved former service nurses, dismissed because of pregnancy, and the Equal Opportunities Commission, which took up their cause, to bring about change.

In November 1993 and April 1994, Anne Spencer and Ruth Montague (the last Directors of the WRNS and WRAF respectively) retired. Their departures also marked the end of the WRNS and reference to the WRAF. Air Commodore Montague was marginal to developments in women's employment opportunities and sought to retain the post of Director. In contrast, leadership provided by senior WRNS officers contributed to the decision to disband their Service. Although they realised that changes would end careers for those who could not or would not adapt, they recognised the imperative to create a fundamentally new career for women in the Royal Navy. The disbanding of the WRAC, mourned by senior retired female officers, was welcomed by Adjutant General Ramsbotham who regarded the Corps as a roadblock to progress for women. The new climate brought an unprecedented opportunity for Brigadier Gael Ramsey as Garrison Commander at Aldershot.

IO

BEYOND INTEGRATION

Marjah district, Helmand Province, Afghanistan, 2008, a British patrol under fire: 'Get some ******* rounds down!' Combat medic Sergeant Chantelle Taylor, fearing she was about to be shot, engaged the enemy. This was her first experience of close quarters combat. The patrol of which she was part was holed up for seven weeks under fire. She was in command of the Company Aid Post for B Company 5 Scots and had a team of four, including another female medic. As the situation became critical, with 66 out of 100 soldiers injured, she served as the number two soldier on a mortar, arming rounds for firing.[1]

Female medics frequently featured in patrols during the conflicts taking place in Iraq and Afghanistan. In March 2009, naval medical assistant Able Seaman Class 1 Kate Nesbitt was also in Marjah district, providing medical support to 3 Commando Brigade. Her patrol coming under fire and with a soldier wounded, Nesbitt ran 60 metres under fire to reach him. She administered aid for about 45 minutes, stemming blood loss and providing him with another airway as his lip, jaw and neck were injured. The casualty was evacuated and survived to tell his tale. Nesbitt's actions were described as exemplary. '... under fire and under pressure her commitment and courage were inspirational and made the difference between life and death'.[2] She was awarded the Military Cross.

The first woman to be awarded the Military Cross was Lance Corporal Michelle Norris. A combat medical technician serving in Iraq in 2006, she was attached to the 1st Battalion Princess of Wales's Royal Regiment in Iraq. Her Warrior patrol vehicle came under fire and the commander was wounded. Norris climbed up to the turret to treat him, coming under fire from a sniper while she gave immediate aid that saved his life.[3]

It had become practice for casualties to be airlifted away from danger to receive emergency (and often life-saving) medical treatment. Helicopter pilot and aircraft captain Flight Lieutenant Michelle Goodman flew missions in Iraq as part of an Incident Reaction Team (IRT). She was the first woman to be awarded the Distinguished Flying Cross. According to the citation, on 1 June 2007 she flew into an extremely dangerous area of Basra City to rescue a casualty:

> Alert to the high risk, but being fully conscious of the importance of providing unfailing IRT support to ground forces, Flight Lieutenant Goodman elected to fly her approach whilst under intense enemy ... fire. ... flying tactically on night vision goggles at very low level across a hostile city, she ... approach[ed] an unfamiliar and dangerous landing site ... undeterred by close friendly covering fire and even closer enemy fire ... This was a bold and daring sortie which undoubtedly saved life.[4]

Within a few years of the 1990s reforms to women's roles in the armed forces, servicewomen were indisputably taking part in combat. Geographic restrictions imposed by Army deployment rules devised for the European theatre were meaningless in the wars of the late twentieth and early twenty-first centuries. Women were contributing to patrols, keeping up with male colleagues, carrying their share of equipment, sustaining effort over weeks of engagement with the enemy and proving capable under fire. Yet some barriers remained. Women could not serve in land warfare units whose primary purpose was to close with and kill an enemy force. This meant exclusion from infantry and armoured corps regiments, the Royal Marines and the RAF Regiment. The Navy also excluded women from submarines. In 2016, the final barriers to women's roles in the armed forces were removed.

The acceptance of change in the late twentieth century and early twenty-first extended beyond servicewomen's roles to social and family circumstances. Equal opportunities offices were established. Anti-bullying campaigns were mounted. A few instances of gender re-assignment occurred. Despite official support, such individuals experienced significant challenges in continuing with their careers.[5] The armed forces also slowly came to terms with the lifting of the ban on homosexuals and lesbians. Like servicewomen's campaign for maternity leave in the late 1980s, this change in policy came about through legal cases mounted by former service personnel dismissed because of their sexual orientation. Although the three men and one woman lost their case in the High Court, a ruling by the European Court of Justice in September 1999 led to the ban being overturned the following year.[6]

Against this background of policy developments, servicewomen were making their careers in integrated units. Competing with men for promotion and with access to maternity leave, how were their careers faring?

Land Warfare

In March 1990, an article in *Soldier* (the magazine of the British Army) reported the achievement of Sergeant Pat Young who had successfully completed a field firing course at the School of Infantry, Warminster. She was quoted as saying 'The part I enjoyed most was low level air defence using GPMGs [general purpose machine guns]'. The course qualified her to run firing ranges used by her unit. She belonged to 2/52 Lowland Volunteers, an infantry battalion of the Territorial Army (TA). A woman had never done the course before so her arrival at Warminster caused some consternation. She was asked whether her unit could not have found someone better to send – presumably a man. Staff checked with the Land Force Headquarters before she was allowed to do the course.[7]

Sergeant Young's story illustrates an important difference between the regular Army and the Territorial. The regular Army was labouring over the implementation of the 1989 Crawford report, allowing women to serve further forward in Germany but not in direct combat roles. The TA signed up whoever volunteered and, if they completed training, used the talents they had. John Drewienkiewicz (Director of Manning for the Army 1993–94) recollected that women were welcomed into TA units in contravention of regular Army policy:

All these TA infantry battalions had been taking on women and had been allowing them to go on the courses and to do the jobs. ... if you've got a TA battalion that needs not only three rifle companies, but a signals platoon, a band, pioneers, transport, clerks in the headquarters. They can all be women. That will allow us to put the men into the rifle platoons. So now we have got the rifle platoons full. And we've got the signalling done by people who are pretty good at it and motivated. We are now at ninety per cent manned, not seventy-two per cent manned. ... then the Director of Infantry had an apoplectic fit. Edicts were issued to say 'Stop doing it'. The women then all had to transfer to other bits of the TA. ... It was pretty grisly ... I thought the TA had got themselves into a muddle. They had got out ahead of the headlights of the collective British Army and you either had to say 'Stop doing it. Or it is a precedent and the rest of the Army will have to catch up'. ... [It] was suddenly an issue because it was a hideous precedent for the rest of the army.[8]

Major General Drewienkiewicz also attributed women's greater opportunities in the TA to the University Officer Training Corps:

> Being universities, ... men and women were equal. The OTC was a part of the university ... and therefore what went on in the university more or less was OK in the OTC. ... [women] became second lieutenants in their third year in the OTC. Then were able to join their local TA unit. If the local TA unit happened to be an infantry unit and here was this ready minted second lieutenant – passed all their exams – pip on their shoulder – good degree from somewhere – jolly keen. Absolute manna from heaven ... happens to be a woman. ... We'll work out what to do with her later. So that was how it came about.[9]

However, it was an unacceptable precedent because it undermined the Army Board's opposition to women serving in the teeth arms – the infantry and the armoured corps. In 1994, the Executive Committee of the Army Board (ECAB) decreed that servicewomen serving in TA infantry units would be given the opportunity to transfer to another unit. If they stayed with their current unit they would not be deployed on operations and promotion chances would be severely curtailed.[10]

In 1996, the ECAB remained under pressure as even the regular Army was not keeping to the rules about the geographic limits to women's employment. The TA still had women serving with infantry and armoured corps units. A new attempt was made to define policy. Three options were presented to the Board: first, keep the current policy that excluded women from units that served forward of brigade headquarters, and from the infantry and armoured corps; second, unrestricted employment; third, open everything except infantry and armoured corps.

With geographic rules already being breached, current policy was described as difficult to sustain. It went against the political imperative to open more roles to women and, anyway, women were successfully doing jobs that in theory were closed. The second option was legally watertight, though it was considered impractical until gender-free assessments were available. General Michael Rose (Adjutant General) thought this outcome was likely eventually, but the Army was not ready. He also believed it would be socially unacceptable. The third option was chosen, although the Board acknowledged that it was not entirely coherent. The policy would result in women serving as far forward in battle as the infantry and armoured corps while excluding them from those 'teeth arm' roles.[11] With this outcome, the Royal Artillery, Royal Engineers and Royal Electrical and Mechanical

Engineers opened fully to women. With the introduction of gender-free assessments in April 1998, 70 per cent of Army jobs were open.[12]

The European Union's Equal Treatment Directive of 1976 required combat policy to be reviewed periodically. Work undertaken by the MOD in 2002 and 2010 to satisfy this requirement crystallised the arguments. 'Ground close combat' was defined as 'combat with the enemy over short range' and the roles described as those that were 'primarily intended and designed with the purpose of requiring individuals on the ground to close with and kill the enemy'. The ability of a unit to carry out its mission was described as 'combat effectiveness' and the 2010 report described cohesion of a unit as a vital factor in achieving combat effectiveness. Three types of cohesion were identified. First, social cohesion which entailed bonds of friendship, caring and closeness among team members. Second, task cohesion in which team members shared a commitment to achieving a common goal. Third was team pride: valuing the team; identifying with the team; and attractiveness of being a team member.[13]

As the 2010 report noted, policies on women's exclusion from close combat roles 'were instigated when there was a clearly defined front-line, but in asymmetric warfare[14] many women in supporting roles found themselves drawn into close combat situations.' This was evident to the Service Chiefs who conceded that women were essential to operational effectiveness, that they won decorations for valour, could act independently and show great initiative. In expressing this sentiment, they echoed views of men and women surveyed for the report. Personnel who had served in Iraq and Afghanistan in combat incidents were mostly of the opinion that mixed gender teams were effective provided that all members were competent. Time spent together developing shared experiences and training together were fundamental to success. However, while a minority of serving men and women surveyed for the report supported the lifting of the ban on close combat roles, most still considered it a step too far.[15]

Meanwhile, some allied nations had opened ground combat roles to women. The MOD thought this had been brought about due to political and legal pressures. Nordic countries were described as the most progressive and Canada was picked out as having opened such roles in the late 1980s. However, only a small number of Canadian women volunteered for combat units. This was attributed to family responsibilities, perceived difficulties in meeting the demands, physical fitness aspects, limited opportunities for career progression in combat units and reported negative attitudes from men towards female combatants.[16]

Taking the 2002 and 2010 conclusions together, evidence considered by the Service Chiefs suggested that some women would be capable of meeting the physical standards required for close combat units. There was no compelling evidence that psychological difference between men and women or the capacity for aggression would be a hindrance. However, there was a question mark over the ability of women to sustain the necessary effort over a period of days or weeks. The 2010 report dismissed reliance on privacy and decency issues, an expression in British sex discrimination law that permitted employers to exclude one gender from a role. It was thought to worry spouses rather than soldiers.

The report also cast doubt on another customary idea – that in contact with the enemy, men would be over-protective of female colleagues and might stop to assist rather than persist with the mission. 'Interviewees consistently said that in contact [with the enemy], training kicks in and everyone just gets on with their job'. The author asked: 'would the training/getting on with the job override these concerns?'[17] The question was left hanging.

It is not clear that leaving casualties where they fell, while continuing with the mission, was the ethos of operations in Iraq or Afghanistan. Considerable effort was made to prevent wounded personnel from falling into the hands of the enemy. In research conducted in 2015 as part of a subsequent review on women in close combat roles, some Army focus groups identified the ability to evacuate a casualty to a point of safety by means of a fireman's [sic] carry as an essential capability.[18] Perhaps this was the latest idea on how to justify exclusion of women – not that men would stop to assist them if they became casualties, but that female soldiers would not have the strength to carry a male colleague to safety.

Despite operational experience gained in the wars of the 1990s and early part of the twenty-first century, it was impossible to generate evidence on female combat soldiers' performance in the ultimate test of military effectiveness – high-intensity warfare. Thus, it was a matter of judgement whether or not to take this step – or risk as it was described in 2010. The Service Chiefs were reluctant and Andrew Robathan (Conservative, south Leicestershire), Minister for Defence Personnel, Welfare and Veterans, was content to side with the military judgement.[19]

The climate changed when Defence Secretary Philip Hammond (Conservative, Runnymede and Weybridge) established the next review in May 2014. In line with a change in American policy made in 2013, this work started with the premise that 'all roles should be open to women unless it could be demonstrated that exclusion was necessary to maintain combat effectiveness'.[20] The report in December 2014 set aside any concerns about cohesion in mixed-gender teams. Cohesion could be developed through leadership, training and competence in roles. The remaining obstacle was health with further research commissioned into mitigating risks of musculoskeletal injury, mental health issues and reproductive health.

The outcome of the further work was prefigured by Prime Minister David Cameron in December 2015 when he was quoted in the *Sunday Telegraph* as saying that he and the Defence Secretary were 'united in wanting to see all roles in our Armed Forces opened up to women in 2016 ... We should finish the job next year and open up ground combat roles to women.'[21] The 2016 report duly highlighted the benefits of opening all remaining roles to women: maximising talent, accessing more talent, equality of opportunity and improving the reputation of the armed forces. Maintaining exclusions would leave Britain 'misaligned with key partners including the US and Australia who had already opened all combat roles to women'. Within the Army, a study of women's roles in recent operations 'identified that commanders wanted more women in their teams especially when operating "amongst the people"'.[22]

There was a suggestion that picking up on experience in America, the Army could introduce a revised system of 'physical employment standards'. These would be designed to match more closely a recruit's capabilities with the role to which they were assigned. There would be an emphasis on training for upper body strength. By better matching individuals to roles, there was an expectation that injuries to men would reduce as well as those to women. Mitigating risk to mental health was more challenging and no clear solution had been identified. Rather, there would be improved training for soldiers and their leaders in an attempt to identify individuals with problems earlier than hitherto. Likewise, there was a lack of evidence in connection with reproductive health for women involved in high-intensity workloads. Comparisons with elite athletes had yielded nothing of note. Nevertheless, the opinion was that health issues should not hold up a change to policy and that more evidence would be gathered over time and further changes implemented when courses of action became clear.[23]

There was also greater clarity on the roles within ground close combat. These were now sub-divided into mounted and dismounted units. Although all units might operate in the dismounted role (i.e. on foot and carrying their equipment), there were so-called heavy units in the Royal Armoured Corps (RAC) that operated primarily in their tanks. These units could provide a starting point for the introduction of women into close combat roles. Female soldiers who had been surveyed expressed a preference for the RAC over the infantry.

The recommendation made to Sir Michael Fallon (Conservative, Sevenoaks), Secretary of State after Philip Hammond, was to lift the exclusion of women from close combat roles progressively, starting with selected units in the RAC (regular and Territorial) and progressing to all units in 2018 when the new physical employment standards should be ready. This policy included the opening of the RAF Regiment and the Royal Marines. Although also projected for 2018, the RAF proceeded with implementation in September 2017.[24] It had been keen to take this step but waited for Army policy to change.

The Army's proposal was far more realistic about the potential number of female recruits into these roles than the RAF's 1989 paper on female aircrew. Taking account of evidence on women's likelihood of passing the physical tests (about 4.5 per cent) and evidence from the USA, the author suggested 10 women per annum would make it into the infantry, 20 into the RAC, perhaps 4 into the Royal Marines and 8 for the RAF Regiment. It also proposed a training package to cover issues of cultural change and leadership. Unlike the RN's hasty introduction of seagoing in 1990, the Army proposal was to prepare the ground – there was to be no 'rushing to failure', a key tenet learned from observing how the USA and Australia were progressing these issues.[25]

Sir Michael Fallon accepted the recommendation and policy was formally announced by David Cameron in July 2016.[26] That is as far as official papers in the public domain take the account, making it seem unproblematic and rational – a systematic and careful assessment of the issues. Behind the scenes, there are suggestions that Army leadership was more reluctant. Like the RN's seagoing decision, political influence was probably important in overcoming the final objections.

Submarines

Once seagoing was established in the early 1990s, the Navy Board turned its attention to the suitability of submarine service for women. Initial thinking was that the Navy needed more experience of employing women in surface ships before considering the more demanding submarine environment.[27] Meanwhile, evidence was collected from the Institute of Naval Medicine on foetal health, a female officer who spent a week at sea in a submarine, and from focus groups of women of all ranks who had served in ships.[28] A paper produced in 1998 concluded that submarines were not suitable for women. There was no doubting the position of the author who introduced his report with a quote from Horace in the original Latin which translates as: 'So that what is a beautiful woman on top ends in a black and ugly fish.'[29] Opening with this sentiment, he made his argument on the basis of inadequate living conditions, health concerns, psychological and social issues, and personnel planning problems. Nor did the women canvassed make a plea for the role to be opened, though some thought it would be inevitable at some point.[30]

Submarines had many more constraints on living conditions compared with surface ships. They always went to sea with a full complement and sometimes with additional personnel for training purposes. In consequence, there were insufficient bunks. It was standard practice in *Trafalgar-* and *Vanguard*-classes of submarines for some crew members to hot bunk, meaning two men were assigned to the same bunk, taking turns of duty and off-duty time. Sometimes camp beds were put up in weapons' storage areas. If women were to have a self-contained sleeping area and ablutions, as in surface ships, there would be a net reduction in space for bunks. The alternative of shared accommodation, accepted in Norway's navy since the 1980s, was deemed unacceptable in British culture.[31]

A key uncertainty concerned women's health and the possibility of a woman being in the early stages of pregnancy. Acceptable radiation and atmospheric pollutant levels were derived from national health and safety regulations. However, unlike industrial workers, submariners lived in the environment as well as working in it and so were exposed to pollutants for protracted periods of time. If a woman was pregnant, the potential harmful effects on a developing foetus of continuous exposure for up to 90 days were unknown. There was also concern that a medical emergency, such as ectopic pregnancy or miscarriage, would be beyond the experience of on-board medical staff.[32] It was not evident from the paper whether these risks were worse than emergencies which might occur for any crew member.

Psychological and social aspects of submarine service were also considered. Serving in nuclear-powered, ocean-going submarines was regarded as more demanding than coastal patrolling as in Norwegian service. Nuclear-powered submarines spent more time submerged because they did not have to surface regularly like conventionally-powered submarines which had to refresh their atmosphere. Nuclear-armed submarines routinely spent 12 weeks submerged. Their crews could only receive family messages weekly and they could not reply. Incoming messages were limited to 40 words, were vetted ashore before transmission and again by the submarine's captain to ensure that they contained no distressing news. There was a fear that women would not adapt to this isolation. In addition, there was recognition that relationships could form between crew members or there could be unwelcome sexual advances. Putting a crew member ashore to defuse an inappropriate, deteriorating or unwelcome relationship, the solution used in the surface fleet, would not be available during a long submarine patrol.[33]

Personnel planning was more complex for submarines than for surface ships. A full complement was achieved through use of an emergency relief pool of men who could be assigned at short notice if a crew member had to be withdrawn before a patrol started. To generate this surplus of trained manpower, men were directed into submarine service. The Navy would have preferred to avoid compulsion, but was unable to attract enough volunteers. Findings from a very limited set of focus group meetings of Navy women suggested that there would also be insufficient female volunteers to sustain jobs assigned to women. This judgement was shared by Lieutenant Hutchings, a female officer who went to sea for a week in a *Trafalgar*-class submarine as part of the research for the 1998 paper. It was thought that the possibility of compulsory service in submarines could deter women from staying in the Navy or, indeed, from joining.[34]

Presenting findings to the Navy Board in October 1998, Admiral Sir John Brigstocke (Second Sea Lord) said he thought accommodation (other than cost of modifications) was not an issue. Nor did he think that normal radiation levels posed a threat. He was not convinced by arguments about the potential for sexual harassment. However, he shared reservations about potential health risks for pregnant women from atmospheric pollutants. Board members agreed that the most compelling argument against opening submarines to women was the difficulties of managing crew complements and the likelihood of compulsory rather than voluntary submarine service. The recommendation to maintain exclusion was accepted.[35]

When further work was undertaken in 2010/11, the Institute of Naval Medicine concluded that health concerns were unfounded, though steps should be taken to avoid pregnant women serving in submarines. Legal advice concluded that submarines should be opened to women to avoid falling foul of the Equality Act (2010).[36] As with surface ships, some physical alterations would be needed in the boats. However, the newer *Astute*-class submarines were fitted with a bunk for each crew member.

By this time, women formed about 9 per cent of the RN and, if they remained excluded from submarines, then this more onerous role would continue to fall exclusively to men. In December 2011, the Navy Board decided to open submarines to women, initially to officers and subsequently to non-commissioned ranks.[37] It was sensible to start with officers before introducing junior ratings in order to minimise issues around integrating a small number of women into the challenging environment of a submarine. The announcement was welcomed by Robert Fox, defence correspondent of the London *Evening Standard*, who claimed that many women were 'the best and brightest and the Navy command [had] recognised this'. For him, women's capabilities outweighed other issues and he called the decision 'the exercise of sheer common sense'.[38]

In 2014, Lieutenants Maxine Stiles (logistics), Alex Olsson (training as a weapons engineering officer) and Penny Thackray (education officer) were the first women to earn their dolphins badge – the symbol of a submariner.[39] All trained aboard the nuclear submarine HMS *Vigilant*.

Women's Careers

With the integration of servicewomen into the armed forces, the female one-star posts of Director were disestablished. Two of the incumbents retired.[40] However, Brigadier Gael Ramsey still had some years to serve. General Ramsbotham (Adjutant General) admired her forthright style and had high hopes that she would go on to reach the two-star rank of major general. To be competitive for promotion with men in the top echelons of the Army, she needed a challenging job. As a former WRAC officer she lacked the operational experience required for many appointments, so General Ramsbotham arranged for her to take command of the Aldershot garrison.[41] She took up the appointment in May 1992 to headlines in the *Daily Mail* of 'Woman to call the tune in home of Army' and following an interview with her, 'I'll command respect and stay a lady, says the blonde brigadier'.[42]

Her appointment was not universally welcomed. As General Ramsbotham recollected:

> Unfortunately, it didn't work. ... Aldershot unfortunately had a lot of diehards – Parachute Regiment and others. I suspect that there was guerrilla warfare against her. I don't know where else we could have put her. I didn't want to put her in a quiet [post] ... perhaps in retrospect Aldershot was unfair. ... we couldn't send her to be a brigade commander in Germany. We couldn't send her to Northern Ireland. I didn't want it only with the [Territorial Army]. ... But perhaps I was wrong and I should have sent her to somewhere quiet like Nottingham.[43]

His view was endorsed by Major General Robin Grist, Director General of the new Adjutant General's Corps. He thought Brigadier Ramsey was seen as a candidate to succeed him in post. He remembered:

> Sending her to Aldershot was a tough call. Gael had some really difficult, desperate problems. And having the Paras [Parachute Regiment] there. I think it was a very hard role for her. ... There were other places that could have been a bit easier for her to have made that transition.[44]

With promotion to major general no longer likely, Gael Ramsey left on redundancy in 1994. It took a further twenty years for women to reach this rank. The first was legal branch Susan Ridge, a professionally qualified officer promoted to the specialist post of Director General Legal Services. Major General Sharon Nesmith was the first mainstream regular service female officer to reach the rank when she was appointed as Director (Personnel) at Army headquarters in March 2019.[45]

The RAF boasts the most senior female officer. The first air vice-marshal was administrator Elaine West, appointed to run defence infrastructure projects in 2013. She was followed a few months later by engineer Air Vice-Marshal Sue Gray who took up responsibility for procurement and maintenance of combat aircraft in the Defence Equipment and Support organisation.[46] She went on to command Number 38 Group (engineering, logistics, communications and medial operational support), also holding the role of Chief Engineer for the RAF. In March 2019, she became Britain's first female three-star officer in the rank of air marshal when appointed as Director General of the Defence Safety Authority.[47]

Policy changes in the 1990s resulted in an increase in the presence of women in the armed forces (Figures 10.1 and 10.2). Comparison with earlier periods is difficult because MOD statistics include figures for armed forces nursing Services, rather than being reported separately, as had been the custom. Numbers can be deceptive because the overall strength of the military was in decline due to budget cuts. However, percentages of women indicate a steady increase in representation. Within each Service, women were less likely to reach the highest commissioned and non-commissioned ranks than men. For officers, the disparity emerged between the ranks of major and lieutenant colonel, or the equivalent ranks in the Navy and RAF (Figure 10.3). For non-commissioned ranks, comparatively few women reached the top rank of warrant officer (Figure 10.4). Nevertheless, more women stayed for full careers and reached these ranks than prevailed prior to the introduction of maternity leave in late 1990.

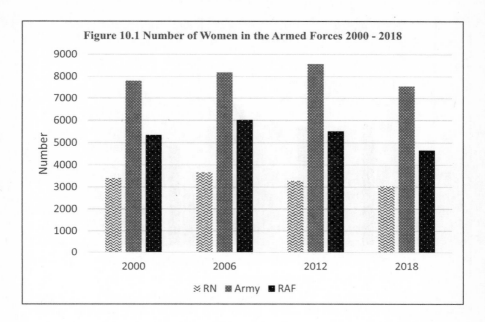

Figure 10.1 Number of Women in the Armed Forces 2000 - 2018

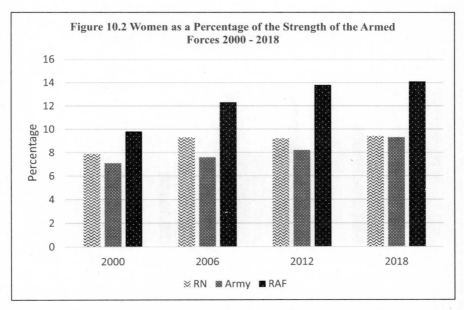

Figure 10.2 Women as a Percentage of the Strength of the Armed Forces 2000 - 2018

Source – Figures 10.1 and 10.2: UK Defence Statistics 2010 and 2012, UK Armed Forces Diversity Statistics 2018. Figures at April. These statistics are not directly comparable with earlier years as nurses are included, resulting in an overstatement of figures compared with those quoted in earlier chapters.

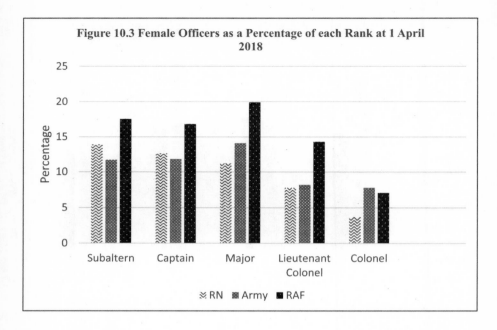

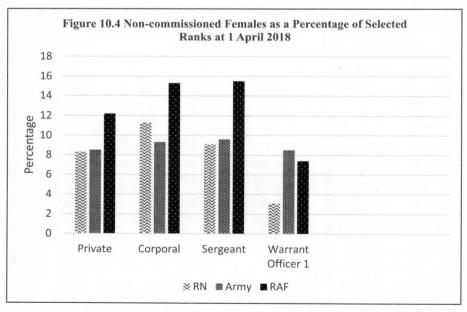

Source – Figures 10.3 and 10.4: UK Armed Forces Diversity Statistics 2018. Figures at 1 April. Army ranks used for illustrative purposes. A guide to equivalent RN and RAF ranks is at Appendix 1.

The introduction of maternity leave and the right to return to duty rather than dismissal in the early months of pregnancy made a significant difference to women's career patterns. However, it took some years for the Services to become used to the presence of serving mothers. Policy was suddenly changed in 1990 (unpaid leave and then paid leave from December 1991) as a result of legal challenges. The move was not universally welcomed as an article in the *RAF News* in February 1992 illustrated. Sergeant Sarah Folley, a clerk serving at RAF Leuchars (Scotland), took unpaid maternity leave in 1991. Married to a sergeant in the RAF Regiment, she and her husband were collocated at RAF Brize Norton (Oxfordshire) after she returned to work. Sarah Folley highlighted the lack of maternity uniform and, on return to work, the absence of child care facilities at her base. She and her husband made private provision, but she thought the lack of help would be problematic for more junior ranks. Nevertheless, she urged women to make the attempt to follow their careers alongside motherhood.[48]

The article prompted correspondence in the *RAF News* for months. Some letter-writers (male and female) claimed that pregnant women could not fulfil their duties, so putting the onus on other personnel to cover for them. Sections were said to be left short-handed when women went on maternity leave. When they returned to work, there were complaints that they took time off at short notice to deal with breakdowns in child-care arrangements or sickness. Women were thought to be given preferential treatment on postings and not sent on detachments. In March, Sergeant Folley's squadron commander wrote in her defence, saying that she fulfilled all the usual commitments and had a plan in place should she be sent on a long-term detachment: 'As one of the first women to remain in the service with a child, she feels she should set an example to others in being able to fulfil her duties.'[49] The following year, Sarah Folley was sent to the Falkland Islands for four months, the standard period of a detachment to the South Atlantic. Her husband remained in the UK and looked after their child. The Sergeants Folley wrote to the *RAF News* to say that they were coping just fine.[50]

While the Services became accustomed to married mothers, with a degree of grumbling, the more contentious issue was that of single mothers. Here, the hasty change of policy left policymakers struggling with the consequences as regulations did not recognise single parenthood (meaning the parents had not married) but only lone parenthood (a parent who had been married but was now widowed, divorced or separated).

The disadvantageous situation of single mothers came to prominence in the *RAF News* and *Soldier* in early 1993.

Sergeant Janice Poole (RAF), a single mother of twins, described the problems of finding accommodation as she was not allowed to apply for a married quarter as a lone parent would have been. Nor could she live in the Sergeants' Mess with her twins. If she was posted abroad, her children would not be entitled to medical care like other dependents. As they grew older, she would not be eligible to claim boarding school allowance as would other parents in the Services. Sergeant Poole thought there were 17 servicewomen across all the Services in the same situation and so allowing them to rent married quarters would be insignificant given the total stock of 75,000 houses.[51] Her theme was taken up in *Soldier* the following month, where children of unmarried mothers were described as 'non-persons' as their existence was not recognised in regulations.[52]

The subsequent flurry of correspondence in the *RAF News* was in the main supportive, though the editor also published letters from those against bringing single parents within the scope of regulations concerning families. Those in favour took up the point that the MOD was probably in breach of the Children Act 1989 and could be vulnerable to law suits, as had occurred with dismissals on pregnancy. There was a sense that it was time for the MOD to catch up with society. Those against raised the question of morality, absent fathers and claimed, by definition, that single mothers could not be entitled to married quarters. It was argued that by conceding that marriage was not an essential qualifying condition in applying for housing, a precedent would be set that would lead on to unmarried couples also claiming eligibility for quarters.[53]

The official response was a review of regulations which took two years to come to the conclusion that single parents should qualify for the same benefits as other parents from 1 January 1995.[54] Married quarters were now referred to as family accommodation. This did not end the controversy as an Army wife warned single women in Service housing not to expect neighbours to rally round to help if they encountered problems.[55]

But the armed forces became accustomed to mothers continuing with their careers and support for families improved, as the case of Commander Catherine Jordan illustrated. She joined the Navy in 1993 – a few weeks before all women transferred to the RN – as a university cadet. After graduating with a law degree from Manchester

University, she qualified top of her course as an observer (navigator and weapons systems operator) on Lynx helicopters and undertook several seagoing tours. She became the first female Lynx flight commander, serving in HMS *St Albans*. Like other naval aviators, she was part of the warfare branch. She qualified as a principal warfare officer and took her bridge warfare officer qualification, enabling her to command ships. Successfully completing tours of duty commanding offshore patrol vessels HMS *Severn* and HMS *Clyde*, she was promoted to the rank of commander and selected to return to HMS *St Albans* as captain. Pregnant with her first baby, her assignment was delayed until she returned from maternity leave.[56]

Support mechanisms were now in place. Her husband, also a senior naval officer, was designated for shore duty while Commander Jordan fulfilled her stint as a frigate captain. They could pay for their daughter Evelyn to attend an on-site nursery at his place of work, simplifying the logistics of child care. Of course, separation from her young daughter was not emotionally easy, but as Commander Jordan explained, 'I had to accept that my husband was very competent – very capable of looking after our daughter.' Although she missed her child, she felt her situation as a parent enabled members of her crew to also talk about dealing with separation. She went on:

> Being at sea, sat in the captain's chair on the bridge, was very comfortable for me. That's what seems normal. I was a working mum. It happened that my work took me a bit further away. In the eighteen months in command, I was away quite a bit but the longest I did away from Evelyn in one go was actually about three and a half, maybe four weeks. I know plenty of other women in the three Services who have done six-month deployments away. Actually, in the grand scheme of things, mine [was] very minor separation.[57]

She also explained that there was a self-help maternity buddies scheme in which serving mothers passed on practical advice to mentor new mothers returning to work. With a second daughter (Vivian) born in 2016 and a son (Aidan) in 2017, she has been well-placed to pass on experience. More formally, the RN started a weekly newsletter on personnel issues, introduced 'keep in touch' days and established dedicated cells in Portsmouth, Plymouth and Scotland to advise on maternity regulations.

Efforts to retain mothers appear to have been successful. MOD statistics for the early years of the twenty-first century show that about 6 per cent of servicewomen took maternity leave in any one year. Figures for 2015 show that about 95 per cent of mothers returned to duty. Of these just over 11 per cent stayed for less than a year, though the MOD was careful not to ascribe decisions to leave to family reasons. Whatever motivated these servicewomen to leave, the figures show that for every 100 women who would previously been lost to the Services, about 84 continued their careers for a further productive period of time.[58] Prolongation of careers is likely to increase the proportion of women reaching the more senior ranks. However, time taken out for maternity leave is likely to have an impact on promotion chances.

Catherine Jordan was unable to take up the opportunity of attending the year-long course at the Joint Service Staff College due to maternity leave. Speaking in 2018, she observed that though the offer was still open, she thought it unlikely she would take it up. She remarked, 'I'm potentially limiting myself for future choice of jobs and chances of promotion unfortunately' but that it was a positive and conscious choice that she made in order to have a family.[59] Nevertheless, she was promoted to the rank of captain in September 2019 when she was appointed to command the training establishment HMS *Collingwood*, including the Maritime Warfare School. She was the first female aviator to attain this rank.

Conclusion

Bringing the account of servicewomen's careers up to the current period inevitably can only result in tentative conclusions. Likewise, the impact of more servicewomen being exposed to the rigours of conflict must be assessed in later years. What is clear for the moment is that women have been proving themselves in operations in Iraq and Afghanistan. In the RAF and the Royal Navy, where combat roles have been opened since the beginning of the 1990s, women have been competing successfully with men for appointments in command of ships and squadrons. The Services have adapted to the introduction of maternity leave and more family friendly policies, such as availability of nursery provision, has aided retention.

By the end of the twentieth century, female soldiers were serving successfully in combat support roles in operational theatres, sharing the risks and responsibilities in facing the enemy alongside male colleagues.

However, the Army was the most reluctant of the Services to permit women to serve in its main combat roles – infantry and armoured corps. It seems unlikely that the generals would have taken this step without being encouraged to do so by Ministers. The Army position was that there is no evidence in favour of women serving in the infantry or armoured corps – and nor could there be short of all-out war. However, the change in American policy put the onus in the other direction – prove that women cannot undertake the roles and, if there is no such evidence, open them. The Army conceded.

I I

CONCLUSION

When considering the post-war configuration of the armed forces, policymakers took a different view in 1946 from their predecessors in 1919. The Second World War was not thought to have been 'the war to end all wars' as had been trumpeted about the Great War. Having defeated fascism, communism was seen as the next threat to peace. A future total war was anticipated. Advances in weaponry meant that a prudent nation would need to be ready for the outbreak of war.

Over the course of the Second World War, hundreds of thousands of women served in the WRNS, ATS or WAAF. Women had been a necessary part of the effort and would be needed again if a further major war occurred. However, readiness for war implied having a core of women around which expansion could take place if the chaos of 1939 was to be avoided. It was these arguments that won the debates in the War Office and the Air Ministry in 1946 when it was decided to offer peacetime regular service careers to women. As planning the post-war strength of the armed forces proceeded and the terms of men's national service were set, employing women as a means of lessening the need for men became a major consideration, particularly for the Army. The Admiralty would have preferred to revert to an all-male, volunteer Service – doing without women or national servicemen. But it felt obliged to go along with what the others were doing and so kept the WRNS.

Organisation was important both for perceptions of servicewomen's roles and for the authority conferred on senior female officers. From the outset of regular service in 1949, the Air Ministry intended that the RAF be integrated in order to eliminate the costly duplication inherent in parallel management of careers for men and women. Women joined the RAF from 1 February 1949, with the term WRAF meant to be an administrative label. The title of Director conferred on the senior woman officer was notional. After Air Commandant Felicity Hanbury oversaw the transition from auxiliary status to regular service between 1946 and 1949, the power and influence of post-holders rapidly waned.

In contrast, Director WRNS was a strong, authoritative figure until her Service folded and women transferred to the Royal Navy in 1993. Nothing happened to Wrens without policymakers seeking the view of the Director. The WRNS had a separate identity from the Royal Navy, epitomised by its use of blue braid rather than naval gold braid and its own rank titles for its officers. But separateness also represented vulnerability, with Directors regularly having to defend the existence of the WRNS.

The Director WRAC was caught between these two positions. The post-holder enjoyed authority as Director of her Corps but found herself at odds with women who worked with other (male) Corps of the Army. Like Director WRNS, she had to be consulted about policies relating to women and she had authority over those women. But she did not exercise full control over careers. Once women could opt to be permanently employed elsewhere, they did.

Unsurprisingly, Directors defended how their own Service did things, each believing that their own system was the best possible way of operating. One issue brought them together. They agreed that motherhood was incompatible with a career in the armed forces with its demands that personnel be available to serve wherever needed, whenever needed.

A Right to be Different

In deciding to offer peacetime careers, post-war policymakers were forward thinkers but there were limits to what they intended. They wanted to retain processes associated with employing women – terms of service, regulations, uniforms, accommodation, training – all issues that had to be re-invented in haste in 1939. They devised short service terms of engagement – longer than undertaken by national servicemen – in periods of four years, that were renewable. They wanted some women to stay for full careers in order to develop senior NCOs and officers to guide junior women and to advise male commanding officers on female matters. To that end, married women could join. Women who married while in the armed forces could stay but they had the right to cut short their service and leave. However, a mother's duty was to her family. Unlike during the war, mothers of school-age children would no longer be allowed to serve. Pregnant women would be dismissed.

Postings for married women needed more consideration than during the war when the needs of the country outweighed consideration of individuals. That approach was more problematic in peacetime. Failure to collocate married couples (where both were in the Services), along with dismissal on pregnancy, resulted in women serving for less than their initial four-year engagement. For decades, policymakers recognised that women leaving on marriage undermined the concept of long-term careers. It called into question the value for taxpayers' money of recruiting, equipping and training servicewomen and was used as a reason for excluding women from roles that required long or expensive training. Service Ministries' aspirations to build up the WRNS, WRAC and WRAF were undermined and women were seen as having a lesser commitment to careers than regular servicemen. Rather than tackling the issues of postings and accommodation, policymakers simply grumbled about the situation.

Servicewomen were treated as single whether that was actually their circumstance or not. If a woman married a man in the same Service, it was likely that she would not be permitted to serve on the same unit as her husband for fear of some disruption to the working environment if a couple worked in close proximity to each other. In the 1970s, the RAF was the first to make more effort to collocate married couples. Retention of airwomen improved as a consequence. The RN introduced the concept of home ports for ships so that families could have time together when ships were in port. The Army struggled. Regiments and corps had their own postings systems. Even if posting authorities knew that a man was married to a female soldier (let alone an airwoman or Wren), consulting WRAC staff was not high on the agenda. When units moved as a collective, like an infantry regiment assigned to West Germany, it was next to impossible to post wives to suitable jobs in the same timeframe, not least because of the geographic restrictions on women's postings. It is no surprise that many former servicewomen think (incorrectly) that they were obliged to leave on marriage.

The crux of the difficulties with servicewomen's careers was motherhood. While laws were enacted in the 1970s to give pregnant women some employment rights – not always respected by employers – the armed forces claimed exemption. Motherhood was seen as incompatible with the onerous commitments of a service career. Senior female officers held to this line as a matter of principle, coupled with a fear about the cost of maternity leave being detrimental to the continuing existence of women's Services. Furthermore, they understood that the law would not allow a distinction to be made between married and unmarried mothers. If maternity leave was conceded for the former, then so the latter would also benefit. Unmarried motherhood was beyond the pale in terms of the standards of behaviour expected of servicewomen. This attitude should be understood in the context of the long history of judgements about the morality of women in the armed forces. Against all the evidence from the First World War onwards that servicewomen had a lower rate of pregnancy outside of marriage than civilian women in the same age group, nevertheless, there was an undercurrent which held to the view that women joined up for the opportunities for sex, not for the challenges of the job.

As senior women officers were not pressing for a change to terms of service, so male policymakers were content to avoid the issue of maternity leave despite interest from the Minister Archie Hamilton. It took two women dismissed because they were pregnant, supported by the Equal Opportunities Commission, to challenge the MOD's policy. The resulting fiasco of needing to pay significant sums in compensation for lost careers made the introduction of paid maternity leave in 1991 problematic – not aided by the haste with which it had to be done. Nevertheless, over the following years family friendly policies were introduced. Housing became family accommodation rather than married quarters, signalling that a family could be other than married man and woman. Some major establishments introduced crèches where service families could pay for child care, as happened with other large civilian employers. Single motherhood, while challenging, was accommodated. The armed forces benefitted as they retained the great majority of women for further productive service rather than losing them as was the case up to the end of 1990.

With longer careers so women had the opportunity to progress to more senior ranks. However, career breaks for more than one child could still hinder the completion of career-enhancing postings and training. Rather than being different from society, the balance between career and family commitments was aligned to those same decisions made in civilian life.

Combat Roles

Major General Jeanne Holm of the United States Air Force summed up discussion about combat and women in the USA's armed forces as akin to Lewis Carroll's character Humpty Dumpty's assertion that 'When I use a word it means just what I choose it to mean, neither more nor less.'[1] So it was in Britain with the contortions over what constituted a combat role.

Ultimately, even if their job was normally in a support trade such as technicians, clerks or cooks, it was a serviceman's duty to pick up a weapon and face the enemy. When peacetime careers were introduced, servicewomen had no such obligation. This was the basis for distinguishing between women and men in Britain's armed forces. It was a self-imposed policy that had no foundation in international law, as was known in the immediate post-war period and re-discovered each time the issue was considered. A situation that had been implicit in the Geneva Conventions was made explicit in revised protocols in 1977. The new text described all members of the armed forces, with the exceptions of padres and medical staff, as combatants and went on to state that this implied having the right to take part in hostilities. There was no requirement to use weapons in order to have combatant status. The Ministry of Defence accepted that women's Services had combatant status, an essential first step towards widening women's roles.

The next move was to arm women so that they had the same fundamental duty as servicemen. Policy change was initiated through pressure from unit commanders who were struggling to meet guarding commitments as complements of servicemen reduced in the 1970s. How the Services tackled the issue reflected their organisations and cultures. After a short trial period, the integrated RAF made it mandatory for recruits. The policy, championed by Air Commodore Joy Tamblin, made airwomen fully interchangeable with airmen. The Army permitted the arming of female soldiers but left it initially to local commanders to decide which women (if any) to train. The Navy declined to join in at the time, saying that it was not necessary for Wrens to be armed.

In agreeing to the arming of women, the MOD was careful to maintain a distinction between men and women's commitments. Women's tasks were restricted to self-defence or to defend their own location, but men could take on offensive action, actively seeking out the enemy. This delineation between defensive and offensive action was needed in order to preserve the exemption from the employment clauses of the Sex Discrimination Act (1975). That exemption was based on combat being men's work – called a genuine occupational qualification. If tasks undertaken by armed servicewomen constituted combat, then exclusion from other roles might no longer be valid.

In the early 1980s, senior male officers were not ready to admit women to the essential functions of their Services – seagoing, flying or land warfare. So, a rifle in the hands of a woman was a defensive weapon. The same rifle in the hands of a man was an offensive weapon. Combat appeared to be narrowed down to offensive action.

Conclusion

Social change from the 1970s onwards began to have an impact on attitudes of men and women in the armed forces. Married men were serving for shorter periods of time because of pressure from families for a more settled life style, reflecting the desire for home ownership, stability for children's education and opportunities for spouses to have careers. Meanwhile, as with other young women who gained more educational qualifications than earlier generations, servicewomen aspired to jobs that reflected their abilities. Like the society from which they were drawn, they married at a later age than earlier generations and were more able to control their own fertility through use of the birth control pill. With deferred motherhood, so women stayed in the armed forces for longer than their predecessors. Women's length of service increased as that of men decreased, weakening the customary argument that women did not provide value for the tax payers' money.

Despite the armed forces' exemption, the Sex Discrimination Act had an important influence on policies. Wanting to be seen to comply with the spirit of the law, exclusion of women subsequently had to be justified, not assumed. Importantly, exemption did not extend to the cadet organisations in universities because they were an educational provision, not employment. Pressure grew from some female undergraduates, student unions, university authorities and MPs until the RAF bowed to external opinion and conceded flying training for selected women at University Air Squadrons. It turned out that some of these young women displayed more aptitude for flying than some of the men alongside whom they trained.

Although it could attract the required number of male volunteers for flying training, the RAF struggled to find sufficient candidates of the right standard. UAS experience, together with evidence from allied nations that already had female aircrew, provided a new pool of talent – young women. Rather than opening all flying to women, the RAF was able to take a piecemeal approach. In Humpty Dumpty fashion, it designated some operational aircraft as non-combat and its female pilots, therefore, as not occupying combat roles – not a description it applied to men flying such aircraft. It managed to preserve elite roles for men while claiming that it was simply observing the 'no combat roles' policy.

Last to decide on peacetime careers in 1946, last to bring women under military law (1977), and last to arm servicewomen (1989), the Navy was the first Service to open its main warfare role to women when it announced and implemented seagoing in warships in 1990. Accepting women for seagoing was a decision on a different scale from that of the RAF and flying because women would live aboard ships. It was a social and cultural challenge, not just about the work. The Navy Board tried all possible arguments to avoid being in the vanguard. It attempted to follow the RAF's example of a small-scale concession but it could not convincingly call any of its ships non-combatant. In addition, its personnel problem was more acute than the RAF's. It was not simply about the quality of male recruits, it was also a failure to retain enough trained men. Separation from ties ashore was inherent in seafaring and so men left to attain more stability for their families. This outflow added to sea time for those who stayed, exacerbating the problem. In turn, it added to the recruitment burden and standards were lowered in order to plug gaps.

None of this made sense to Archie Hamilton who saw for himself that women were proving to be capable sailors in other navies. Admiral Oswald could not devise a coherent proposal for limited seagoing. While Admiral Brown continued to argue for confining Wrens to a restricted list of ships, Admiral Oswald's view was influenced by younger officers around him and the revelation that there was no formal government policy bar on women in combat roles. He was faced also by a determined Archie Hamilton who was unwilling to accept any solution other than women at sea. The time had come and he would not take 'no' for an answer.

Timing and the publicly stated reasons for the new seagoing policy were important. Explaining it as embracing a policy of equality implied that when defence cuts were put in hand later that same year, the decision could not be reversed even had that been an aspiration. Although an overt agenda of equality had not driven the decision, using it as part of the publicity ensured it stayed in force, despite the lessening of the need for service personnel. Although quality was the essence of the decision, equality enabled it to survive the early turbulent period.

The Royal Navy was driven to concede combat roles to women, and RAF flying policy was brought into line soon thereafter as a consequence. The focus shifted to the Army, which had managed to stay out of the fray until this point. There was dismay among some male army officers as they sought assurances that the word combat would not be used to describe new roles for Wrens. With echoes of the Second World War's policy in terms of which women could aim but not fire anti-aircraft artillery guns, there was even a plea that the Navy should not allow women to fire naval guns – as though only the act of firing a naval gun constituted a combat role aboard a warship. It was fruitless to suppose that the Navy would abandon its all-of-one-company philosophy for a ship's complement. Army language was revised. Female soldiers were said to be excluded from close combat, later ground close combat. These were functions that could bring women into contact with enemy soldiers, as distinct from the Navy and RAF's combat at a distance.

The Army's defence of its exclusion of women from close combat was centred on an assumed disruption to unit cohesion and hence an adverse impact on combat effectiveness, which had the rather circular definition of how effective units were in combat. The idea was that women would not cope physically or mentally, men would not cope with having women present, men might neglect their duty to assist a female colleague, and women lacked physical strength and stamina. Yet allowing women into combat support roles such as intelligence, engineering, signalling and combat medics had the effect of undermining the Army's own analysis. As operations in Iraq and Afghanistan proved, units remained effective when female soldiers were attached for these specialist functions.

Until evidence emerges into the public record, the nature of the debate within the Executive Committee of the Army Board cannot be fully assessed. It seems likely that the change of policy in the USA, where the armed forces came under political pressure to remove remaining exclusions, also influenced the British situation. It has the same feel about it as the Navy's angst over seagoing. Plus, it has echoes of the RAF's decision about female pilots. There was a view that not many women would become fast jet pilots, but more were likely to be adept as navigators, as has been proved. The same is said about women in infantry regiments and the armoured corps. Fewer are thought to be capable of the former while more might be attracted to tanks. That assessment, and the success of the new policy, must await the passage of time. However, small numbers of women in predominantly male units will find it a harder challenge than female aircrew whose operational bases provided a less gender-skewed environment.

'Lessening the need for men', a customary explanation for employing women, was often about the quality of male recruits rather than the number of young men in the population being insufficient and so opening the way for women. Needing only a very small percentage of young women to volunteer, the women's Services could (and did) set higher entry standards than were used for men and still have their pick of recruits. The persisting limitation for women's participation is the wartime idea of an acceptable level of dilution – the percentage of a

Service that is allowed to be female without 'weakening' effectiveness. This perception of women as less effective and less reliable than men remains a mind-set. The government has set a target for women as a proportion of the armed forces at 15 per cent, just lower than the figure achieved by the WAAF in 1943.

Women are now free to choose a career in the armed forces as men do – applying for a role according to their capabilities. The risk of dying in war is widely shared. The aspect that troubled policymakers the most when determining roles for women was whether they would willingly kill the enemy in close combat. But as Mary Tyrwhitt argued in 1948, women in the Army would prefer to trust their own skills with a rifle rather than rely on the chivalry of an enemy. So it proved for combat medic Chantelle Taylor, believed to be the first female soldier to shoot an enemy at close quarters in Afghanistan. On patrol in Helmand province, she recollected that she could feel rounds of ammunition pinging around her Land Rover. She preferred to face the danger rather than be killed in the back of the vehicle:

> The world erupted – it was really close ... I got eyes on the insurgent and fired seven rounds ... I fired until he dropped. ... I never thought about having to kill someone. But all the courses I had done – I was prepared. I was a soldier. It was between him and me at the time.[2]

APPENDIX 1

RANK TITLES

Commissioned Officers

Royal Navy	Women's Royal Naval Service	Army and WRAC**	Auxiliary Territorial Service	Royal Air Force	Women's Auxiliary Air Force (1939–1949)	Women's Royal Air Force (1949)
Admiral of the Fleet		Field Marshal		Marshal of the Royal Air Force		
Admiral		General		Air Chief Marshal		
Vice Admiral		Lieutenant General		Air Marshal		
Rear Admiral		Major General	Chief Controller	Air Vice-Marshal	Air Chief Commandant	
Commodore	Commandant	Brigadier	Senior Controller	Air Commodore	Air Commandant	Air Commandant*
Captain	Superintendent	Colonel	Controller	Group Captain	Group Officer	Group Officer*

(Continued)

235

Royal Navy	Women's Royal Naval Service	Army and WRAC**	Auxiliary Territorial Service	Royal Air Force	Women's Auxiliary Air Force (1939–1949)	Women's Royal Air Force (1949)
Commander	Chief Officer	Lieutenant Colonel	Chief Commander	Wing Commander	Wing Officer	Wing Officer*
Lieutenant Commander	First Officer	Major	Senior Commander	Squadron Leader	Squadron Officer	Squadron Officer*
Lieutenant	Second Officer	Captain	Junior Commander	Flight Lieutenant	Flight Officer	Flight Officer*
Sub Lieutenant	Third Officer	Lieutenant	Subaltern	Flying Officer	Section Officer	Flying Officer
		Second Lieutenant	Second Subaltern	Pilot Officer	Assistant Section Officer	Pilot Officer

*Women joined the RAF from 1 February 1949 but for administrative purposes were designated as 'WRAF'. Reference to 'WRAF' ceased in 1994. In 1968 WRAF officers were given the same rank titles as RAF officers.

**The highest rank achieved in the Women's Royal Army Corps was brigadier.

Unlike the RAF's rank of air commodore, commodore was not a substantive rank in the Royal Navy. It was a temporary rank associated with particular appointments. It became a substantive rank in 1997.

Non-commissioned Ranks

Royal Navy	Women's Royal Naval Service	Army	Auxiliary Territorial Service	Royal Air Force (1949)	Women's Auxiliary Air Force	Women's Royal Air Force (1949)
Warrant Officer		Warrant Officer Class I	Warrant Officer Class I	Warrant Officer	Warrant Officer	Warrant Officer
		Warrant Officer Class II	Warrant Officer Class II			
Chief Petty Officer	Chief Petty Officer	Staff Sergeant	Staff Sergeant	Flight Sergeant	Flight Sergeant	Flight Sergeant
Petty Officer	Petty Officer	Sergeant	Sergeant	Sergeant	Sergeant	Sergeant
Leading Seaman	Leading Wren	Corporal	Corporal	Corporal	Corporal	Corporal
Able Seaman	Wren, Able rate	Private including lance corporal	Private including lance corporal	Leading Aircraftman	Leading Aircraftwoman	Leading Aircraftwoman
Ordinary Seaman	Wren (Trained)			Aircraftman 1st Class	Aircraftwoman 1st Class	Aircraftwoman 1st Class
	Wren, Ordinary			Aircraftman, 2nd Class	Aircraftwoman 2nd Class	Aircraftwoman 2nd Class

Air Force: Non-commissioned aircrew ranks have been omitted. Technician ranks were introduced later. Aircraftman 1st and 2nd class were later renamed as leading aircraftman and aircraftman. The former leading aircraftman rank became senior aircraftman. Women's rank titles used aircraftwoman in place of aircraftman.

APPENDIX 2

DIRECTORS OF THE WOMEN'S SERVICES

WRNS

Vera Laughton Mathews	1939–46
Jocelyn Woollcombe	1946–50
Mary Lloyd	1950–54
Nancy Robertson	1954–58
Elizabeth Hoyer-Millar	1958–61
Jean Davies	1961–64
Margaret Drummond	1964–67
Marion Kettlewell	1967–70
Daphne Blundell	1970–73
Mary Talbot	1973–76
Vonla McBride	1976–79
Elizabeth Craig McFeely	1979–82
Patricia Swallow	1982–86
Marjorie Fletcher	1986–88
Anthea Larken	1988–91
Anne Spencer	1991–93

ATS/WRAC

Helen Gwynne-Vaughan	1938–41
Jean Knox	1941–43
Leslie Whateley	1943–46
Mary Tyrwhitt	1946–51
Frances Coulshed	1951–54
Mary Railton	1954–57
Mary Colvin	1957–61
Jean Rivett-Drake	1961–64
Joanna Henderson	1964–67
The Hon. Mary Anderson	1967–70
Sheila Heaney	1970–73
Eileen Nolan	1973–77
Anne Field	1977–82
Helen Meechie	1982–86
Shirley Nield	1986–89
Gael Ramsey	1989–92

WAAF/WRAF

Katherine Jane Trefusis-Forbes	1939–43
Ruth Mary Eldridge Welsh	1943–46
Felicity Hanbury	1946–50
Nancy Salmon	1950–56
Henrietta Barnet	1956–60
Anne Stephens	1960–63
Jean Conan Doyle	1963–66
Felicity Hill	1966–69
Philippa Marshall	1969–73
Molly Allott	1973–76
Joy Tamblin	1976–80
Helen Renton	1980–86
Shirley Jones	1986–89
Ruth Montague	1989–94

NOTES

Chapter 1: Introduction

1. J M Cowper, *The Auxiliary Territorial Service* (War Office, 1949), p.48. Official history of the ATS.
2. Ibid, Appendix VI.
3. Air Historical Branch [henceforward AHB]: WRAF/WAAF Miscellaneous papers, The WAAF in Balloon Command, not dated.
4. For a detailed description of this role, known as 'Operation Outward', *see* Hannah Roberts, *The WRNS in Wartime: The Women's Royal Naval Service 1917–45* (London: I.B. Tauris, electronic book, 2018), Chapter 6.
5. Beryl E Escott, *The Heroines of SOE F Section: Britain's Secret Women in France* (Stroud: The History Press, 2010). Escott's book gives brief biographies of 40 women who worked for F Section.
6. General Sir Frederick Pile, *Ack-Ack: Britain's Defence against Air Attack during the Second World War* (London: George G. Harrap, 1949), pp.193–4.
7. The Sexual Offences Act (1967) applied in England and Wales. It allowed consenting men, over the age of twenty-one and acting in private not public space, to engage in a same-sex relationship.
8. For example, Beryl E. Escott, *Women in Air Force Blue: The Story of Women in the Royal Air Force from 1918 to the Present Day* (Wellingborough, Northamptonshire: Patrick Stephens, 1989), Ursula Stuart Mason, *Britannia's Daughters: the Story of the WRNS* (Barnsley: Pen and Sword Books, 2011), Lucy Noakes, *Women in the British Army: War and the Gentle Sex, 1907–1948* (London and New York: Routledge, 2006), Jo Stanley, *Women and the Royal Navy* (London: I. B. Tauris, 2017), Roy

240

Terry, *Women in Khaki: the Story of the British Woman Soldier*, (London: Columbus Books, 1988), and Rachel Woodward and Trish Winter, *Sexing the Soldier: The Politics of Gender and the Contemporary British Army* (London and New York: Routledge, 2007).

9. www.icrc.org, Articles 22 & 24 to the First Geneva Convention 1949, accessed 16 Apr 2010.

10. For example, Christopher Dandeker and Mady Wechsler Segal, 'Gender Integration in Armed Forces: Recent Policy Developments in the United Kingdom', *Armed Forces & Society*, Vol.23, No.1, Fall 1996 pp.37–40 and Kate Muir, *Arms and the Woman* (Sevenoaks: Coronet Books – Hodder and Stoughton, 1993).

Chapter 2: *'Doubtful Wisdom'*

1. House of Commons Debates [henceforward HC Deb], 5th Ser., Vol. 423, Col.1338, 30 May 1946. The Women's Auxiliary Air Force existed from 1939 to January 1949. WRAF, the First World War title, was re-introduced on 1 February 1949.

2. Vera Laughton Mathews, *Blue Tapestry*. (London: Hollis & Carter, 1948), p.276.

3. The USA's 1948 legislation limited women to 2 per cent of the strength. Martin Binkin and Shirley J Bach, *Women and the Military*, (Washington D.C.: The Brookings Institution, 1977), pp.10–11. For Canada, *see* www.forces.gc.ca Newsroom Backgrounder 'Women in the Canadian Forces' (accessed 19 Mar 2009); for Australia, *see* www.defence.gov.au (accessed 22 Nov 2008).

4. Imperial War Museum, London [henceforward IWM]: Recruitment Poster, accession number PST 0759.

5. The National Archive, Kew [henceforward TNA]: ADM 167/127, A. V. Alexander, 4 Mar 1946.

6. Army statistics from Terry, *Women in Khaki*, p.83; WRNS data from M. H. Fletcher, *The WRNS: A History of the Women's Royal Naval Service* (Annapolis: Naval Institute Press, 1989), p.11; WRAF statistics from Escott, *Women in Air Force Blue*, p.295.

7. TNA: AIR 6/14 Air Council Minutes, 18 Mar 1919.

8. TNA: AIR 8/1741 Future of the WRAF, not dated but circa early 1919.

9. TNA: WO/33/3156, Report of the Women's Reserve Committee, 13 Dec 1920.

10. TNA: WO/32/10649, Minute, 7 Jun 1921.

11. J M Cowper, *The Auxiliary Territorial Service*, p.201.

12. National Museum of the Royal Navy, Portsmouth [henceforward NMRN]: 1988.350.18.47, *The Wren*, Feb 1960.

13. Cowper, *The Auxiliary Territorial Service*, p.7.

14. TNA: ADM 116/5102, Meeting with Judge Advocate General, 23 May 1940.

15. TNA: ADM 234/219, Women's Royal Naval Service 1939-45 (Official History), 1956, p.41.

16. Fletcher, *The WRNS*, pp.150-1. As in the RAF, work for officers was organised in branches. The word categories designated work of non-commissioned ranks; the RAF used trades.

17. TNA: ADM 234/219, Women's Royal Naval Service 1939–45 (Official History), 1956, pp.76–7 and p.84; Mathews, *Blue Tapestry*, p.202 and p.206.

18. Escott, *Women in Air Force Blue*, pp.298–9.

19. Royal Air Force Museum, Hendon [henceforward RAFM]: AP3234, *The Women's Auxiliary Air Force 1939–1945*, 1953, p.86.

20. Second Officer Archdale and thirty Wren ratings were evacuated from Singapore to Columbo on 3 Feb 1942 to escape from the Japanese forces. Fletcher, *The WRNS*, pp.41–2.

21. NMRN: 1988.350.1–5, BR1077 Regulations and Instructions for the WRNS, 1943.

22. RAFM: AP3234, *The Women's Auxiliary Air Force 1939–1945*, 1953, p.105.

23. Cowper, *The Auxiliary Territorial Service*, p.114 and Appendix VI.

24. Violet R Markham, *Return Passage, the Autobiography of Violet Markham, C.H.*, (London: Geoffrey Cumberlege, Oxford University Press, 1953), p.154 and p.225.

25. *Report of the Committee on Amenities and Welfare Conditions in the Three Women's Services*, Cmd. 6384, (London: HMSO, 1942), p.14.

26. TNA: CAB 66/38, Report of the Committee on the Women's Services, 24 Jun 1943.

27. Ibid.

28. Ibid.

29. HC Deb, 5th Ser., Vol.391, Col. 1072–1073, 22 Jul 1943.

30. TNA: AIR 2/7824, Committee on Manning the Post-War RAF – Sixth Interim Report, Dec 1944.

31. TNA: AIR 14/1009, Sandford to Secretary Royal Commission on Equal Pay, 5 Jun 1945.

32. TNA: AIR 2/7824, Future of the WAAF, Note to Air Council, 31 Jan 1945 and Post-War Planning Committee Conclusions, 7 Feb 1945.

33. TNA: AIR 2/7824, Future of the WAAF, Note for the Air Council, 20 Jun 1945.

34. TNA: AIR 6/75, Air Council Conclusions 7(45), 17 Jul 1945.
35. TNA: WO 32/13160, Brief for Secretary of State – Women's Services Post-War, 19 Feb 1944 and Army Committee on Post-War Problems, Minutes, 24 Feb 1944.
36. TNA: WO 163/97, Provision of a Permanent Regular Women's Service as Part of the Post-War Army, 4 Aug 1945.
37. Ibid, Executive Committee of the Army Council, Minutes, 10 Aug 1945.
38. TNA: AIR 6/75, Air Council Conclusions, 2 Oct 1945.
39. Ibid.
40. TNA: ADM 1/18884, Statement for Royal Commission on Equal Pay, 3 Oct 1945.
41. TNA: ADM 167/124, Admiralty Board Minutes, 21 Dec 1945.
42. NMRN: 1988.350.57, Permanent Service, 28 Mar 1946.
43. TNA: AIR 6/82, Future of the WAAF AC3(46), 11 Jan 1946.
44. TNA: AIR 6/76, Air Council Conclusions, 15 Jan 1946.
45. TNA: WO 32/13160, Appendix A to PICB/P(46)3, 1 Apr 1946. The figure included in the final paper for the Cabinet was 8,000, Cabinet Paper DO(46)63, 8 May 1946.
46. TNA: ADM 167/127, Minute by Mr Alexander, 4 Mar 1946.
47. Ibid., Minute by Mr Dunn, 7 Mar 1946.
48. TNA: PREM 8/835, Ismay to Prime Minister, 26 Mar 1946.
49. Ibid. and CAB 131/1, Cabinet Defence Committee Conclusions, 27 Mar 1946.
50. TNA: ADM 116/5725, Signal, First Lord to Sir Henry Markham, 17 Apr 1946.
51. Ibid., Signal, Sir Henry Markham to First Lord, 17 Apr 1946 and ADM 167/126, Board Minutes, 17 Apr 1946.
52. TNA: CAB 131/2, Organisation of the Women's Services in Peace, 8 May 1946.
53. TNA: CAB 131/1, Cabinet Defence Committee Conclusions, 17 May 1946.

Chapter 3: No 'Little Olgas'

1. TNA: DEFE 7/559, Brief for Minister of Defence for Cabinet meeting on 9 Dec 1948.
2. Private papers of Dame Felicity Peake (née Hanbury) [henceforward Peake papers]: Box 3, Hanbury letter.
3. TNA: T 213/288, Monk-Jones (Air Ministry) to Clough (Treasury), 2 Nov 1948.
4. NMRN: 1988.350, BR1077 Regulations & Instructions for the WRNS, 1947, Chapter 1.
5. TNA: ADM 116/5102, Note by Sir Henry Markham, 15 Mar 1941, War Cabinet Conclusions 33(41), 31 Mar 1941 and Disciplinary Status of the WRNS, 8 Apr 1941.

6. Ibid., Minute by Director WRNS, 27 Jan 1944; Commander-in-Chief The Nore (13 Mar 1944). His letter was supported by: Commander-in-Chief Rosyth, Islands Command, Dover and Naval Air Stations. Plymouth, Portsmouth and Western Approaches opposed introducing the NDA; Minute by Second Sea Lord, 6 Jun 1944.
7. NMRN: 1988.350.57, Permanent Service, Head of Naval Law to DWRNS, 12 Jun 1946.
8. TNA: ADM 167/127, Admiralty Board – Disciplinary Status of the WRNS, 26 Sep 1946.
9. Ibid.
10. NMRN: 1988.350.57, Permanent Service, Head of Naval Law to DWRNS, 12 Jun 1946.
11. Ibid and TNA: ADM 167/127, Admiralty Board – Disciplinary Status of the WRNS, 26 Sep 1946.
12. TNA: AIR 30/281, King's Order, 10 Jan 1949.
13. TNA: ADM 167/129, Admiralty Board Minutes, 2 Jun 1947.
14. NMRN: 1988.350.28.1–4, Minutes of Conference, 18 Jul 1947.
15. TNA: ADM 1/21217, Commander-in-Chief Plymouth to Secretary of the Admiralty, 23 Sep 1948.
16. Ibid.
17. Ibid., Mr Samuel to Second Sea Lord, 1 Oct 1948.
18. TNA: WO 163/101, P(46)159 Regular Women's Service, 13 Dec 1946.
19. TNA: WO 163/299, P(46)10 Draft Interim Report, circa Sep 1946.
20. TNA: WO 163/101, P(46)159 Regular Women's Service, 13 Dec 1946.
21. National Army Museum, London [henceforward: NAM]: 1992-11-97-6, Women with the British Army, War Office, May 1956.
22. Gwynne-Vaughan, *Service with the Army*, p.137.
23. TNA: ADM 1/20316, Prime Minister's Personal Minute, 4 Nov 1946 and Titles of the Women's Services, 6 Mar 1947.
24. HC Deb, 5th Ser., Vol.435, Col.98, 17 Mar 1947. Parkin was speaking during the Air Estimates debate.
25. TNA: AIR 6/76, Air Council Meetings 6/47, 15 May 1947 and 10/47, 24 Jul 1947.
26. TNA: PREM 8/835, Alexander to Attlee, 19 Jan 1948, handwritten note by Clement Attlee, 10 Feb 1948 and Note to Prime Minister, 10 Feb 1948.
27. TNA: WO 32/12618, Title of the Regular Women's Service, correspondence and minutes, Feb 1947–Feb 1948.
28. Ibid, Army Council minutes, 6 Jan 1948.
29. Quoted in Roy Terry, *Women in Khaki,* p.173.
30. TNA: WO 32/13163, Army Council P(48)4, 15 Apr 1948.
31. Ibid, letter dated 20 March 1950.

32. TNA: AIR 6/77, Air Council Conclusions, 2 Sep 1948 and AIR 6/87, Air Council Paper – Rank Titles for Women Officers, 20 Jan 1950.

33. TNA: AIR 6/79, Air Council Conclusions, 26 Jan 50. Remaining WRAF rank titles were made the same as men's in 1968 (TNA: AIR 6/160, Air Council Conclusions, 22 Jan 1968).

34. TNA: AIR 6/87, Air Council Paper – Rank Titles for Women Officers, 20 Jan 1950.

35. TNA: AIR 6/79, Air Council Conclusions, 26 Jan 50.

36. TNA: ADM 116/5579, Minute by Director WRNS, 30 Jan 1947.

37. TNA: WO 32/13689, Hull to McCandlish, 14 Jun 1949.

38. TNA: WO 32/13173, correspondence, Apr 1948–Nov 1948 including Tyrwhitt to Adjutant General, 22 Apr 1948.

39. TNA: AIR 24/1645, Minute to AMP, Appendix 10 to Operations Record Book, 24 Nov 1941.

40. TNA: ADM 167/118, WRNS Disciplinary Status, 10 Feb 1943.

41. TNA: WO 32/13173, Minute to Brigadier AG Co-ord, 28 May 1948 and Minutes of Meeting on Defensive Role of WRAC in War, 8 Nov 1948.

42. TNA: WO 32/13160, Secretary of State Air to Secretary of State War, 31 Mar 1947. This letter was in the context of women officers' authority under disciplinary codes being adopted for regular service.

43. TNA: AIR 20/6531, Future of the RAF Regiment, 1 Dec 1945 and AIR 6/80, Air Council Conclusions, Apr 1951.

44. TNA: AIR 10/5614, Queen's Regulation number 877.

45. TNA: WO 32/13155, Brief on Powers of Command, 3 Nov 1959.

46. TNA: AIR 8/793, Leigh-Mallory to Under Secretary of State for Air and Chief of Air Staff, 3 Jan 1944.

47. TNA: AIR 19/331, Sinclair to Stafford Cripps, 13 Dec 1943 and correspondence between Secretary of State's office and Air Marshals Portal, Sutton and Courtney Dec 1943–Feb 1944.

48. Ibid.

49. TNA: T 162/741, Admiralty to Treasury, 9 Mar 1943 and Air Ministry response, 8 Jun 1943.

50. TNA: AIR 14/1009, Third Interim Report of the Substitution Committee, Nov 1942.

51. Anne Mettam, 'The Flying Nightingales' in A E Ross (ed.), *Through Eyes of Blue: Personal Memories of the RAF from 1918,* (Shrewsbury: Airlife Publishing, 2002), pp.164–7.

52. Recollections of female mechanics in Escott, *Women in Air Force Blue,* pp.173–176.

53. HC Deb, 5th Series, Vol.435, Col.106, 17 Mar 1947. He was speaking during the debate on the Air Estimates.

54. TNA: AIR 8/793, Flying Employment for Members of the Permanent Women's Service, Jun 1947, and Air Council Standing Committee Minutes, Jun 1947; Peter Elliott, 'The RAF's First Women Pilots', *Air Clues*, May 1990, pp. 170–174. *Air Clues* is a professional journal for the RAF.

55. Peter Elliott, 'The RAF's First Women Pilots', *Air Clues*, p.172.

56. TNA: AIR 20/8985, McGlennon to Private Secretary to Air Member for Personnel, 24 Sep 1952 and Brief for Auxiliary and Reserve Forces Committee Meeting, 30 Nov 1953.

57. TNA: AIR 6/90, Air Council Standing Committee Conclusions, 11 Oct 1946.

58. TNA: AIR 6/136, Air Council Standing Committee Memoranda, Pilot and Navigator Training, Aug 1946 and AIR 6/90, Air Council Standing Committee Conclusions, 4 Sep 1946. There were three further stages (applied training, crew training and operational conversion unit) before pilots reached operational squadrons.

59. TNA: AIR 8/1591, Sandford to Sir Maurice Dean (MOD), 3 Jul 1950.

60. HC Deb, 5th Ser., Vol.387, Col.769–770, 10 Mar 1943.

61. TNA: WO 32/13160, Cabinet Defence Committee Paper DO(46)63, Organisation of the Women's Services in Peace, 8 May 1946.

62. TNA: WO 163/101, P(46)159, Regular Women's Service, 13 Dec 1946 and ECAC Minutes, 20 Dec 1946.

63. TNA: WO 32/13160, P(47)62, Regular Women's Service, 7 May 1947 and Minutes of the ECAC, 16 May 1947.

64. TNA: WO 32/12613, ECAC Minutes, 20 Dec 1946.

65. TNA: ADM 167/126, Admiralty Board Minutes, 14 Oct 1946.

66. TNA: WO 163/325, PWS(47)6, Permanent Women's Services: Comparative Statement of Schemes, 19 Nov 1947.

67. NMRN: 1988.350.57, Permanent Service (305B), AFO 6356a/46, WRNS Ratings Allocation for December 1946, 18 Oct 46.

68. According to naval historian Eric Grove, the Fleet Air Arm employed 24,000 men in shore establishments in 1947. Eric J. Grove, *Vanguard to Trident: British Naval Policy since World War II* (London: Bodley Head, 1987), p.27.

69. TNA: ADM 1/19887, Naval Air Personnel Committee Report, Feb 1946.

70. NMRN: 1988.350.1–5, Structure and Conditions of Service for the Permanent WRNS: Ratings' Paper, Jul 1947 and BR 1077(47) Regulations and Instructions WRNS, Appendices 3 and 4, 31 Dec 1947.

71. NMRN: 1988.350.58–9, Director WRNS to Assistant Chief of Naval Personnel, 30 May 1946, Permanent WRNS Officer Force, 20 Aug 1946 and Minutes of Meeting, 23 Aug 1946.

72. TNA: WO 32/13160, Structure and Conditions of Service for the Permanent WRNS Officer Corps, Oct 1946.

73. TNA: AIR 19/808, Air Member for Personnel to Secretary of State, 5 Jan 1949; AIR 2/10626, Report of the Trade Structure Committee, Part I, Mar 1949.

74. TNA: AIR 2/10237, Meeting on the Field of Trades Open to WAAF, 21 Oct 1948.

75. TNA: AIR 20/6538, S11 to DWAAF, 5 Mar 1947. Apprentices were aged 15½ to 17 on entry. Women could not join until they were 17½ to 18.

76. Ibid, Employment of WAAF Officers in the Technical Branch, Apr 1947. The technical branch included engineering, signals and armaments. Of approximately 417 female officers employed in signals during the war, the vast majority were part of the administration and special duties branch. Only about 45 were commissioned in the technical branch.

77. TNA: WO 32/13160, Comparative Statement of Draft Schemes 16 Aug 1947.

78. TNA: WO 163/325, PWS(47)6, Permanent Women's Services: Comparative Statement of Schemes, 19 Nov 1947.

Chapter 4: 'They Are After All Women'

1. NMRN: 1988.350.28, letter dated 3 Jun 1948.

2. Ibid., Senior WRNS Officer Portsmouth to DWRNS, 21 Jun 1948.

3. RAFM: X002.5638,Woodhead/Welsh Papers, Constance Woodhead, unpublished manuscript, Ch.XIII, pp.7–8.

4. Helen Gwynne-Vaughan, *Service with the Army*, p.94.

5. Lesley Thomas, 'Mathews, Dame Elvira Sibyl Maria Laughton (1888–1959)', Oxford Dictionary of National Biography [henceforward ODNB].

6. Mathews, *Blue Tapestry*, p.53.

7. It was not until 1941 that it became policy to accept mothers with school-age children. TNA: T 162/688, Notes of a meeting, 23 Jan 1941.

8. ODNB: Lesley Thomas, 'Woollcombe, Dame Jocelyn May (1898–1986)'.

9. Molly Izzard, *A Heroine in Her Time: a Life of Dame Helen Gwynne-Vaughan 1879–1967*, (London: Macmillan, 1969), p.342.

10. Gwynne-Vaughan, *Service with the Army*, p.149.

11. J M Cowper, *The Auxiliary Territorial Service*, (The War Office, 1949), p.42.

12. TNA: WO 32/10038, Adjutant General to Permanent under Secretary, 26 Jul 1941.

13. TNA: WO 138/68, undated memorandum.

14. ODNB: Roy Terry, 'Dame Leslie Violet Lucy Evelyn Whateley'.

15. TNA: WO 138/68, Whateley to Adjutant General, Feb 1946.

16. ODNB: Tessa Stone, 'Forbes, Dame (Katherine) Jane Trefusis (1899–1971)'.

17. RAFM: AC 72/17 Box 3, handwritten note by Trefusis-Forbes, 3 Nov 1942.
18. Christ Church, Oxford [henceforward ChCh]: Portal Papers, Box C, File 4, Minute from AMP to Secretary of State, 3 Sep 1943. Trefusis-Forbes left the Service after completing tours to Canada, the USA and India. She regretted not being involved in the establishment of regular service and offered her services again in 1948 during the crisis over Berlin. Her offer was declined. RAFM: AC 72/17/3 Box 2, letter from Air Ministry to Trefusis-Forbes, 19 Jul 1948.
19. ChCh: Portal Papers, Box D, File 5, AMP to CAS, 9 Jun 1943.
20. TNA: AIR 6/62, Air Council Memoranda, WAAF Administration, 16 Oct 1942.
21. ChCh: Portal Papers, Box D, File 5, Freeman to Portal, 11 Jun 1943.
22. Peake Papers: Box 6, Record of Service.
23. ChCh: Portal Papers, Box C, File 4, Freeman to Portal, 5 Sep 1943.
24. ChCh: Portal Papers, Box C, File 3, CAS to Secretary of State, 16 Sep 1943.
25. Ibid.
26. ChCh: Portal Papers, Box D, File 3, correspondence between Freeman and Portal, Mar and Apr 1944; Box C, File 6, papers on the case against Hanbury, May 1944 and Portal to AMP May and Jun 1944.
27. RAFM: C. G. Burge (ed.), 'White Paper on Post-War Pay, Allowances and Service Pensions and Gratuities for Members of the Forces below Officer Rank' and Post-War Code of Pay, Allowances, Retired Pay and Service Gratuities for Commissioned Officers', *Royal Air Force Quarterly,* Vol.17, 1945–46, pp.111–16 and 177–79. Pre-war qualifying ages were: junior ranks 25 (RN), 26 (Army and RAF); officers age 30.
28. TNA: ADM 116/5579, Minute by DWRNS, 31 Mar 1947.
29. TNA: AIR 6/76, Air Council Conclusions, 13 Feb 1947.
30. TNA: AIR 2/12605, Minute to Secretary of State, 20 Aug 1948.
31. TNA: T 213/305, Interdepartmental Committee on Post-war Pay, Allowances and Pensions, Minutes, 27 Jul 1948, Minute to Secretary of State, 20 Aug 1948 and Minute by Secretary of State, 1 Sep [1948].
32. TNA: ADM 116/5723, Minute by Dunn, 13 Sep 1948 and Minutes of Service Ministers' Meeting, 24 Sep 1948.
33. TNA: T 213/489, Pay of the Women's Services, record of discussion between Chancellor and Treasury officials, 6 Aug 1948 and Cripps to Alexander, 8 Sep 48.
34. TNA: AIR 6/76, Air Council Conclusions, 30 Apr 1947.
35. TNA: T 213/489, Pay of the Women's Services, record of discussion between Chancellor and Treasury officials, 6 Aug 1948 and Cripps to Alexander, 8 Sep 48.

36. Ibid, Remuneration of the Permanent Women's Services – Draft Cabinet Paper, Aug 1948. Treasury officials recognised RAF tradesmen as being employed 'behind the fighting line' and Royal Army Pay Corps men as being employed in non-combatant duties.

37. *Royal Commission on Equal Pay 1944–46 Report*, Cmd. 6937, (London: HMSO, 28 October 1946), p.17. The Commission questioned the 'reality' of this liability.

38. David French, *Military Identities: The Regimental System, the British Army, and the British People, C.1870–2000* (Oxford: Oxford University Press, 2005), p.314.

39. TNA: T 213/489, Clough to Padmore, 23 Jul 1948 and Alexander to Cripps, 22 Oct 1948.

40. Ibid, Pay of the Women's Services, 6 Aug 1948, Clough to Padmore, 25 Aug 1948 and Remuneration of the Permanent Women's Services – Draft Cabinet Paper, Aug 1948.

41. TNA: T 213/489, Freeman to Cripps, 29 Sep 1948.

42. TNA: T 213/489, Haslett to Cripps 20 Oct 1948 and 28 Oct 1948.

43. Institute of Engineering and Technology: NAEST 33/14.3, Haslett to Lady Cripps, 6 Dec 1948.

44. TNA: T 213/490, Handwritten Note on Brief on Pay, Pensions and Retiring Gratuities, initialled by Cripps 3 Dec 1948.

45. TNA: CAB 129/31, Rates of Pay, Pensions and Gratuities for the Permanent Women's Forces, Cabinet Papers (48)295 (Ministry of Defence) and (48)296 (Treasury), 7 Dec 1948.

46. TNA: CAB 195/6, Sir Norman Brook's Diaries, 9 Dec 1948.

47. TNA: CAB 128/13, Cabinet Meeting Conclusions, 9 Dec 1948.

48. TNA: T 213/69, Notes to Text of Parliamentary Reply on Pay for Women's Services for Minister of Defence, 14 Dec 1948.

49. TNA: T 213/489, Minute to Sir Edward Bridges, 23 Jul 1948.

50. TNA: DEFE 7/559, Minutes of Service Ministers Meeting, 30 Nov 1948.

51. TNA: T 213/489, Retired Pay, Pensions and Gratuities, Post-War Pension Code Paper (48)2, 1948.

52. TNA: T 213/479, Notes, 12 Mar 1947 and Curtis to Sandford, 17 Mar 1947.

53. TNA: T 213/489, Retired Pay, Pensions and Gratuities for Officers and Other Ranks of the Permanent Women's Services, PWPC(48)2, 1948 and Notes on Revised Scales of Pay for the Permanent Women's Services, 25 Aug 1948.

54. TNA: CAB 129/31, Rates of Pay, Pensions and Gratuities for the Permanent Women's Forces, CP(48) 296, 7 Dec 1948.

55. TNA: CAB 195/6, Sir Norman Brook's Diaries, 9 Dec 1948.

56. TNA: T 162/741, Correspondence between Humphrey-Davies and Le Maitre, 17 May 1940 and 21 May 1940.

57. TNA: T 213/305, correspondence from Apr 1949 concluding with a handwritten note by Chancellor, 19 May 1950.

58. AHB: WAAF/WRAF Directorate Files, Box 3, DWRAF 213, Equal Pay, Minute by Campbell, 24 May 1950.

59. TNA: T 162/688, Notes of a meeting, 23 Jan 1941.

60. A survey of employers (local government, banks, railway companies, an airline, the BBC, and five large manufacturers), that had pre-war marriage bars but employed married women during the war, showed that those that had decided a post-war policy mostly intended to re-introduce a marriage bar. *Marriage Bar in the Civil Service*, Cmd. 6886, (London: HMSO, 1946), pp.19–22.

61. TNA: AIR 2/7824, Committee on Policy for Manning Post-War RAF, meetings 14 Apr 1944 and 3 Nov 1944, 6th Interim Report, Dec 1944.

62. TNA: AIR 6/76, Air Council Conclusions, 13 Feb 1947.

63. TNA: AIR 2/7824, Conditions of Service and Emoluments of Women Employed in the RAF, Apr 1947.

64. TNA: AIR 2/9278, WAAF Liability for Overseas Service, Air Member for Personnel, 22 Jul 1947 and Henderson to Alexander, 22 Nov 1947. The period of national service was expected to be 12 months. It was increased to 18 months and, due to the outbreak of the Korean War in 1950, it became 2 years.

65. TNA: AIR 6/76, Air Council Conclusions, 24 Jul 1947.

66. NMRN: 1988.350.58–9, Notes of a Meeting, 19 Jun 1946 and Director WRNS to Secretary to Second Sea Lord, 30 Sep 1946.

67. TNA: WO 163/299, Minutes of the Regular Women's Service Committee, 12 Sep 1946 and WO 163/325, Inter-Service Working Party, minutes 29 Aug 1947.

68. Peake, Felicity, *Pure Chance* (Shrewsbury: Airlife Publishing, 1993), p.172.

69. TNA: AIR 19/808, AMP to Commanders in Chief, 24 Jun 1950. The earlier letter (Air Marshal Sir John Slessor, May 1945) was written when there was concern about an increase in pregnancy in single women.

70. Research covering a 2.5 year period to June 1949 recorded 318 discharges of unmarried, pregnant airwomen (TNA: AIR 32/298, WRAF Wastage by Marriage and Pregnancy, Sep 1949).

71. NMRN: 1988.350.28, Notes from Conference of Senior Women Officers, 25 Oct 1949.

72. TNA: WO 163/101, ECAC Minutes, 20 Dec 1946.

73. TNA: WO 32/13160, The Position of the Pregnant Officer, 29 Jan 1947.
74. Ibid, ECAC Minutes.

Chapter 5: *Early Years of Regular Service*

1. From a speech at the Association of Wrens Annual Meeting, May 1947 (NMRN: 1988.350.18.5, *The Wren*, No.177, Oct 1947).
2. TNA: CAB 131/2, Cabinet Defence Committee paper DO(46)63, 8 May 1946.
3. David French, *Army, Empire, and Cold War: the British Army and Military Policy, 1945–1971* (Oxford: Oxford University Press, 2012), p.156.
4. *Defence: Outline of Future Policy*, Cmnd. 124, (London: HMSO, April 1957).
5. Air Commodore Joan Hopkins, May 2009.
6. Commandant Anthea Larken (née Savill), Mar 2010.
7. TNA: INF 12/72, meeting 48(6), Jul 1948.
8. TNA: INF 2/89, Advertisements 1952–3 campaign.
9. TNA: INF 2/75, Advertisements 1947–1951.
10. TNA: INF 2/86, Advertisement 1952.
11. TNA: AIR 19/808, WRAF Policy, Booklet 'Your daughter and the WRAF'.
12. TNA: AIR 77/421, Report on WRAF Recruiting, Jan 1950; AIR 32/400, Characteristics of WRAF Recruits, Jul 1951; AHB: WRAF Files Box 3 Hist/21, The 1958 Internal recruiting Survey (WRAF), Apr 1958.
13. TNA: WO 163/380, Committee on the WRAC – Report, Jul 1952.
14. Ibid.
15. TNA: WO 32/13160, papers on Future of the Women's Services, Mar 1945 – Aug 1947 and Comparative Statement of Draft Schemes, Aug 1947.
16. *Annual Abstract of Statistics*, No. 103, (London: HMSO, 1966), Table 13; David Coleman, 'Population and Family', in A.H. Halsey and Josephine Webb (eds.), *Twentieth-Century British Social Trends* (Basingstoke: Macmillan, 2000), p.43.
17. TNA: WO 123/471, Army Orders – Supplementary, Feb 1949.
18. NMRN: 1988.350.1–5, BR1077 Regulations and Instructions for the WRNS, 1951.
19. TNA: AIR 10/5614, Queen's Regulations 334 and 564, 1956.
20. *Report of the Advisory Committee on Recruiting*, Cmnd. 545, (London: HMSO, October 1958), p.15.
21. Quotes from NMRN: 1988.350.28.5, Letter to Director WRNS, 20 Jul 1960.
22. Quotes from TNA: AIR 2/15707, WRAF Recruiting Advisory Panel, 1(59), 10 Dec 1959 & Minutes of Officer and Aircrew Manning Committee

Working Party, 24 Feb 1960. This committee was not responsible for non-commissioned ranks. The extent of collocation for airwomen was unlikely to be better than for officers as fewer RAF stations accepted non-commissioned women.

23. NMRN: 1988.350.28.1–4, Conference of Senior WRNS officers March 1952, Manning State; NAM: 1997-10-153, Director WRAC's Liaison Letter, Sep 1955; TNA: AIR 19/808, Proposed Policy and Conditions of Service for an Immobile Section of the WRAF, 25 Jul 1957.

24. TNA: DEFE 7/592, Report of Inter-Service Working Party on Size and Shape of the Armed Forces, 28 Feb 1949 (Harwood Report).

25. TNA: ADM 167/132, Board Minutes, 12 Apr 1949.

26. Ursula Stuart Mason, *Britannia's Daughters: the Story of the WRNS* (Barnsley: Pen and Sword Books, 2011), pp.101–2.

27. Ibid, p.102.

28. M. H. Fletcher, *The WRNS: A History of the Women's Royal Naval Service* (Annapolis: Naval Institute Press, 1989), pp.100–103.

29. TNA: WO 163/380, Minutes of the Committee on the WRAC, 26 May 1952.

30. TNA: WO 163/59, Organisation of the WRAC, 25 Mar 1952.

31. TNA: WO 32/16814, WRAC in the Long term Army, 27 Jun 1958.

32. Ibid, Employment of WRAC in 'Y' Services, 9 Dec 1959.

33. Ibid, Letter to Deputy Chief of the Imperial General Staff, 9 Mar 1960.

34. TNA: WO 163/59, Army Council Minutes, 11 Sep 1952.

35. TNA: AIR 6/129, Progress and Problems of the WRAF Local Service Scheme, Air Council Paper AC(60)48, 9 Sep 60.

36. TNA: AIR 2/15789, Extract from Air Council Conclusions, 5 Oct 1960 & Normal and Local Service - WRAF Future Policy, 26 Apr 1962.

37. Air Commodore R. M. B. Montague, 'Women in the RAF', in Tony Ross (ed.), *75 Eventful Years: A Tribute to the Royal Air Force* (London: Lockturn, 1993), p.226. Jurby was used for male officer candidates who did not qualify for the elite cadetship at RAF College Cranwell.

38. Peake Papers: Box 3, Minutes of WRAF Officers' Conference, 12 May 1950. The War Office approved Staff College places for women in October 1959, a move not copied for the WRNS until the 1970s.

39. British Library Sound Archive: C465/03/06 (F1894), Air Commandant Jean Conan Doyle, interviewed by Cathy Courtney, 24 Jul 1991 and *Air Force List*, (London: HMSO, 1954 and 1955 editions).

40. TNA: AIR 2/16595, Future Location of the WRAF Depot, 29 Oct 1963.

41. AHB: WRAF Directorate Files, Box 1, DWRAF/Hist/102, Disestablishment of WRAF Posts in Operational Units 2nd TAF, 14 Jun 1952.

42. Ibid, Foster to Air Ministry, 21 Mar 1952.

43. Ibid, Minute 26 Jan 1952.

44. TNA: AIR 19/808, Air Member for Personnel to Under Secretary of State, 25 Nov 1955.

45. AHB: WRAF Directorate Files, Box 1, DWRAF/Hist/102, letter 2nd TAF to Air Ministry, 27 Aug 1955.

46. TNA: AIR 19/808, Air Member for Personnel to Under Secretary of State, 25 Nov 1955.

47. The trade was later re-named air loadmaster.

48. Crew members received a pay supplement for flying as distinct from flying pay which was payable as an addition to pay whether the person was on flying duties or not. Flying badges are more commonly known as brevets. TNA: AIR 2/11672, AQMs, Note by Transport Command, 8 Apr 1960. There were 12 pence to the shilling and 20 shillings to the pound. When decimal coinage was introduced, a shilling became 5p.

49. Private papers of Vera Beale, by kind permission of her stepson Mr Tony Ranson.

50. TNA: AIR 2/15813, Minutes of a meeting to consider the recruitment of AQMs, 8 Oct 1957.

51. Ibid.

52. Sgt Celia Watkins (later Reed), 7 Dec 2015.

53. TNA: AIR 2/15707, Status and Conditions of Service of Air Quartermasters, Sep 1960.

54. TNA: AIR 2/15501, Dutt (Manning 3) to Director of Manning 1, 19 May 1960.

55. TNA: AIR 6/131 Air Council Meeting 4(61) Conclusions, Paper AC(61)12 – New Conditions of Service for Air Quartermasters, 23 Feb 1961.

56. TNA: AIR 2/15501, handwritten note, 4 Oct 1961; AIR 2/16376, S10(Air) to AUS(P)(Air), referring back to 1961, 3 May 1965; AIR 2/16320, Flying Duties as AQMs, Air Ministry Pamphlet, Sep 1962 and AIR 2/15789, DWRAF to DGPS, WRAF Shortage of NCOs, 18 Feb 1963.

57. WO 32/13160, Comparative Statement of Draft Schemes, 16 Aug 1947. Women were to be given the opportunity to join the Reserves but would not be compelled to do so.

58. TNA: ADM 116/5579, Notes of a Meeting, Conditions of Service for the WAAF, circa Jul 1947.

59. TNA: AIR 2/1158, Future Policy for Ground Branches and Trades in the RAF Volunteer Reserve, May 1952.

60. TNA: WO 32/13171, correspondence 1947–1951.

61. *Daily Express*, 9 Apr 1957, p.7.

62. HC Deb, 5th Ser., Vol.568, Col.2007, 17 Apr 1957.

63. TNA: DEFE 7/1918, H. L. Lawrence Wilson to Newling, 14 Mar 1957.

64. TNA: ADM 1/27371, Long Term Defence Policy – the 75 Fleet, paper for Vice Chief of Naval Staff, 17 Feb 1957.

65. TNA: DEFE 7/1177, Defence Expenditure 1956 – Memorandum by the Admiralty, 10 Oct 1956.

66. TNA: DEFE 7/1918, H. L. Lawrence Wilson to Chilver, 28 May 1957.

67. TNA: AIR 19/808, correspondence between MOD and Air Ministry Jul 1957.

68. TNA: DEFE 10/354, Further Interim Report of Ministerial Committee on Recruiting, DM/P(57)16, Defence Ministers Committee, 25 Jul 1957.

69. TNA: DEFE 10/354, Recruiting – Report by Defence Administration Committee, 26 Sep 1957.

70. *Report of the Advisory Committee on Recruiting*, Cmnd. 545, (London: HMSO, October 1958), Appendix A, [henceforward Grigg Report].

71. Grigg Report, p.46.

72. Ibid, p.47.

73. *Recruiting: Government Comments on Report of the Advisory Committee on Recruiting (Cmnd. 545)*, Cmnd. 570, (London: HMSO, November 1958). 'Manpower' here intended to mean men and women.

74. Grigg Report, p.45.

75. Ibid, all quotes from p.44.

76. HC Deb, 5th Ser., Vol.703, Col.28, 30 Nov 1964.

Chapter 6: A Right to be Different?

1. *Daily Mail*, 14 Nov 1979. Women were about 6 per cent of the total US Army strength. However, as they were excluded from fighting units, they were closer to 30 per cent of the strength of support units.

2. Although new roles were opened to women, postings remained restricted. Combat posts were for men; women were assigned to what were described as non-combatant posts. Major General Jeanne Holm, *Women in the Military: an Unfinished Revolution* (Novato, Ca: Presidio, 1992 edition), pp.289–304, 317–21, and 337–45.

3. Ibid, p.151.

4. TNA: DEFE 10/1250, Sex Equality in the Armed Forces, Sep 1978. Portugal, Greece, Italy, Luxembourg and Iceland did not employ servicewomen. The paper noted that Belgium had only recently started to include women and their status was not covered. West Germany only employed women as medics. The Dutch were in the process of removing the right to leave on marriage.

5. TNA: DEFE 10/1250, Sex Equality in the Armed Forces, Sep 1978. This was a joint Services committee. Membership included the senior personnel officers: Second Sea Lord for the RN, Adjutant General for the Army and Air Member for Personnel for the RAF.

6. Ibid and DEFE 10/1249, PPO Minutes, 15 Nov 1978.

7. TNA: DEFE 49/19, Mr Taylor to Deputy Under-Secretary, 3 Dec 1968.

8. TNA: DEFE 49/19, Family Planning, Policy Letter 17/67, 17 Jul 1967.

9. Ibid, Chief Officer Mary Talbot, National Health Service (Family Planning) Act 1967, 9 Oct 1968 and Chief Officer Talbot 28 Mar 1969, Annex to Report for PPO Committee, National Health Service (Family Planning) Act 1967, 22 May 1969.

10. Ibid, Chaplain of the Fleet, 16 Jun 1969, Principal Chaplain Church of Scotland and Free Churches (Naval), 16 Jun 1969, Principal Roman Catholic Chaplain, (Naval), 12 Jun 1969.

11. TNA: DEFE 49/19, Principal Personnel Officers' Minutes, 2 Jul 1969.

12. Ibid, Hattersley to Second Sea Lord, 3 Nov 1969.

13. Ibid, Guidance to Service Medical Officers on Family Planning, 14 Nov 1969.

14. TNA: DEFE 71/50, Abortion Act 1967, Policy letter 12/69, 16 Dec 1969.

15. TNA: AIR 10/5614, Queen's Regulations, 4th edition, regulations 629 and 630; DEFE 71/50, Termination of Pregnancy, Deputy Director WRAF, 19 Jan 1977 and Abortions for Servicewomen, Mr Stevens, 14 Sep 1977.

16. AHB: WRAF Directorate Files Box 2, Senior Women Officers' Conferences, 13th meeting, Nov 1970.

17. TNA: DEFE 71/50, Pregnancy in WRAF Personnel, Soutar to MOD, Dec 1976.

18. Ibid.

19. Ibid, Abortions for Servicewomen, T M P Stevens, 14 Sep 1977 and draft revised regulations, 23 Sep 1977.

20. AHB: WRAF Directorate Files Box 2, WRAF 164 Part III – Medical Policy, Sex Education, 13 Aug 1968.

21. Ibid and Report on Family Planning, 21 May 1968 and notes of a meeting, 23 Sep 1968.

22. NMRN: 1988.350.28, Senior Women Officers Conference, 1974.

23. Ibid.

24. TNA: BA 19/515, Unmarried Mothers, 27 Jul 1970.

25. Parliamentary Archive, London [henceforward PA]: HL/PO/PU/4/213, Employment Protection Act 1975, clause 34.

26. TNA: DEFE 71/50, Deputy Director WRAF to S10(Air), 16 Dec 1974.

27. AHB: WRAF Directorate Files Box 1, AF/5762/72 Part II, Deputy Director to S10, Jan 1976.

28. NAM: 1998–11–54, WRAC Conferences, Mar 1977 and Feb 1979.

29. AHB: WRAF Directorate Files Box 2, WRAF Conference, 1975.

30. AHB: WRAF Directorate Files Box 2, DWRAF 25, Re-entry of Officers, correspondence 1968. Subsequent career traced in *Air Force Lists*. Her name last appeared in 1970.

31. TNA: DEFE 47/36, Brief for Secretary of State, Mar 1970. The Merchant Navy was also excluded from the terms of the Act if personnel were serving in UK-registered ships.

32. TNA: AIR 2/13859, Unnatural Relationships Between Women, *circa* 1960.

33. Ibid.

34. Ibid.

35. TNA: DEFE 24/1318, Homosexuality in the Armed Forces, 26 Feb 1980.

36. TNA: AIR 2/18644, Air Commodore Marshall (DWRAF) to Air Officer Commanding Training Command, 25 Oct 1971.

37. TNA: DEFE 47/36, Army, RN and RAF instructions, 29 Jan 1968, 16 May 1969 and Dec 1970; AIR 2/18644, Disposal of Cases of WRAF Personnel Who Have Unnatural or Abnormal Sexual Tendencies, 3 Dec 1971.

38. Commandant Anne Spencer, 12 Jan 2011.

39. TNA: DEFE 24/1318, correspondence, 1979 to 1980.

40. Lesley Merryfinch, *Spare Rib*, No.104, Mar 1981. The article was written in the context of rumours of conscription for women in some NATO countries and weapons training for women in the British Army.

41. Jan Parker, *Spare Rib,* No.119, Jun 1982, 'What the Women's Army is Really Like – from the inside'.

42. Ibid.

43. Ibid.

44. TNA: DEFE 49/1, Press Conference, 16 Jun 1969.

45. *Annual Abstract of Statistics*, Table 152, Vol.103, 1966 and *Service Pay and Pensions*, Cmnd. 2903, Feb 1966.

46. The Ministry of Defence subsumed the Admiralty, War Office and Air Ministry in a 1964 reorganisation.

47. *Standing Reference on the Pay of the Armed Forces Third Report*, Cmnd. 4291 (London: HMSO, 1970).

48. TNA: DEFE 10/1207, Draft Evidence to Armed Forces Pay Review Body, 1 Nov 1977.

49. *Standing Reference on the Pay of the Armed Forces Third Report*, Cmnd. 4291 (London: HMSO, 1970).

50. PA: HL/PO/PU/4/199, Equal Pay Act (1970), Clause 7.

51. *Armed Forces Pay Review Body (AFPRB) Fourth Report*, Cmnd. 6063, (London: HMSO, 1975).

52. NAM: 1192-11-98, liaison letter 34, Mar 1973 and 1998-11-54, Annual Conference, 1975.

53. AHB: WRAF Directorate Files Box 1, AF/5762/72 Part I, Draft Paper on MOD position, 16 Oct 1972.

54. PA: HL/PO/PU/4/212, Sex Discrimination Act 1975, clause 85.

55. TNA: DEFE 71/309, S10 to staff, 9 Jul 1975.

56. Ibid, S10 to Air Force Department, 3 Nov 1975.

57. Women married before joining were not entitled to leave under these regulations unless they could prove material change of circumstances.

58. TNA: DEFE 71/309, S10 to Air Force Department, 3 Nov 1975 and S10 to DS14, Mar 1976.

59. AHB: WRAF Directorate Files, Box 1, AF/5762/72 Part I, Record of Meeting, March 1975 and Wing Commander Weighall to S10, 14 Aug 1974.

60. AHB: WRAF Directorate Files, Box 1, AF/5762/72 Part II, Director WRAC, Jun 1975 and correspondence Aug–Oct 1975.

61. TNA: DEFE 70/24, Mr Howell (Head of Naval Personnel Division 2), 30 Nov 1977.

62. Ibid, correspondence Nov–Dec 1977.

63. TNA: DEFE 10/1250, Sex Equality in the Armed Forces, Sep 1978 and DEFE 10/1249, PPO Minutes, 15 Nov 1978.

64. Liddell Hart Archive, King's College London [henceforward LHA]: Meechie Papers. *The Lioness*, No.2 1980, pp.44–5.

65. TNA: DEFE 71/309, Sex Equality in the Armed Forces, S10(Air) to DS 14, 18 Oct 1977.

Chapter 7: Combatant Status

1. Quoted in Roy Terry, *Women in Khaki: the Story of the British Woman Soldier*, (London: Columbus Books, 1988), p.216.

2. TNA: DEFE 69/1366, Brief for Second Sea Lord, 3 Aug 1973. Despite this theoretical ceiling, actual trained strength in 1973 was 265 officers and 2,380 ratings.

3. Ibid.

4. Ibid, correspondence Sep – Dec 1973.

5. TNA: ADM 105/99, WRNS Study Group Report, Nov 1974.

6. TNA: ADM 167/178, Admiralty Board Minutes, 13 Feb 1975.

7. TNA: ADM 105/99, WRNS Study Group Report, Nov 1974.

8. TNA: ADM 167/178, Admiralty Board Minutes, 13 Feb 1975 and 3 Mar 1975.

9. NMRN: 1988.350.28.20, Minutes of Conference, 27 Oct 75.

10. NMRN: *Naval Review*, 'View from the Nest', by 'Snapdragon', 75th Anniversary issue, 1988, p.38.

11. Commander Jackie Mulholland, 14 Nov 2011.

12. NMRN: 1988.350.28.23, Senior Women Officers' Conference, 20 Nov 1978.

13. www.icrc.org, Article 43 to Protocol I to the Geneva Convention of 12 August 1949, dated 8 Jun 1977, accessed 18 Jul 2007.

14. TNA: DEFE 24/1301, Brief for Secretary of State, Mar 1978.

15. NAM: 2004-09-157-1, Working Party Report, Nov 1976.

16. TNA: WO 163/756, Future Employment of the WRAC, 14 Jun 1977 and Army Board Minutes, 30 Jun 1977.

17. NAM: 1992-11-97-6, Women with the British Army, War Office, May 1956.

18. NAM: 1192-11-98-30 DWRAC Newsletter Jun 1980.

19. *Daily Mail*, 23 Feb 1972 and 12 Jun 1974.

20. Air Commodore Tamblin, 26 May 2009.

21. Ibid.

22. TNA: DEFE 71/226, Draft Air Force Board Paper, 6 Sep 1978.

23. Ibid.

24. TNA: AIR 2/10539, WRAF Commissions in the fighter control branch, 3 Nov 1950.

25. TNA: DEFE 71/31, Arming of WRAF Personnel, Mr West, 21 Apr 1978.

26. TNA: DEFE 71/226, Director of Security, 25 May 1978.

27. Ibid, Director Training (Ground), 2 Nov 1978.

28. TNA: DEFE 71/31, Arming of WRAF Personnel and Air Force Board Conclusions, 9 Nov 1978.

29. TNA: DEFE 71/31, Principal Personnel Officers' Committee Minutes, 13 Dec 1978.

30. Ibid, Draft Air Force Board Paper, 6 Sep 1978.

31. Freedom of Information [henceforward FOI] MOD: AB/P(79)13, Wider Employment of the WRAC, 16 Mar 1979 & TNA: WO 163/758 Army Board minutes, 30 Mar 1979.

32. FOI AHB: ID3/110/21, VCDS (Personnel & Logistics) to Secretary of State, 5 Jun 1980.

33. *Daily Mail*, 13 Mar 1979.

34. FOI AHB: ID3/110/21, VCDS (P&L) to Secretary of State, 5 Jun 1980.

35. Ibid, Arming of Servicewomen, McDonald to PS/Secretary of State, 4 Jul 1980.

36. Ibid, Note by AMP, 30 Sep 1983.

37. NAM: 1192-11-98, DWRAC News Bulletin, March 1982.

38. FOI MOD: Army Board P(79)13, Wider Employment of the WRAC, 16 Mar 1979 & TNA: WO 163/758, Army Board Minutes, 30 Mar 1979.

39. TNA: DEFE 70/1295, Brigadier Field 2 Dec 1981.

40. LHA: Meechie papers, Box 3, *The Lioness*, Vol. LXII, No.1, 1989.

41. TNA: DEFE 69/1556. File on arming of the WRNS.

42. TNA: DEFE 71/226, Arming of WRAF Personnel – X-Factor, 5 Jun 1979.

43. *AFPRB Eleventh Report*, Cmnd. 8549, (London: HMSO, 1982), p.8. The differential was justified on the grounds that other terms of service for women were more favourable than those of men.

44. Ibid, p.8.

45. TNA: DEFE 69/1366, DGNMT on draft terms of reference 9 Oct 1973.

46. Ibid. Talbot to DGNMT 12 Sep 1973.

47. TNA: ADM 105/99, WRNS Study Group Report, Nov 1974.

48. For example, Captain Read to Pritchard, 3 Feb 1976 (TNA: DEFE 69/689, Seagoing Service for WRNS).

49. TNA: ADM 105/99, WRNS Study Group Report, Nov 1974.

50. TNA: ADM 167/179, Admiralty Board Minutes, 1 Jul 1976.

51. Ibid. It took until 1981 to implement the decision.

52. Commandant Anthea Larken, 29 Mar 2010. Larken (née Savill) ran the final course at Greenwich and the first at Dartmouth in 1976.

53. TNA: DEFE 13/1342, Second Sea Lord to Under Secretary of State (Navy) 11 Aug 1976 and MOD News Release, No.36, 1976. Staff training prepared officers for work at MOD or Headquarters. Chief Officer Swallow and Major Meechie WRAC were the first military women to attend the National Defence College.

54. TNA: ADM: 167/178, Admiralty Board Minutes, 13 Feb 1975 and 5 Mar 1975; DEFE 13/1342, Second Sea Lord to Under Secretary of State (RN), 23 Jun 1976.

55. TNA: ADM 167/176, Admiralty Board Paper, 24 Feb 1975.

56. TNA: DEFE 69/689, Seagoing Opportunities for the WRNS, 10 Jun 1975.

57. Ibid.

58. TNA: DEFE 69/689, Minutes 7 Jul 1975 and Seagoing Opportunities for WRNS, 20 Dec 1977.

59. Ibid, Captain Read to Pritchard, 3 Feb 1976.

60. Ibid, Rear Admiral Janion to Pritchard, 11 Nov 1975.

61. Ibid, Minutes, 7 Jul 1975.

62. TNA: DEFE 13/1342, Second Sea Lord to Under Secretary of State (RN), 23 Jun 1976.

63. TNA: DEFE 69/689, Seagoing Opportunities for WRNS, 20 Dec 1977.

64. DEFE 69/1366, Minute 4 Jan 1978 and DGNPS 30 Jan 1978.

65. Ibid, and DUS (Navy) to Under Secretary of State (RN), 8 May 1978.

66. TNA: ADM 167/178, Admiralty Board Minutes, 5 Mar 1975.

67. TNA: DEFE 69/689, Seagoing Opportunities for the WRNS, Superintendent Sherriff, 28 Sep 1977.

68. NMRN: Judith Sherratt Collection, 2009.103.14, recording of a speech by Commandant McBride, 14 Oct 1978.

69. NMRN: 1988.350.28, Senior Women Officers' Conference, 5 Oct 1979.

70. Ibid, 27 Oct 1975 and 25 Oct 1976.

71. North Sea industries employed 400 helicopter pilots in 1980 compared with 206 in 1976 (FOI Fleet: Employment of Women as Pilots, Second Sea Lord, 12 Sep 80).

72. TNA: DEFE 69/689 AUS(NP) to Secretary to Second Sea Lord, 16 Feb 1978.

73. Ibid.

74. TNA: DEFE 69/1198, Capt Briggs to DNMP 13 Feb 1980.

75. FOI Fleet: Admiralty Board Sub-Committee Minutes, 25 Sep 1980.

76. TNA: DEFE 69/1198, Craig-McFeely, 4 Sep 1980.

77. NAM: 1998-11-54-3, WRAC Conference 1972.

78. TNA: WO 163/756, Future Employment of the WRAC, 14 Jun 1977 and Minutes, 6 Jul 1977.

79. FOI MOD: AB/P(79)13, Wider Employment of the WRAC, 16 Mar 1979. Officers with the Royal Signals could not progress beyond the rank of major due to the lack of field experience.

80. NAM: 1998-11-54-8, WRAC Conference 1978.

81. The paper did not give examples. However, there was a trend towards integration. Canada had disestablished separate corps. The USA had integrated Navy women (1973) and Air Force women (1976). It approved army integration in 1975, taking until 1978 to implement the decision. Norway's integration plans were also coming to fruition in 1977. The Netherlands still had separate women's corps and was studying integration. (TNA: AIR 2/19195, Minutes of NATO Women's Conference 1977).

82. TNA: WO 163/756, Future Employment of the WRAC, 14 Jun 1977.

83. Ibid and Minutes, 6 Jul 1977.

84. FOI MOD: Wider Employment of the WRAC, 16 Mar 1979.

85. NAM: 2001-05-593, Wider Employment of the WRAC, HQ BAOR to MOD, 18 Nov 1977.

86. FOI MOD: Wider Employment of the WRAC, 16 Mar 1979.

87. TNA: DEFE 70/149, Brigadier Thursby, 16 Oct 1972.

88. TNA: DEFE 70/148, Northern Ireland Headquarters to MOD, 5 Sep 1972.

89. Ibid, Heaney, 17 May 1973.

90. Ibid, UDR Women, 8 Aug 1973.

91. NAM: 2001-05-595, Recruitment of Women into the Infantry, 26 Sep 1973 and 6 Jun 1974.
92. NAM: 1998-11-54-7, Annual Conference, Mar 1977.
93. Ibid.
94. NAM: 1998-11-54-9, Annual Conference, Feb 1979.
95. Ian F. W. Beckett, *Territorials: a Century of Service*, (Plymouth: DRA Publishing, 2008), p.213.
96. NAM: 1192-11-98, Liaison Letters, Jun 1980 and Mar 1982.
97. Major General Robin Grist, 7 Oct 2015.
98. FOI AHB: ID3/92/32 Part 5, brief for Chief of Air Staff, 24 Aug 1977.
99. Ibid.
100. The Navy was the first American service to train female pilots. Six women were awarded wings in 1973. The Army followed in 1974. The US Air Force agreed to open some flying to women in 1975. Holm, *Women in the Military*, pp.317–21.
101. FOI AHB: V/9/962, Women Pilots in the RAF, 28 Sep 1978 and AMP, 22 Sep 1978.
102. Ibid, Women pilots in the RAF, AMP, 22 Sep 1978.
103. AHB: Sebastian Cox, *History of the University Air Squadrons*, quoting The Future of the University Air Squadron, AMP, 17 May 1971.
104. TNA: DEFE 71/379, Air Vice-Marshal Ness to S1ok(Air), 30 Nov 1977; Harcourt-Smith to Ness, 27 Jul 1978.
105. Ibid.
106. TNA: DEFE 24/1599, Female Volunteer Reserve Membership of UASs, Director General of Training, 13 Aug 1979.
107. TNA: DEFE 71/379, Head of Finance2(Air), 22 Aug 1979.
108. TNA: DEFE 24/1599, DS9 to DGT, 21 Aug 1979; DGPS to DGT, 17 Aug 1979.
109. TNA: DEFE 71/379, handwritten note on Women VR Membership, 2 Oct 1979.
110. C. G. Jefford, *Observers and Navigators: and Other Non-pilot Aircrew in the RFC, RNAS and RAF* (Shrewsbury: Airlife Publishing, 2001), p.216.
111. FOI AHB: ID3/900/36, Nimrod AEW Manning Policy, 1 Dec 1980.
112. Ibid, Borrett, 26 Jan 1981.
113. Ibid, Head of S10(Air), 5 Mar 1981.
114. Ibid, Nimrod AEW Manning Policy, AMSO, 16 Dec 1980. Manning came under AMSO until 1984 when responsibility transferred to AMP.
115. Ibid, Nimrod AEW Crew, 30 Mar 1981 and note of action, 1 Apr 1981.
116. FOI AHB: ID3/110/21, Hayr to VCAS, 30 Apr 1981.
117. Ibid, handwritten note not dated.

118. TNA: DEFE 71/443, AMP, 3 Jan 1978. Master Air Loadmaster Joy McArthur worked on passenger-cum-freight flights from the mid-1960s. McArthur 15 Dec 2015.
119. TNA: DEFE 71/443, AMP, 3 Jan 1978.
120. Ibid.
121. Ibid.
122. Ibid, handwritten note on AMSO copy of 3 Jan 1978 letter.
123. Ibid, WRAF Air Loadmasters, 6 Feb 1978.

Chapter 8: Combat Roles

1. National Audit Office [henceforward NAO], *Ministry of Defence: Control and Use of Manpower*, (London: HMSO, 1989). Research was conducted in 1986/87 and a draft report circulated in 1988.
2. Larken, 29 Mar 2010.
3. NAM: 1998.11.52: Nield to WRAC senior officers, 10 May 1988.
4. Drewienkiewicz, 24 Apr 2015.
5. NAM: 1192-11-98, News Bulletin, Mar 1982 & 1998-11-38, *Corps Today*, 1988.
6. NAM: 1998-11-38, *Corps Today*, 1985.
7. Officer training moved to Sandhurst in 1984. This was collocated not integrated training.
8. Flight Lieutenant Wendy Nichols, 11 Feb 2012.
9. TNA: DEFE 68/1217, Minutes, Principal Personnel Officers' Committee, 18 Jan 1989 and FOI MOD: MARILYN Report, 1988. The report's title – Manning and Recruiting in the Lean Years of the Nineties – was chosen to create a memorable acronym.
10. Ibid.
11. NAO, *Control and Use of Manpower.*
12. FOI MOD: Long Term Role and Employment of Women in the Army [henceforward Crawford Report], Mar 1989.
13. NAM: 1998-11-52-10, DWRAC to DGAMR, 21 Apr 1988.
14. TNA: DEFE 70/1701, Nield to Crawford, 1 Sep 1988.
15. Crawford Report.
16. Ibid.
17. FOI MOD: ECAB/P(89)20, Long Term Role and Employment of Women in the Army, 6 Jul 1989.
18. NAM: 1998-11-52-41, Brigadier Nield, Oct 1989.
19. Pascoe, 11 Sep 2015.

20. *Employment Gazette*, Vol.98, No.5, (London: HMSO, 1990), p.276. CSE grade 1 was equivalent to a GCE O level pass at grade C.

21. Purvis, 15 Jun 2010.

22. Wilkinson, 11 May 2011.

23. FOI MOD: Employment of WRNS Personnel in the RN, Jan 1990.

24. Captain Coates' papers: Employment of Women's Royal Naval Service Personnel in the Royal Navy, Mar 1989 [Henceforward: West Report].

25. FOI Fleet: Headmark 2000, 11 Nov 1987.

26. Prior to the study, Alan West spent seventeen years in ships and did one tour at MOD. Admiral Lord West, 5 Jun 2007.

27. West Report.

28. West, 5 Jun 2007.

29. West Report.

30. Ibid.

31. Ibid.

32. West, 5 Jun 2007.

33. Ibid.

34. Admiral Sir Brian Brown, 1 Apr 2010.

35. IWM Sound Archive: Admiral Sir Julian Oswald, Dec 2004, accession number 27454, reel 31.

36. FOI Fleet: The WRNS Study, Second Sea Lord, 11 Apr 1989.

37. FOI Fleet: Correspondence: 'Employment of WRNS Personnel in the RN', Naval Home Command, NP3 (Discipline), Fleet Headquarters and ACNS, Sep – Oct 1989.

38. FOI Fleet: The WRNS Study, Controller of the Navy, 22 May 1989; FOI Fleet: Correspondence: 'Employment of WRNS Personnel in the RN', DGNMT, 29 [Sep] 1989 and Director WRNS, 3 Oct 1989.

39. FOI MOD: NAVB/P(90)1 Employment of WRNS Personnel in the RN, 24 Jan 1990.

40. FOI Fleet: The WRNS Study, Second Sea Lord, 11 Apr 1989; FOI Fleet: Correspondence: 'Employment of WRNS Personnel in the Royal Navy', Nav Sec, DGNPS, DGST(N), Fleet Headquarters and Director WRNS, Sep – Oct 1989.

41. FOI Fleet: Correspondence: 'Employment of WRNS Personnel in the Royal Navy', AUS(NP), 16 Aug 1989.

42. Larken, 29 Mar 2010.

43. Ibid and Chief Officer (later Commander) Wilson, 4 Jun 2007.

44. FOI Fleet: Correspondence: 'Employment of WRNS Personnel in the RN', Director WRNS, 3 Oct 1989.

45. TNA: DEFE 69/1616, Head of Naval Manning and Training, 16 Nov 1989.
46. West Report.
47. Larken, 29 Mar 2010.
48. Roy Clare, 9 Mar 2011 and correspondence 8 Mar 2019.
49. NMRN Oral History Collection: Lord Hamilton interviewed by Katy Elliott, track 4; Clare, 9 Mar 2011.
50. Hamilton, 6 Apr 2011.
51. Clare, 9 Mar 2011 and Wilkinson, 1 May 2011.
52. Lippiett, 4 Apr 2011.
53. Wilkinson, 1 May 2011.
54. FOI MOD: Navy Board, Employment of WRNS Personnel in the RN, Second Sea Lord, Jan 1990.
55. FOI Fleet: Correspondence: Employment of WRNS Personnel in the Royal Navy, AUS(NP), DN Plans and Programmes, DGST(N), FONAC and Nav Sec, Aug – Oct 1989.
56. FOI Fleet: Employment of Women in Combat, 20 Nov 1989.
57. FOI Fleet: Brief for Minister for the Armed Forces, 1 Dec 1989, handwritten annotation.
58. Clare, 9 Mar 2011.
59. Correspondence Lord West/author 3 Mar 2019.
60. Correspondence Nick Wilkinson/author 5 Mar 2019. Recollections based on a private diary.
61. Ibid.
62. TNA: DEFE 24/3130, WRNS Study, 14 Dec 1989 and Moss to 2nd Permanent-under-Secretary, 25 Jan 1990.
63. TNA: DEFE 69/1616, Second Sea Lord to Navy Board colleagues, 9 Jan 1990.
64. Ibid, Roy Clare to Secretary/Second Sea Lord, 9 Jan 1990.
65. TNA: DEFE 24/3130, Principal Personnel Officers' Committee minutes, 10 Jan 1990.
66. Correspondence Nick Wilkinson/author 5 Mar 2019. Recollections based on a private diary.
67. TNA: DEFE 24/3130, Moss to 2nd Permanent-under-Secretary, 25 Jan 1990.
68. FOI MOD: Employment of WRNS Personnel in the RN, Jan 1990.
69. FOI MOD: WRNS Study, minute to Navy Board members, 15 Jan 1990.
70. FOI Treasury: DM – DSPA/AT/0046/002 Part A, correspondence 29 Jan 1990 and 30 Jan 1990.
71. TNA: DEFE 24/3130, Had of Naval Manpower & Training, 24 Jan 1990.

72. NMRN Oral History Collection: Lord Archie Hamilton of Epsom interviewed by Katy Elliott, 4 Jul 2006, accession number 2006.65, track 5.

73. HC Deb, 6th Series, Vol.166, Col.734, 5 Feb 1990. Reaction recollected by Hamilton, interviewed by Katy Elliott, NMRN Oral History Collection, track 14.

74. FOI MOD: VCAS File 111/1 Part 7, Draft – Nimrod AEW manning, 18 Nov 1983.

75. TNA: AIR 29/4666, Manning Plans Aug 1977, May 1979 and Jun 1980.

76. FOI AHB: 'Nimrod AEW – Employment of WRAF Personnel', Vice Chief of Air Staff, 8 May 1984 and brief for Chief of Air Staff, 19 Jun 1984.

77. FOI AHB: Employment of WRAF Personnel on Nimrod AEW, 9 Jul, 1984.

78. FOI AHB: ID6/1006, Employment of WRAF Personnel on the E-3 [Sentry], 6 Jun 1988.

79. TNA: AIR 8/3577, papers 1983–4 and Chief of the Air Staff to Air Member for Personnel, 4 Jan 1984.

80. FOI MOD: AFBSC(89)11, Female Aircrew in the Royal Air Force, Jun 1989.

81. FOI AHB: Female Aircrew in the RAF, Air Vice-Marshal Honey, 1 Mar 1989.

82. FOI AHB: ID6/1006, Conference on Pilot Shortages, 21 Dec 1988.

83. *RAF News*, 20 Jan 1989, p.1.

84. FOI AHB: Female Aircrew in the RAF, Air Vice-Marshal Honey, 1 Mar 1989.

85. FOI AHB: Correspondence on Female Aircrew, Air Vice-Marshal Austin, 13 Mar 1989. Roger Austin went on to become Deputy Chief of Defence Staff (Systems) in the rank of air marshal.

86. Ibid.

87. Ibid, Air Commodore Garden, Air Vice-Marshal Macey, Air Commodore Farrer and Air Vice-Marshal Mills, Mar 1989. Engine failure or damage to control surfaces could result in unusual (asymmetric) forces on the aircraft that required the pilot to exert greater than normal effort to operate the controls.

88. FOI AHB: Female Aircrew in the RAF, Air Vice-Marshal Honey, 1 Mar 1989.

89. FOI AHB: Correspondence on Female Aircrew, Air Vice-Marshal Mills, 30 Mar 1989.

90. Ibid, Air Commodore Jones, 28 Mar 1989.

91. FOI AHB: Correspondence on Female Aircrew, Air Vice-Marshal Thomson, 28 Mar 1989.

92. FOI MOD: AFBSC(89)11, Female Aircrew in the Royal Air Force, Jun 1989.

93. FOI AHB: ID3/A/18/1 Part 3, Air Force Board Standing Committee, 27 Jun 1989.

94. FOI Fleet: Employment of Female Aircrew in the RN, Second Sea Lord, Oct 1990.

95. FOI Fleet: NAVB P(91)4 Post Options Restructuring of the RN, 22 Mar 1991.

96. FOI AHB: Correspondence on Female Aircrew, Air Member for Personnel, 21 Dec 1990.

97. FOI MOD: Major General Lytle (Director Army Air Corps), 15 Mar 1994.

98. The first women to complete training joined squadrons in 1991.

99. FOI AHB: Correspondence on Female Aircrew, Air Member for Personnel, 3 Jul 1991.

100. Ibid. Deputy Controller Aircraft, Assistant Chief of Air Staff and 2nd Permanent Under-Secretary, Jul 1991.

101. FOI AHB: Air Force Board Standing Committee, Conclusions, 24 Sep 1991.

102. FOI AHB: Correspondence on Female Aircrew, Air Member for Personnel, 27 Nov 1991.

103. Ibid.

104. Ibid, Director of Public Relations, 2 Dec 1991.

105. Ibid, Air Member for Personnel, 6 Dec 1991.

106. Ibid, Air Marshal Sir John Thomson, 2 Dec 1991.

107. Ibid, PSO to Chief of Air Staff, 6 Dec 1991.

108. Ibid, Air Member for Personnel, 6 Dec 1991.

109. Hamilton, 17 May 2007.

Chapter 9: Integration

1. Gibson Papers: University of London Air Squadron letter, 5 Nov 1981 and Jerry Wiggin (Under-Secretary of State Armed Forces) to Peter Mills MP, 30 Nov 1981.

2. Flight Lieutenant Julie Gibson, 20 Jul 2010.

3. Unnamed female applicant, recounted by Commander Rosie Wilson, 11 Jan 2011. WRNS officers adopted RN ranks from 1 December 1990. To avoid confusion, only RN rank titles are used in this chapter with the exception of the Director who retained her title of Commandant.

4. Colonel Fiona Walthall, correspondence with the author, Aug 2018.

5. *Armed Forces Pay Review Body Twentieth Report*, Cm. 1414, (London: HMSO, Jan 1991).

6. FOI MOD: Employment of WRNS Personnel in the RN, Second Sea Lord, Jan 1990.

7. FOI MOD: Minute to Navy Board members, Secretary to First Sea Lord, 15 Jan 1990.

8. FOI Fleet: WRNS Personnel Sea Service – Ship Accommodation, 29 Mar 1990 and Wilson, 11 Jan 2011.

9. Larken, 29 Mar 2010.

10. *Navy News*, Mar 1990, reported 20–30 women participating in protests in both Plymouth and Portsmouth. The Portsmouth local paper reported fewer than 40 marchers (*The News*, 16 Feb 1990).

11. Margaret Aldred, 13 Jul 2007.

12. *Navy News*, Apr 1990.

13. FOI Fleet: WRNS Sea Service Feedback, 19 Apr 1990.

14. West Report.

15. *Navy News*, Mar 1990; Lieutenant Commander Elaine Smith, 10 Aug 2010.

16. FOI MOD: Minute to Navy Board Members, Secretary to First Sea Lord, 15 Jan 1990.

17. FOI Fleet: WRNS Sea Service – Volunteers for Sea Service, 7 Feb 1990.

18. Ibid and WRNS Sea Service Feedback, 19 Apr 1990.

19. FOI Fleet: WRNS Personnel – Service at Sea, 28 Mar 1990.

20. FOI Treasury: Pay for the Women's Royal Naval Service, 11 Jun 1990.

21. FOI Fleet: WRNS Sea Service – Situation Report, 13 Dec 1990. One Wren and 30 nurses of the Queen Alexandra's Royal Naval Nursing Service were also serving in Royal Fleet Auxiliary *Argus,* a casualty receiving ship for the Gulf War. Figures for female officers were not quoted.

22. FOI MOD: Integration of Sea Service: Report on the Integration of the WRNS into the RN, Lyn Bryant, Joan Chandler and Tracey Bunyard, University of Plymouth, Oct 1995.

23. FOI Fleet: Integration of Sea Service – Continuation Study: Ship-board Survey, Lyn Bryant, Tracey Bunyard, Joan Chandler and Commander J. L. Wakeling, University of Plymouth, Oct 1995, and Commodore John Hart, 7 Jun 2011.

24. West Report.

25. Smith, 10 Aug 2010.

26. Cobbold, 18 Jun 2007. Cobbold handed over to Captain Toby Elliott in December 1990.

27. *The Times*, 14 Jun 1991.

28. *The Sun*, 14 Jun 1991.

29. *Daily Mirror*, 30 Sep 91.

30. FOI Fleet: University of Plymouth reports, Oct 1995.

31. FOI Fleet: Integration of Sea Service – Continuation Study of Seagoing Personnel, 4 Dec 1995.

32. Commandant Anne Spencer, 12 Jan 2011; Hart, 7 Jun 2011; Rear Admiral Clare, 9 Mar 2011.

33. Spencer, 12 Jan 2011.

34. FOI Fleet: Integration of Sea Service – Continuation Study of Seagoing Personnel, 4 Dec 1995; Spencer.

35. Hart, 7 Jun 2011.

36. *Navy News*, Jul 1992.

37. FOI Fleet: Women at Sea, Minute to Minister Armed Forces' Office, 14 Feb 1994.

38. 'Ricochet', 'Amazons at Sea', in *Naval Review*, Vol.82, No.3, 1994, p.221.

39. Ibid.

40. IWM Sound Archive: Admiral Sir Ben Bathurst, reel 11.

41. FOI MOD: Female Aircrew in the Royal Air Force, Jun 1989.

42. TNA: AIR 58/452, Aircrew Size Limitations, Institute of Aviation Medicine, Jan 1986.

43. FOI AHB: Correspondence: Female Aircrew in the RAF, Mills to Air Secretary, 30 Mar 1989.

44. G. M. Turner, RAF Institute of Aviation Medicine, 'Application of USAF Female Anthropometric Data to Identify Problems with the Introduction of Female Aircrew into the RAF', AGARD conference proceedings, Apr 1990.

45. Flight Lieutenant Dawn Hadlow, 14 Mar 2012.

46. FOI MOD: Female Aircrew in the Royal Air Force, Jun 1989.

47. Ibid.

48. *Annual Abstract of Statistics*, Vol.132 (London: HMSO, 1996), Table 7.1.

49. Hadlow, 14 Mar 2012. Rather than wait for fast jet training, she became an instructor.

50. Squadron Leader Helen Gardiner, 21 Oct 2011.

51. FOI DASA: RAF and RN Aircrew Statistics, 27 Nov 2007. These official statistics were rounded to the nearest 10.

52. G. M. Turner, 'Some Equipment Problems Associated with the Introduction of Female Aircrew into the Royal Air Force', Apr 1990.

53. Gibson, 20 Jul 2010.

54. Flight Lieutenant Keren Watkins, 21 Oct 2011.

55. Nichols, 11 Feb 2012.

56. Bettyann Holtzman Kevles, *Almost Heaven*, (Cambridge Massachusetts and London: MIT Press, 2006), p.75.

57. Squadron Leader Redmore, 'Female Aircrew in the Royal Air Force', *Royal Air Force '90*, p.7.

58. AHB: WAAF/WRAF Miscellaneous Papers, Press Release, 10 Aug 89.

59. G. M. Turner, 'The Application of USAF Female Anthropometric Data to Identify Problems with the Introduction of Female Aircrew into the RAF', Apr 1990.

60. Gibson, 20 Jul 2010.

61. Air Vice-Marshal Honey, 25 May 2011.

62. Gibson Papers: valedictory letter, 1 May 2001.

63. Gibson, 20 Jul 2010.

64. Watkins, 21 Oct 2011.

65. Flight Lieutenant Jo Salter, 20 Sep 2007.

66. Hadlow, 14 Mar 2012.

67. *Daily Mail*, 4 Mar 1992, *Daily Telegraph*, 4 Mar 1992, *Sunday Times*, 8 Mar 1992.

68. London's *Evening Standard*, 4 Mar 1992.

69. Ibid, 5 Mar and 9 Mar 1992.

70. FOI AHB: Correspondence: 'Employment of Female Aircrew', Thomson to Air Marshal Palin, 2 Dec 1991.

71. Gardiner and Watkins, 21 Oct 2011.

72. *RAF News*, 20 Aug 93.

73. Gardiner, 21 Oct 2011.

74. *RAF News*, 22 Mar 1991. Anne-Marie Dawe was the first to complete training. She joined a Hercules (transport aircraft) squadron.

75. FOI AHB: Correspondence: Employment of Female Aircrew, 3 Jul 1991. Nimrod had reconnaissance and maritime patrol roles.

76. RAFM: X008-4753, Group Captain Anne-Marie Houghton, interviewed by Ewan Burnet, 23 Nov 2017. In 2018, Houghton was the parade commander for the RAF's 100th anniversary parade in London.

77. Air Commodore Ruth Montague, 29 August 2007. Ruth Montague's promotions to group captain and then to air commodore were specifically to fill the Deputy Director and, subsequently, Director posts. She was the last officer to be promoted on this 'WRAF' basis.

78. TNA: DEFE 24/3130, correspondence, Feb 1990.

79. FOI MOD: ECAB, Deployment Rules for Women, paper and minutes of meetings, 31 Jul 1990, 16 Aug 1990 and 16 Jan 1991.

80. NAM: 1998-11-38-13, *The Corps Today*, Dec 1989.

81. FOI MOD: Deployment Rules for Women, 31 Jul 1990, ECAB Minutes, 16 Aug 1990 and 16 Jan 1991.

82. FOI MOD: ECAB papers on employment of women, 14 Jun 1991, 24 Apr 1992, 4 Nov 1992, 26 Feb 1993, 5 Nov 1993 and 10 Nov 1994.

83. Major General Drewienkiewicz, 24 Apr 2015.

84. FOI MOD: ECAB paper, Long-term Role and Employment of Women – Progress Report, 14 Jun 1991.

85. FOI MOD: ECAB, Formation of the Adjutant General's Corps, Implementation, Volume 1, Part 4, Aug 1991.

86. Colonel Fiona Walthall, correspondence with the author, Aug and Sep 2018.

87. FOI MOD: ECAB, Formation of the Adjutant General's Corps, Implementation, Volume 2, Paper 8, Aug 1991.

88. General Pascoe, 11 Sep 2015.

89. *Soldier*, 14 May 1990.

90. NAM: Anne Field papers.

91. General David Ramsbotham, 13 July 2015.

92. *Soldier Magazine*, 20 April 1992.

93. Spencer, 12 Jan 2011.

94. FOI Fleet: WRNS Sea Service – Situation Report, 13 Dec 1990.

95. NMRN: 2007.15.6, *The Wren*, No. 316, Feb 1993.

96. FOI Fleet: WRNS Integration with the RN, 21 May 1991.

97. Wilson, 11 Jan 2011.

98. NMRN: 2007.15.9, *The Wren*, No. 319, Feb 1994.

99. *Navy List,* (London: HMSO, 2003 and 2005 editions).

100. FOI: MOD, reply to author, 29 Nov 2018.

101. FOI AHB: Air Commodore Montague to Air Member for Personnel, Jan 1992.

102. FOI AHB: Further Integration of Women, 19 Nov 1993.

103. *RAF News*, 19 Nov – 2 Dec 1982.

104. Air Commodore Joan Hopkins, May 2009.

105. AHB: WAAF/WRAF Miscellaneous Papers, Brief for Minister Armed Forces, 28 Jan 94.

106. *Armed Forces Pay Review Body Seventeenth Report*, Cm.357 (London: HMSO, 1988) and *Twentieth Report*, Cm.1414 (London: HMSO, 1991).

107. FOI Treasury: Pay for Seagoers in the Women's Royal Naval Service, 1 Feb 1990 and Pay for the Women's Royal Naval Service, 16 Feb 1990.

108. FOI Treasury: Pay of WRNS Ratings, Chairman Armed Forces Pay Review Body to Prime Minister, 26 Mar 1990 and reply, 25 Apr 1990.

109. TNA: DEFE 69/1617, Pay for Seagoers in the WRNS, 9 Feb 1990.

110. FOI Treasury: Correspondence AUS(P)(Air)/Mr Fox, 29 Jun 1989 and 7 Jul 1989.

111. FOI AHB: ID3/A/18/1 Part 3, Nine Year Notice Engagement, 15 Jun 1989.

112. *RAF News*, 29 Jul 94.

113. *Armed Forces Pay Review Body Twentieth Report*, Cm.1414 (London: HMSO, 1991).

114. West Report. FOI AHB: ID3/A/18/1 Part 3, Air Member for Personnel Liaison Team Report, 28 Jul 1987 and Maternity Leave and Exit on Pregnancy, 3 Feb 1988.

115. Air Commodore Cynthia Fowler, 25 May 2007.

116. Larken, 29 Mar 2010.

117. FOI AHB: ID3/A/18/1 Part 3, Maternity Leave and Exit on Pregnancy, 3 Feb 1988.

118. Larken, 29 Mar 2010.

119. FOI Treasury: Female Aircrew, AUS(P)Air to Mr Fox, 29 Jun 1989.

120. TNA: DEFE 71/827, minute 9 Jan 1990.

121. Ibid, Study into Terms of Service for Women – Pregnancy, 16 Mar 1990.

122. Ibid, Management and Return to Work of Pregnant Servicewomen, 3 Jul 1990.

123. Ibid.

124. Ibid.

125. FOI Treasury: Defence Council Instructions – Royal Navy 261/90, Oct 1990.

126. *Navy News*, Feb 1992.

127. FOI MOD: Chief Claims Officer, Annual Report 1997/1998, Oct 1998.

128. *The Times*, 25 Mar 1994 and 8 Apr 1994 reported awards of £172,000 and £150,000 to two former WRAF officers and £300,000 to a former major in the army. *RAF News,* letters, 26 Nov 93, 9 Sep 94 and 18 Nov 94. *Soldier*, 11 Dec 1995.

129. *The Sun*, 9 Apr 1994.

130. FOI MOD: Chief Claims Officer, Annual Report 1998/1999, Jul 1999.

131. Commander Maggie Robbins, 27 Jul 2011. She attended some tribunals on behalf of the RN; *Daily Telegraph*, 9 Apr 94; *The Times*, 8 Sep 94.

Chapter 10: Beyond Integration

1. Chantelle Taylor, *Battleworn – the Memoir of a Combat Medic in Afghanistan* (iUniverse, 2016), Preface and Chapter 5.

2. MOD statement quoted in *Daily Mail*, 11 Sep 2009.

3. Danny Danziger, *We Are Soldiers: Our Heroes, Their Stories* (London: Sphere, 2010), p.57.

4. www.rafmuseum.org.uk/research/online-exhibitions/women-of-the-air-force/ women-in-the-raf-today/citation-and-distinguished-flying-cross-awarded-to- flight-lieutenant-michelle-goodman.aspx accessed 24 Oct 2018.

5. *See* Caroline Paige, *True Colours* (London: Biteback Publishing Ltd, 2007). Having joined the RAF in 1980 to become a navigator, she made her transition in 1999. She continued to serve until 2014.

6. Wing Commander Phil Sagar, spokesman for the MOD, BBC Radio 4, '*Cleaning out the Camp*', broadcast 21 and 28 Jun 2007.

7. *Soldier*, 5 March 1990 and LHA: Meechie papers, *Lioness*, No.2, 1990.

8. Major General John Drewienkiewicz, 24 Apr 2015.

9. Ibid.

10. FOI MOD: ECAB P(94)18, Revised Employment Policy for Women in the Army, 10 Nov 1994 and Minutes dated 30 Nov 1994.

11. FOI MOD: ECAB P(96)5, Future Employment Policy for Women in the Army, 3 Jun 1996 and Minutes, 24 Jun 1996.

12. FOI MOD: ECAB Minutes, 3 Mar 1998.

13. www.mod.uk, MOD Report, Women in the Armed Forces, May 2002 and Review of the Exclusion of Women from Ground Close-Combat Roles, Nov 2010 and Berkshire Consultancy Ltd, Qualitative Report for the Study of Women in Combat, 13 Nov 2009, accessed 8 Dec 2010.

14. Warfare in which the belligerents have significantly different military resources. The weaker party uses unconventional weapons or tactics to exploit vulnerabilities of the stronger party.

15. www.mod.uk, Review of the Exclusion of Women from Ground Close-Combat Roles, Nov 2010 and Berkshire Consultancy Ltd, Qualitative Report for the Study of Women in Combat, 13 Nov 2009, accessed 8 Dec 2010.

16. Ibid. Canada, Denmark, France, the Netherlands, Norway, Israel and Germany were named in the report.

17. www.mod.uk, Qualitative Report for the Study of Women in Combat, 13 Nov 2009, p.65, accessed 8 Dec 2010.

18. www.mod.uk Interim Report on the Health Risks to Women in Ground Close combat Roles, 2016, accessed 25 Jul 2016.

19. www.mod.uk, MOD Report, Review of the Exclusion of Women from Ground Close-Combat Roles, Nov 2010, accessed 8 Dec 2010.

20. www.mod.uk Women in Ground Close Combat Roles, 17 May 2016, accessed 25 Jul 2016.

21. *Sunday Telegraph*, 20 Dec 2015.

22. www.mod.uk Women in Ground Close Combat Roles, 17 May 2016, accessed 25 Jul 2016.

23. Ibid.

24. www.gov.uk/government/news 13 Jul 2017, accessed 1 Sep 2017.

25. www.mod.uk Women in Ground Close Combat Roles, 17 May 2016, accessed 25 Jul 2016.

26. www.gov.uk/government/news 8 Jul 2016, accessed 8 Jul 2016.

27. FOI Fleet: Mixed Gender Manning of Submarines: a feasibility study – annex on 1993 report, Flag Officer Submarines, 31 Mar 1998.

28. FOI Fleet: Mixed Manning in Submarines: Foetal Health, Institute of Naval Medicine, Dec 1997 and Mixed Gender Manning of Submarines: a feasibility study, Flag Officer Submarines, 31 Mar 1998; FOI MOD: Women in Submarines Feasibility Study: Focus Groups reports, Defence Analytical Services, Jan 1998.

29. FOI Fleet: Mixed Gender Manning of Submarines: a feasibility study, Flag Officer Submarines, 31 Mar 1998. Translation of Horace from Elizabeth Knowles (ed.), *Oxford Dictionary of Quotations,* (Oxford: Oxford University Press, 2009, 7th edition), p.408.

30. FOI MOD: Women in Submarines Feasibility Study Focus Groups Report, Defence Analytical Services Agency, Jan 1998.

31. FOI Fleet: Mixed Gender Manning of Submarines: a feasibility study, Flag Officer Submarines, 31 Mar 1998, Annex A – Conclusions and Recommendations from 1993 Feasibility Study and Rear Admiral Lippiett 4 Apr 2011, on attitudes towards privacy.

32. FOI Fleet: Mixed Gender Manning of Submarines: a feasibility study, Flag Officer Submarines, 31 Mar 1998. Only nuclear-armed submarines carried a doctor; others had a medical assistant.

33. Ibid.

34. Ibid.

35. FOI Fleet: Employment of Women in Submarines, Minutes of a Navy Board meeting, 1 Oct 1998.

36. FOI Fleet: Mixed Manning in Submarines – NAVB Update, 9 Jun 2011.

37. www.mod.uk/DefenceInternet/DefenceNews 9 Dec 2011.

38. *Evening Standard*, London, 9 Dec 2011.

39. www.gov.uk/government/news/female-submariners-make-history 5 May 2014.

40. Commandant Anne Spencer and Air Commodore Ruth Montague retired in November 1993 and April 1994 respectively.

41. Lord Ramsbotham, 13 Jul 2015.

42. *Daily Mail*, 11 Apr and 17 Apr 1992.

43. Lord Ramsbotham, 13 Jul 2015.

44. Major General Robin Grist, 7 Oct 2015.

45. *The Times*, 8 Jul 2015 (Susan Ridge) and Mar 2019 (Sharon Nesmith – late Royal Signals).

46. www.gov.uk/government/news 23 Aug 2013 and 30 Dec 2013, accessed 5 May 2014.

47. www.gov.uk/defence-and-armed-forces, news story, 20 Feb 2019, accessed 21 Feb 2019.

48. *RAF News*, 7 Feb 1992.

49. Ibid, 20 Mar 1992.

50. Ibid, 15 Oct 1993.

51. *RAF News*, 8 Jan 1993.

52. *Soldier*, 22 Feb 1993.

53. *RAF News*, 5 Feb 1993 and 5 Mar 1993.

54. *Soldier*, 23 Jan 1995.

55. Ibid, 15 May 1995.

56. Commander Jordan, 6 Feb 2018.

57. Ibid and correspondence 18 Mar 2019.

58. Based on statistics from UK Armed Forces Biannual Diversity Statistics 1 Oct 2017, published 30 Nov 2017.

59. Catherine Jordan, 6 Feb 2018 and correspondence Sep 2019.

Chapter 11: Conclusion

1. Holm, *Women in the Military*, p.398, quoting from Lewis Carroll, *Through the Looking Glass*.

2. National Army Museum: Oral History interview with Chantelle Taylor, 25 Jan 2016, accession number National Army Museum 2016-09-17.

BIBLIOGRAPHY

Departments Releasing Documents under the Freedom of Information Act (2000)
Air Historical Branch, Ministry of Defence
Defence Analytical Services and Advice, Ministry of Defence
Department of Work and Pensions
Fleet Information Cell, Royal Naval Headquarters
Ministry of Defence
Treasury

Archives
Air Historical Branch
Cox, Sebastian, *Note on the History of University Air Squadrons* (Air Historical Branch, 28 July 2005)
WAAF/WRAF Miscellaneous Papers (File)
WRAF Directorate Files
British Library Sound Archive
C465/03/06 (F1894), Air Commandant Jean Conan Doyle, interviewed by Cathy Courtney, 24 July 1991
Christ Church Oxford: Portal papers.
Imperial War Museum Sound Archive
Admiral Sir Ben Bathurst, interviewed 2004, accession number 27084
Admiral Sir Julian Oswald, interviewed December 2004, accession number 27454
Institute of Engineering and Technology: Caroline Haslett Papers
Liddell Hart Archive (King's College London): Brigadier Meechie papers including *Lioness*
National Archive, Kew: Series ADM, AIR, BA, CAB, DEFE, INF, PREM, T, WO

National Army Museum, London
Anne Field papers
Video interview with Chantelle Taylor, 25 Jan 2016, accession number 2016-09-17
WRAC papers
National Museum of the Royal Navy, Portsmouth
Ricochet (pseudonym), 'Amazons at Sea', *Naval Review*, Vol.82, No.3, 1994, pp.221–3
Judith Sherratt Collection, 2009.103.14, recording of a speech by Commandant McBride, 14 Oct 1978
WRNS papers
National Museum of the Royal Naval Oral History Collection, Portsmouth
Admiral Sir Brian Brown interviewed by Dr Chris Howard Bailey, 6 December 1993, accession number 1993/456
Lord Archie Hamilton of Epsom interviewed by Katy Elliott, 4 July 2006, accession number 2006.65
Commandant Anthea Larken interviewed by Katy Elliott, 24 July 2006, accession number 2006.74
Commander Rosie Wilson, interviewed by Katy Elliott, 14 August 2006, accession number 2006
Parliamentary Archive: Lord Royle papers.
Royal Air Force Museum Hendon
Air Publication 3234, *The Women's Auxiliary Air Force 1939–1945*, Air Historical Branch, 1953
Group Captain Anne-Marie Houghton, interviewed by Ewan Burnet, 23 Nov 2017, accession number X008-4753
Dame Katherine Watson-Watts (also known as Jane Trefusis-Forbes) papers
Woodhead/Welsh Papers, X002.5638

Privately Held Papers
Sergeant Vera Beale (RAF)
Captain Caroline Coates (RN)
Flight Lieutenant Julie Gibson (RAF)
Dame Felicity Peake (RAF) (known during WAAF/WRAF service as Felicity Hanbury)

Interviewees and Correspondents

Margaret Aldred
Admiral Sir Brian Brown
Rear Admiral Roy Clare
Captain Caroline Coates
Rear Admiral Richard Cobbold
Major General John Drewienkiewicz
Air Commodore Cynthia Fowler
Squadron Leader Helen Gardiner
Flight Lieutenant Julie Gibson
Major General Robin Grist
Flight Lieutenant Dawn Hadlow
Lord Archie Hamilton of Epsom
Commodore John Hart
Air Vice Marshal Robert Honey
Air Commodore Joan Hopkins
Commander Catherine Jordan
Commandant Anthea Larken
Rear Admiral John Lippiett
Master Air Loadmaster Joy McArthur
Air Commodore Ruth Montague
Commander Jackie Mulholland
Flight Lieutenant Wendy Nichols
General Sir Robert Pascoe
Vice Admiral Sir Ned Purvis
General Lord Ramsbotham
Commander Maggie Robbins
Flight Lieutenant Jo Salter
Lieutenant Commander Elaine Smith
Commandant Anne Spencer
Air Commodore Joy Tamblin
Colonel Fiona Walthall
Sergeant Celia Watkins
Flight Lieutenant Keren Watkins
Admiral Lord Alan West of Spithead
Rear Admiral Nick Wilkinson
Commander Rosie Wilson

Command Papers

Armed Forces Pay Review Body Reports (London: HMSO)
Defence: Outline of Future Policy, Cmnd. 124 (London: HMSO, April 1957)

Marriage Bar in the Civil Service, Cmd. 6886 (London: HMSO, August 1946)

Ministry of Labour and National Service Reports (London: HMSO)

Pay and Marriage Allowances of Members of the Armed Forces (other than the Women's Services), Cmd. 7588 (London: HMSO, Dec 1948)

Pay, Retired Pay, Service Pensions and Gratuities for Members of the Women's Services, Cmd. 7607 (London: HMSO, Jan 1949)

Recruiting: Government Comments on Report of the Advisory Committee on Recruiting (Cmnd. 545), Cmnd. 570 (London: HMSO, November 1958)

Report of the Advisory Committee on Recruiting, Cmnd. 545 (London: HMSO, October 1958)

Report of the Committee on Amenities and Welfare Conditions in the Three Women's Services, Cmd.6384 (London: HMSO, 1942)

Royal Commission on Equal Pay 1944–46 Report, Cmd.6937 (London: HMSO, 28 October 1946)

Service Pay and Pensions, Cmnd. 2903 (London: HMSO, Feb 1966)

Standing Reference on the Pay of the Armed Forces Third Report, Cmnd. 4291 (London: HMSO, February 1970)

Other Official Publications

Air Force List

Annual Abstract of Statistics (London: HMSO)

Burge, C. G. (ed), 'White Paper on Post-War Pay, Allowances and Service Pensions and Gratuities for Members of the Forces below Officer Rank', *The Royal Air Force Quarterly*, Vol.17, 1945–46, pp.111–116

'Post-War Code of Pay, Allowances, Retired Pay and Service Gratuities for Commissioned Officers', *The Royal Air Force Quarterly*, Vol.17, 1945–46, pp.177–179

Employment Gazette, Vol.98, No.5, (London: HMSO, 1990)

Hansard: House of Commons Debates

National Audit Office, '*Ministry of Defence: Control and Use of Manpower*', (London: HMSO, April 1989)

Navy List

Redmore, M., 'Female Aircrew in the Royal Air Force', *Royal Air Force '90* (an RAF publication), pp.6–8

Turner, G. M., RAF Institute of Aviation Medicine, 'The Application of USAF Female Anthropometric Data to Identify Problems with the Introduction of Female Aircrew into the RAF', *Recruiting, Selection, Training and Military Operations of Female Aircrew*, AGARD Conference Proceedings No.491, April 1990 (AGARD, August 1990), pp.17.1–17.3

'Some Equipment Problems Associated with the Introduction of Female Aircrew into the Royal Air Force, AGARD, *Recruiting, Selection, Training and Military Operations of Female Aircrew*, AGARD Conference Proceedings No.491, April 1990 (AGARD, August 1990), pp.20.1–20.3

Newspapers and Periodicals

Daily Express
Daily Mail
Daily Mirror
Daily Telegraph
London Evening Standard
Navy News
RAF News
Soldier
Spare Rib
Sunday Telegraph
Sunday Times
The News (Portsmouth)
The Times
The Sun

Professional Magazine

Elliott, Peter, 'The RAF's First Women Pilots', *Air Clues*, May 1990, pp.170–174

Other Contemporary Published Sources

Cowper, J. M., *The Auxiliary Territorial Service* (War Office, 1949)
Gwynne-Vaughan, Helen, *Service with the Army* (London: Hutchinson, 1942)
Holm, Major General Jeanne, *Women in the Military: an Unfinished Revolution* (Novato, Ca: Presidio, 1992 edition)
Peake, Felicity, *Pure Chance* (Shrewsbury: Airlife Publishing, 1993)
Pile, General Sir Frederick, *Ack-Ack: Britain's Defence against Air Attack* (London: George G. Harrap, 1949)
Markham, Violet R., *Return Passage, the Autobiography of Violet Markham, CH* (London: Geoffrey Cumberlege, Oxford University Press, 1953)
Mathews, Vera Laughton, *Blue Tapestry* (London: Hollis and Carter, 1948)
Mettam, Anne, 'The Flying Nightingales', in Ross, A. E. (ed.), *Through Eyes of Blue: Personal Memories of the RAF from 1918* (Shrewsbury: Airlife Publishing, 2002), pp.164–167

Montague, Air Commodore R. M. B., 'Women in the RAF', in Ross Tony (ed.), *75 Eventful Years: A Tribute to the Royal Air Force* (London: Lockturn, 1993), pp.225–229

Taylor, Chantelle, *Battleworn – the Memoir of a Combat Medic in Afghanistan* (iUniverse, 2016)

Secondary Sources
Books
Beckett, Ian F. W., *Territorials: a Century of Service* (Plymouth: DRA Publishing, 2008)

Binkin, Martin and Bach, Shirley J., *Women and the Military* (Washington D.C.: The Brookings Institution, 1977)

Coleman, David, 'Population and Family', in Halsey, A.H. and Webb, Josephine (eds.), *Twentieth-Century British Social Trends* (Basingstoke: Macmillan, 2000)

Danziger, Danny, *We Are Soldiers: Our Heroes, Their Stories* (Plymouth: DRA Publishing, 2008)

Escott, Beryl E., *The Heroines of SOE F Section: Britain's Secret Women in France* (Stroud: The History Press, 2010)

Women in Air Force Blue: The Story of Women in the Royal Air Force from 1918 to the Present Day (Wellingborough, Northamptonshire: Patrick Stephens, 1989)

Fletcher, M. H., *The WRNS: A History of the Women's Royal Naval Service* (Annapolis: Naval Institute Press, 1989)

French, David, *Army, Empire, and Cold War: the British Army and Military Policy, 1945–1971* (Oxford: Oxford University Press, 2012)

Military Identities: The Regimental System, the British Army, and the British People, C.1870–2000 (Oxford: Oxford University Press, 2005)

Grove, Eric J., *Vanguard to Trident: British Naval Policy since World War II* (London: Bodley Head, 1987)

Izzard, Molly, *A Heroine in Her Time: a Life of Dame Helen Gwynne-Vaughan 1879–1967* (London: Macmillan, 1969)

Jefford, C. G., *Observers and Navigators: and Other Non-pilot Aircrew in the RFC, RNAS and RAF* (Shrewsbury: Airlife Publishing, 2001)

Kevles, Bettyann Holtzman, *Almost Heaven: The Story of Women in Space* (Cambridge Massachusetts and London: The MIT Press, 2006)

Mason, Ursula Stuart, *Britannia's Daughters: the Story of the WRNS* (Barnsley: Pen and Sword Books, 2011)

Muir, Kate, *Arms and the Woman* (Sevenoaks: Coronet Books – Hodder and Stoughton, 1993)

Noakes, Lucy, *Women in the British Army: War and the Gentle Sex, 1907–1948* (London and New York: Routledge, 2006)

Paige, Caroline, *True Colours* (London: Biteback Publishing Ltd, 2007)

Roberts, Hannah, *The WRNS in Wartime: The Women's Royal Naval Service 1917–45* (London: I.B. Tauris, 2017)

Stanley, Jo, *Women and the Royal Navy* (London: I. B. Tauris, 2017)

Terry, Roy, *Women in Khaki: the Story of the British Woman Soldier* (London: Columbus Books, 1988)

Woodward, Rachel and Winter, Trish, *Sexing the Soldier: The Politics of Gender and the Contemporary British Army* (London and New York: Routledge, 2007)

Articles

Dandeker, Christopher and Segal, Mady Wechsler, 'Gender Integration in the Armed Forces: Recent Policy Developments in the United Kingdom', *Armed Forces and Society,* Vol.23, No.1, Fall 1996, pp.29–47

Oxford Dictionary of National Biography (www.oxforddnb.com):

Stone, Tessa, 'Forbes, Dame (Katherine) Jane Trefusis (1899–1971)'

Terry, Roy, 'Dame Leslie Violet Lucy Evelyn Whateley'

Thomas, Lesley, 'Mathews, Dame Elvira Sibyl Maria Laughton (1888–1959)'

'Woollcombe, Dame Jocelyn May (1898–1986)'

Broadcast

BBC Radio 4, '*Cleaning out the Camp*', broadcast 21 and 28 Jun 2007

Websites

www.defence.gov.au

www.forces.gc.ca

www.gov.uk/government/news

www.icrc.org

www.mod.uk

www.mod.uk/DefenceInternet/DefenceNews

www.rafmuseum.org.uk/research/online-exhibitions/women-of-the-air-force/
women-in-the-raf-today

INDEX